*Go Web Programming*

Ref

forums.mannig.com/forums/go-web-programming
www.calhoun.io/using-postgresql-with-golang

# *Go Web Programming*

SAU SHEONG CHANG

MANNING
SHELTER ISLAND

For online information and ordering of this and other Manning books, please visit www.manning.com. The publisher offers discounts on this book when ordered in quantity. For more information, please contact

Special Sales Department
Manning Publications Co.
20 Baldwin Road
PO Box 761
Shelter Island, NY 11964
Email: orders@manning.com



Manning Publications Co.
20 Baldwin Road
PO Box 761
Shelter Island, NY 11964

Development editor: Marina Michaels
Technical development editors: Glenn Burnside, Michael Williams
Review editor: Ozren Harlovic
Project editor: Kevin Sullivan
Copyeditor: Liz Welch
Proofreader: Elizabeth Martin
Technical proofreader: Jimmy Frasché
Typesetter: Marija Tudor
Cover designer: Marija Tudor

ISBN: 9781617292569
Printed in the United States of America
1 2 3 4 5 6 7 8 9 10 – EBM – 21 20 19 18 17 16

# brief contents

# contents

# *preface*

Web applications have been around in one form or another since the beginning of the World Wide Web in the mid-1990s. They started by only delivering static web pages but soon escalated and evolved into a dizzying variety of dynamic systems delivering data and functions. My own journey in developing applications for the web started around the same time, in the mid-1990s, and I eventually spent the larger part of my professional career designing, developing, and managing teams in developing large-scale web applications. Over the same period of time, I have written web applications in numerous programming languages and using various frameworks including Java, Ruby, Node.js, PHP, Perl, Elixir, and even Smalltalk.

I stumbled on Go a few years ago, and what worked very well for me is the simplicity and refreshing directness of the language. I was even more impressed when I realized that I could quickly write complete web applications (and services) that are fast and scalable with only the Go standard libraries. The code is direct, easy to understand, and can be quickly and easily compiled into a single deployable binary file. I no longer need to throw in application servers to scale or to make my web application production-capable. Needless to say, all of these elements made Go my new favorite language for writing web applications.

Writing web applications has changed dramatically over the years, from static content to dynamic data over HTTP, from HTML content delivered from the server to client-side single-page applications consuming JSON data over HTTP. Almost as soon as the first web applications were written, web application frameworks appeared, making it easier for programmers to write them. Twenty years on, most programming languages have at least one web application framework—and many have dozens—and most applications written today are web applications.

While the popular web application frameworks made it easier to write web applications, they also concealed a lot of the underlying plumbing. It became increasingly common to find programmers who don't even understand how the World Wide Web works writing web applications. With Go I found a great tool to teach the basics of web application programming, properly. Writing web applications is direct and simple again. Everything's just there—no external libraries and dependencies. It's all about HTTP again and how to deliver content and data through it.

So with that in mind, I approached Manning with an idea for a Go programming language book that focuses on teaching someone how to write web applications from the ground up, using nothing except the standard libraries. Manning quickly supported my idea and green-lighted the project. The book has taken a while to come together, but the feedback from the early access program (MEAP) was encouraging. I hope you will gain much and enjoy reading this book as much as I enjoyed writing it.

# *acknowledgments*

This book started with an idea to teach the basics of web programming with Go, using nothing more than the standard libraries. I wasn't sure if that would work, but the readers who paid hard-earned money to buy my MEAP along the way gave me encouragement and motivation to push the idea through. To my readers, thank you!

Writing books is a team effort, and though my name appears on the front cover of this one, it only exists because of the efforts of a large number of people:

- Marina Michaels, my hardworking and efficient editor from the other side of the world, worked tirelessly alongside me, ever ready to accommodate her schedule to our dramatically different time zones
- The Manning extended team: Liz Welch, copyeditor, and Elizabeth Martin, proofreader, who with their eagle eyes helped spot my mistakes; Candace Gillhoolley and Ana Romac, who helped me market and promote this book; and Kevin Sullivan and Janct Vail, who worked to take my raw manuscript and make it into a real book
- Jimmy Frasché, who gave the manuscript a full technical proofread, and my reviewers, who gave valuable feedback at four stages of manuscript development: Alex Jacinto, Alexander Schwartz, Benoit Benedetti, Brian Cooksey, Doug Sparling, Ferdinando Santacroce, Gualtiero Testa, Harry Shaun Lippy, James Tyo, Jeff Lim, Lee Brandt, Mike Bright, Quintin Smith, Rebecca Jones, Ryan Pulling, Sam Zaydel, and Wes Shaddix
- My friends from the Singapore Go community who helped me spread the word on my new book as soon as the MEAP came out, especially Kai Hendry, who made a long video from his comments on my book

I'd also like to thank the creators of Go—Robert Griesemer, Rob Pike, and Ken Thompson—as well as contributors to the net/http, html/template, and other web standard libraries, especially Brad Fitzpatrick, without whom I probably wouldn't have anything to write about!

Last but certainly not least, I'd like to thank my family—the love of my life, Wooi Ying, and my taller-than-me-now son, Kai Wen. I hope that in writing this book, I will be an inspiration to him and he will soon pick up my book proudly and learn from it.

# *about this book*

This book introduces the basic concepts of writing a web application using the Go programming language, from the ground up, using nothing other than the standard libraries. While there are sections that discuss other libraries and other topics, including testing and deploying web applications, the main goal of the book is to teach web programming using Go standard libraries only.

The reader is assumed to have basic Go programming skills and to know Go syntax. If you don't know Go programming at all, I would advise you to check out *Go in Action* by William Kennedy with Brian Ketelsen and Erik St. Martin, also published by Manning (www.manning.com/books/go-in-action). Another good book to read is *The Go Programming Language* (Addison-Wesley 2015), by Alan Donovan and Brian Kernighan. Alternatively, there are plenty of free tutorials on Go, including the A Tour of Go from the Go website (tour.golang.org).

## *Roadmap*

The book includes ten chapters and an appendix.

Chapter 1 introduces using Go for web applications, and discusses why it is a good choice for writing web applications. You'll also learn about key concepts of what web applications are, including a brief introduction to HTTP.

Chapter 2 shows you how to build a typical web application with Go, taking you step by step through the creation of a simple internet forum web.

Chapter 3 gets into the details of handling HTTP requests using the `net/http` package. You'll learn how to write a Go web server to listen to HTTP requests and how to incorporate handlers and handler functions that process those requests.

Chapter 4 continues with the details of handling HTTP requests—specifically, how Go allows you to process the requests and respond accordingly. You'll also learn how to get data from HTML forms and how to use cookies.

Chapter 5 delves into the Go template engine provided in the `text/template` and `html/template` packages. You'll learn about the various mechanisms provided by Go and about using layouts in Go.

Chapter 6 discusses storage strategies using Go. You'll learn about storing data in memory using structs, in the filesystem using CSV and the gob binary format as well as using SQL and SQL mappers to access relational databases.

Chapter 7 shows you how to create web services using Go. You'll learn how to create and parse XML as well as JSON with Go, and how a simple web service can be written using Go.

Chapter 8 gives insight into the ways you can test your Go web application at various levels, including unit testing, benchmark testing, and HTTP testing. This chapter also briefly discusses third-party testing libraries.

Chapter 9 talks about how you can leverage Go concurrency in your web application. You'll learn about Go concurrency and how you can improve the performance of a photo-mosaic web application using Go concurrency.

Chapter 10 wraps up the book by showing how you can deploy your web application. You'll learn how to deploy to standalone servers and to the cloud (Heroku and Google App Engine), as well as in Docker containers.

The appendix provides instructions for installing and setting up Go on different platforms.

## Code conventions and downloads

This book contains many examples of source code both in numbered listings and inline with normal text. In both cases, source code is formatted in a `fixed-width font like this` to separate it from ordinary text. Sometimes code is in bold to highlight code that has changed from previous steps in the chapter or code that is discussed in surrounding text.

Also, colors are used to highlight code commands and code output:

```
curl -i 127.0.0.1:8080/write
HTTP/1.1 200 OK
Date: Tue, 13 Jan 2015 16:16:13 GMT
Content-Length: 95
Content-Type: text/html; charset=utf-8

<html>
<head><title>Go Web Programming</title></head>
<body><h1>Hello World</h1></body>
</html>
```

Print book readers who want to see this color code highlighting (and all figures in color) can go to www.manning.com/books/go-web-programming to register and get their free eBook in PDF, ePub, and Kindle formats.

Code samples used throughout the book are also available at www.manning.com/books/go-web-programming and at github.com/sausheong/gwp.

### About the author

SAU SHEONG CHANG is now the Managing Director of Digital Technology at Singapore Power. Before that, he was a Director of Consumer Engineering at PayPal. He is active in the Ruby and Go developer communities, and has written books, contributed to open source projects, and spoken at meetups and conferences.

### Author Online

Purchase of *Go Web Programming* includes free access to a private web forum run by Manning Publications; you can make comments about the book, ask technical questions, and receive help from the author and from other users. To access the forum and subscribe to it, point your web browser to www.manning.com/books/go-web-programming. This page provides information on how to get on the forum after you're registered, what kind of help is available, and the rules of conduct on the forum.

Manning's commitment to our readers is to provide a venue where a meaningful dialogue between individual readers and between readers and the author can take place. It's not a commitment to any specific amount of participation on the part of the author, whose contribution to the forum remains voluntary (and unpaid). We suggest you try asking the author some challenging questions lest his interest stray!

The Author Online forum and the archives of previous discussions will be accessible from the publisher's website as long as the book is in print.

# *about the cover illustration*

The figure on the cover of *Go Web Programming* is captioned "Man in Medieval Dress." The illustration by Paolo Mercuri (1804–1884) is taken from "Costumes Historiques," a multivolume compendium of historical costumes from the twelfth, thirteenth, fourteenth, and fifteenth centuries assembled and edited by Camille Bonnard and published in Paris in the 1850s or 1860s. The nineteenth century saw an increased interest in exotic locales and in times gone by, and people were drawn to collections such as this one to explore the world they lived in—as well as the world of the distant past.

The colorful variety of Mercuri's illustrations in this historical collection reminds us vividly of how culturally apart the world's towns and regions were a few hundred years ago. In the streets or in the countryside people were easy to place—sometimes with an error of no more than a dozen miles—just by their dress. Their station in life, as well as their trade or profession, could be easily identified. Dress codes have changed over the centuries, and the diversity by region, so rich at one time, has faded away. Today, it is hard to tell apart the inhabitants of one continent from another, let alone the towns or countries they come from, or their social status or profession. Perhaps we have traded cultural diversity for a more varied personal life—certainly a more varied and faster-paced technological life.

At a time when it is hard to tell one computer book from another, Manning celebrates the inventiveness and initiative of the computer business with book covers based on the rich diversity of regional life of many centuries ago, brought back to life by Mercuri's pictures.

# Part 1

# Go and web applications

Web applications are probably the most widely used type of software application today and if you're connected to the internet, you would hardly pass a day without using one. Even if you're mostly on a mobile device, you still are using web applications. Many mobile applications that look like native applications are hybrids that have portions that built on web technologies.

Knowing HTTP is the foundation to learning how to write web applications, so these first two chapters will introduce HTTP. I will also explain why using Go for writing web applications is a good idea. I will jump straight into showing you how to write a simple internet forum using Go and show you a bird's-eye view of writing a web application.

# 1 Go and web applications

***This chapter covers***

- Defining web applications
- Using Go to write web applications: the advantages
- Understanding the basics of web application programming
- Writing the simplest possible web application in Go

Web applications are ubiquitous. Take any application you use on a daily basis, and likely it's a web application or has a web application variant (this includes mobile apps). Any language that supports software development that interfaces with human beings will inevitably support web application development. One of the first things developers of a new language do is build libraries and frameworks to interact with the internet and the World Wide Web. There are myriad web development tools for the more established languages.

Go is no different. Go is a relatively new programming language created to be simple and efficient for writing back end systems. It has an advanced set of features and focuses on programmer effectiveness and speed. Since its release, Go has gained tremendous popularity as a programming language for writing web applications and *-as-a-Service systems.

In this chapter, you'll learn why you should use Go for writing web applications and you'll learn all about web applications.

## 1.1 Using Go for web applications

So why should you use Go for writing web applications? My guess is, having bought this book, you have an inclination to find out the answer. Of course, as the author of a book that teaches Go web programming, I believe there are strong and compelling reasons to do so. As you continue reading this book, you'll get a sense of Go's strengths in web application development and, I hope, agree with me about the usefulness of Go.

Go is a relatively new programming language, with a thriving and growing community. It is well suited for writing server-side programs that are fast. It's simple and familiar to most programmers who are used to procedural programming, but it also provides features of functional programming. It supports concurrency by default, has a modern packaging system, does garbage collection, and has an extensive and powerful set of built-in standard libraries.

Plenty of good-quality open source libraries are available that can supplement what the standard libraries don't have, but the standard libraries that come with Go are quite comprehensive and wide-ranging. This book sticks to the standard libraries as much as possible but will occasionally use third-party, open source libraries to show alternative and creative ways the open source community has come up with.

Go is rapidly gaining popularity as a web development language. Many companies, including infrastructure companies like Dropbox and SendGrid, technology-oriented companies such as Square and Hailo, as well as more traditional companies such as BBC and *The New York Times*, have already started using Go.

Go provides a viable alternative to existing languages and platforms for developing large-scale web applications. Large-scale web applications typically need to be

- Scalable
- Modular
- Maintainable
- High-performance

Let's take a look at these attributes in detail.

### 1.1.1 Scalable web applications and Go

Large-scale web applications should be *scalable*. This means you should be able to quickly and easily increase the capacity of the application to take on a bigger volume of requests. The application should scale also linearly, meaning you should be able to add more hardware and process a corresponding number of requests.

We can look at scaling in two ways:

- *Vertical scaling*, or increasing the amount of CPUs or capacity in a single machine
- *Horizontal scaling*, or increasing the number of machines to expand capacity

Go scales well vertically with its excellent support for concurrent programming. A single Go web application with a single OS thread can be scheduled to run hundreds of thousands of *goroutines* with efficiency and performance.

Just like any other web applications, Go can scale well horizontally as well as by layering a proxy above a number of instances of a Go web app. Go web applications are compiled as static binaries, without any dynamic dependencies, and can be distributed to systems that don't have Go built in. This allows you to deploy Go web applications easily and consistently.

### 1.1.2 Modular web applications and Go

Large-scale web applications should be built with components that work interchangeably. This approach allows you to add, remove, or modify features easily and gives you the flexibility to meet the changing needs of the application. It also allows you to lower software development costs by reusing modular components.

Although Go is statically typed, it has an interface mechanism that describes behavior and allows dynamic typing. Functions can take interfaces, which means you can introduce new code into the system and still be able to use existing functions by implementing methods required by that interface. Also, with a function that takes an empty interface, you can put any value as the parameter because all types implement the empty interface. Go implements a number of features usually associated with functional programming, including function types, functions as values, and closures. These features allow you to build more modular code by providing the capability of building functions out of other functions.

Go is also often used to create *microservices*. In microservice architecture large-scale applications can be created by composing smaller independent services. These services are interchangeable and organized around capabilities (for example, a systems-level service like logging or an application-level service such as billing or risk analysis). By creating multiple small Go services and composing them into a single web application, you enable these capabilities to be swappable and therefore more modular.

### 1.1.3 Maintainable web applications and Go

Like any large and complex applications, having an easily maintainable codebase is important for large-scale web applications. It's important because large-scale applications often need to grow and evolve and therefore you need to revisit and change the code regularly. Complex, unwieldy code takes a long time to change and is fraught with risk of something breaking, so it makes sense to keep the source code well organized and maintainable.

Go was designed to encourage good software engineering practices. It has a clean and simple syntax that's very readable. Go's package system is flexible and unambiguous, and there's a good set of tools to enhance the development experience and help programmers to write more readable code. An example is the Go source code formatter (*gofmt*) which standardizes the formatting of Go code.

Go expects documentation to evolve along with the code. The Go documentation tool (*godoc*) parses Go source code, including comments, and creates documentation in a variety of formats such as HTML and plain text. It's very easy to use—just write the documentation above the source code itself and *godoc* will extract it along with the code to generate the documentation.

Testing is built into Go. *gotest* discovers test cases built into the same package and runs functional and performance testing. Go also provides web application testing tools by emulating a web client and recording responses generated by the server.

### 1.1.4 High performing web applications and Go

High performance means being able to process a large volume of requests within a short period of time. It also means being able to respond to the client quickly and making operations faster for end users.

One of Go's design goals is to approach the performance of C, and although it hasn't reached this goal, the current results are quite competitive. Go compiles to native code, which generally means it's faster than other interpreted languages and frameworks. As described earlier, Go also has great concurrency support with goroutines, which allows multiple requests to be processed at the same time.

I hope I've convinced you that Go is at least worth looking into as a useful language and platform for developing web applications. But before we jump into any Go code, let's get in sync on what web applications are and how they work. This will be important as you read through the next few chapters.

## 1.2 How web applications work

Ask a room full of programmers what a web application is and you'll likely get a wide range of answers (plus looks of scorn and amazement for asking such a basic question). But as you get your answers from the assembled technologists, you might realize that the common understanding of what a web application is might not be as straightforward. For example, is a web service also a web application? Many would consider them different, primarily because web services are consumed by other software whereas web applications are used by humans. But if a web application produces data that's readable by humans but is only consumed by other software (as with an RSS feed), is it a web service or still a web application?

If an application returns only an HTML page without any processing, is it a web application? Is a Adobe Flash program running on a web browser a web application? How about an application only written in HTML5, running on your browser but that resides on your laptop? If the application doesn't use HTTP to send requests to a server, is it still a web application? At a higher level, most programmers understand what a web application is. Down at a lower, implementation level, though, things get fuzzy and gray.

In a purist and narrow sense, a web application is a computer program that responds to an HTTP request by a client and sends HTML back to the client in an HTTP response. But isn't this what a web server is? From this definition, there *is* no difference between a web server and a web application. The web server is the web application (see figure 1.1).

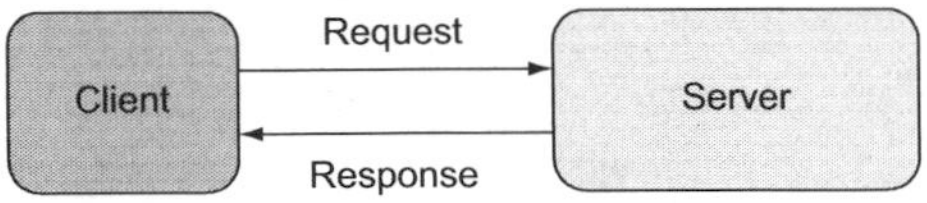


**Figure 1.1 The basic request response structure of a web application**

The only consideration is probably that a web server like *httpd* or Apache looks at a particular directory (in Apache this is the *docroot*) and returns files in that directory when requested. In comparison, a web application doesn't simply return files; it processes the request and performs operations that are programmed into the application (see figure 1.2).

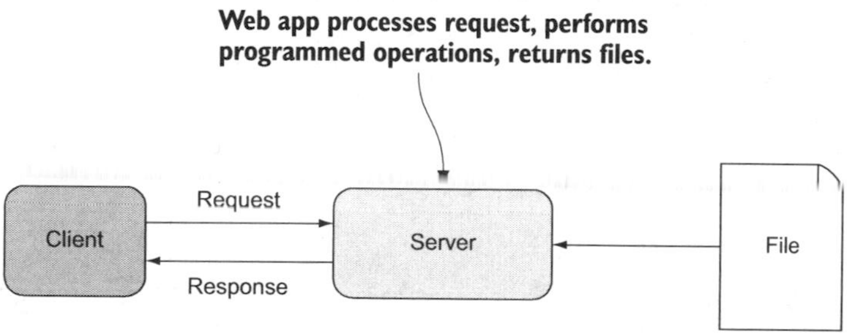


**Figure 1.2 How a web application works**

From this point of view, you can probably consider a web server to be a specialized type of web application that returns only files that are being requested. In a broader sense, many users would consider any application that uses a browser as the client to be a web app. This includes Adobe Flash applications, single-page web applications, and even applications that aren't served over HTTP but that reside on your desktop or laptop.

In the context of this book, we need to draw the line somewhere. Let's consider first what an *application* is.

An *application* is a software program that interacts with a user and helps the user to perform an activity. This includes accounting systems, human resource systems, desktop publication software, and so on. A *web application* is then an application that's deployed and used through the web.

In other words, a program needs to fulfill only two criteria to be considered a web app:

- The program must return HTML to a calling client that renders HTML and displays to a user.
- The data must be transported to the client through HTTP.

As an extension of this definition, if a program doesn't render HTML to a user but instead returns data in any other format to another program, it is a *web service* (that is, it provides a service to other programs). We'll get into web services in chapter 7.

Although this is probably a narrower definition than what most programmers would likely define as a web application, it's a useful one for our discussion in this book. It cuts through all the fuzziness and makes web applications much easier to understand. As we progress, things will start to make a lot more sense. But first, let's understand how HTTP came to be the way it is today.

## 1.3 A quick introduction to HTTP

HTTP is the application-level communications protocol that powers the World Wide Web. Everything that you see on a web page is transported through this seemingly simple text-based protocol. HTTP is simple but surprisingly powerful—since its definition in 1990, it has gone through only three iterative changes. HTTP 1.1 is the latest version, and HTTP 2.0 is in draft form.

The first version of HTTP (HTTP 0.9), created by Tim Berners-Lee, was a simple protocol created to help adoption of the World Wide Web. It allows a client to open a connection to a server, issue an ASCII character string request, and terminate with a carriage return (CRLF). The server then responds with only the HTML (no other metadata).

The explosion of features came with different implementations of HTTP. Eventually the multitude of features consolidated as HTTP 1.0 in 1996, followed by HTTP 1.1 in 1999, which is the most common version in use today. HTTP 2.0 (or HTTP/2) is in draft, so in this book we'll concentrate on HTTP 1.1 only.

Let's start defining what HTTP is first (this is my simplified definition):

**HTTP** HTTP is a stateless, text-based, request-response protocol that uses the client-server computing model.

*Request-response* is a basic way two computers talk to each other. The first computer sends a *request* to the second computer and the second computer *responds* to that request. A *client-server* computing model is one where the requester (the *client*) always initiates the conversation with the responder (the *server*). As the name suggests, the server provides a *service* to the client. In HTTP, the client is also known as the *user-agent* and is often a web browser. The server is often called the *web server*.

HTTP is a stateless protocol. Each request from the client to the server returns a response from the server to the client, and that's all the protocol remembers. Subsequent requests to the same server have absolutely no idea what happened before. In comparison, connection-oriented protocols like FTP or Telnet (also request-response and client-server) create a persistent channel between the client and the server. Having said that, HTTP 1.1 does persist connections to improve performance.

HTTP sends and receives protocol-related data in plain text (as opposed to sending and receiving in binary), like many other internet-related protocols. The rationale behind this is to allow you to see what goes on with the communications without a specialized protocol analyzer, making troubleshooting a lot easier.

HTTP was originally designed to deliver HTML only and HTTP 0.9 had only one method: GET. Later versions expanded it to be a generic protocol for distributed collaborative systems, including web applications, which we'll get into next.

## 1.4 The coming of web applications

Not long after the World Wide Web was introduced to the world at large, people started to realize that just serving files is great but it'd be even better if the content served was dynamically created. One of the early attempts to do this was the *Common Gateway Interface* (CGI).

In 1993, the National Center for Supercomputing Applications (NCSA) wrote a specification for calling command-line executable programs called the CGI. The NCSA included it in its popular NCSA *httpd*. Despite its name, it never became an internet standard.

CGI is a simple interface that allows a web server to interface with a program that's running separately and externally to the web server process. This program, usually called a CGI program, can be written in any language (hence, *common*), and in the earlier years that was mostly Perl. Input to the CGI program is done through environment variables, and anything the CGI program produces into standard output is returned to the client through the server.

Another technology from the same period is *server-side includes* (SSI), which are directives you can include in an HTML file. These directives are executed when the HTML file is requested and the contents from the execution of these directives are included in the spot where the directive was, before the final content is delivered to the client. One of the most popular uses of SSI is to include a frequently used file in another, or to embed header and footer snippets that are common throughout the site.

As an example, the following code includes the contents of the navbar.shtml file in the location you placed the directive:

```
<html>
  <head><title>Example SSI</title></head>
  <body>
    <!--#include file="navbar.shtml" -->
  </body>
</html>
```

The eventual evolution of SSI was to include more complex code in the HTML and use more powerful interpreters. This pattern grew into highly successful engines for building sophisticated web applications such as PHP, ASP, JSP, and ColdFusion. This also became the basis for web template engines like Mustache, ERB, Velocity, and many others.

As you can see, web applications originated as delivery of customized, dynamic content to the user through HTTP. To figure out how web applications operate, you need to know how HTTP works and understand HTTP requests and responses.

## 1.5 HTTP request

HTTP is a request-response protocol, so everything starts with a request. The HTTP request, like any HTTP message, consists of a few lines of text in the following order:

1. Request-line
2. Zero or more request headers
3. An empty line
4. The message body (optional)

This is how a typical HTTP request looks:

```
GET /Protocols/rfc2616/rfc2616.html HTTP/1.1
Host: www.w3.org
User-Agent: Mozilla/5.0
(empty line)
```

In this request, the first line is the *request-line*:

```
GET /Protocols/rfc2616/rfc2616.html HTTP/1.1
```

The first word in the request-line is the *request method*, followed by the *Uniform Resource Identifier* (URI) and the version of HTTP to be used. The next two lines are the request *headers*. Notice the last line is an empty line, which must exist even though there's no message body. Whether the message body exists depends on the request method.

### 1.5.1 Request methods

The request method is the first word on the request-line and indicates the action to be done on the resource. HTTP 0.9 had only one method: GET. HTTP 1.0 added POST and HEAD. HTTP 1.1 added another five—PUT, DELETE, OPTIONS, TRACE, and CONNECT—and opened the possibility for adding more methods (and many promptly did).

Interestingly, HTTP 1.1 specifies that GET and HEAD must always be implemented while all other methods are optional (this means even POST is optional).

- *GET*—Tells the server to return the specified resource.
- *HEAD*—The same as GET except that the server must not return a message body. This method is often used to get the response headers without carrying the weight of the rest of the message body over the network.
- *POST*—Tells the server that the data in the message body should be passed to the resource identified by the URI. What the server does with the message body is up to the server.
- *PUT*—Tells the server that the data in the message body should be the resource at the given URI. If data already exists at the resource identified by the URI, that data is replaced. Otherwise, a new resource is created at the place where the URI is.
- *DELETE*—Tells the server to remove the resource identified by the URI.
- *TRACE*—Tells the server to return the request. This way, the client can see what the intermediate servers did to the request.
- *OPTIONS*—Tells the server to return a list of HTTP methods that the server supports.
- *CONNECT*—Tells the server to set up a network connection with the client. This method is used mostly for setting up SSL tunneling (to enable HTTPS).
- *PATCH*—Tells the server that the data in the message body modifies the resource identified by the URI.

### 1.5.2 Safe request methods

A method is considered *safe* if it doesn't change the state of the server—that is, the server provides only information and nothing else. GET, HEAD, OPTIONS, and TRACE are safe methods because they aren't supposed to change anything on the server. In comparison, POST, PUT, and DELETE methods do change the state of the server; for example, after a POST request is sent, data at the server is supposed to be changed.

### 1.5.3 Idempotent request methods

A method is considered *idempotent* if the state of the server doesn't change the second time the method is called with the same data. Safe methods by definition are considered idempotent as well (though obviously not the other way around).

PUT and DELETE are idempotent but not safe. This is because PUT and DELETE don't change the state of the server the second time they're called. PUT with the same resource will result in the same actions being taken by the server, because after the first request the resource at the URI is either already updated or created. DELETE with the same resource might result in an error by the server, but the state doesn't change.

POST is neither a safe nor an idempotent method because subsequent POST requests to the server might (or might not) result in a state change, depending on the server. Idempotency is an important idea that we'll revisit when we talk about web services in chapter 7.

### 1.5.4 Browser support for request methods

GET is the most fundamental HTTP method, and it's supported with all browsers because it's how you actually get content from the server. POST support started with HTML 2.0 with the addition of HTML forms. The HTML `form` tag has an attribute, `method`, that accepts either the value `get` or `post` that indicates which HTTP method you want to use.

HTML doesn't support any other HTTP methods besides GET and POST. In early drafts of HTML5, PUT and DELETE support were added as values in the HTML form `method` attribute, but it was taken out again.

Modern browsers do more than just HTML, though. To support PUT and DELETE, you can use XMLHttpRequest (XHR). XHR is a set of browser APIs (actually, it's mostly just a browser object called XMLHttpRequest) with JavaScript code usually wrapped around it. XHR allows programmers to send HTTP requests to the server and, despite its name, isn't limited to using XML only. Requests and responses can be sent in any format, including JSON and text files.

### 1.5.5 Request headers

Although the HTTP request method defines the action requested by the calling client, other information on the request or the client is often placed in HTTP request headers. Request headers are colon-separated name-value pairs in plain text, terminated by a carriage return (CR) and line feed (LF).

A core set of HTTP request fields is standardized in RFC 7231 (which is a part of the set of HTTP 1.1 RFCs). In the past, nonstandard HTTP request fields conventionally started with `X-`, but this practice has been discontinued.

HTTP request headers are mostly optional. The only mandatory header in HTTP 1.1 is the Host header field. But if the message has a message body (which is optional, depending on the method), you'll need to have either the Content-Length or the Transfer-Encoding header fields. Some common request headers you'll see appear in table 1.1.

**Table 1.1 Common HTTP request headers**

| Header field | Description |
|---|---|
| Accept | Content types that are acceptable by the client as part of the HTTP response. For example, `Accept: text/html` signals to the server that the client wants the response body's content type to be in HTML. |
| Accept-Charset | The character sets required from the server. For example, `Accept-Charset: utf-8` tells the server that the client wants the response body to be in UTF-8. |
| Authorization | This is used to send Basic Authentication credentials to the server. |
| Cookie | The client should send back cookies that were set by the calling server. If the server had set three cookies at the browser previously, the Cookie header field will contain all three cookies in a semicolon-delimited name-value pair string. For example:<br>`Cookie: my_first_cookie=hello; my_second_cookie=world` |
| Content-Length | The length of the request body in octets. |
| Content-Type | The content type of the request body (when there's a request body). When a POST or a PUT is sent, the content type is by default `x-www-form-urlen-coded`. But when uploading a file (using the HTML input tag with the type attribute set to `file`, or otherwise) the content type should be `multipart/form-data`. |
| Host | The name of the server, along with the port number. If the port number is omitted, it will be resolved as port 80. |
| Referrer | The address of the previous page that linked to the requested page. |
| User-Agent | Describes the calling client. |

## 1.6 HTTP response

An HTTP response message is sent every time there's a request. Like the HTTP request, the HTTP response consists of a few lines of plain text:

- A status line
- Zero or more response headers
- An empty line
- The message body (optional)

You probably realized that an HTTP response is structured the same way as an HTTP request. This is how a typical HTTP response looks like (shortened in the interest of saving trees):

```
200 OK
Date: Sat, 22 Nov 2014 12:58:58 GMT
Server: Apache/2
  Last-Modified: Thu, 28 Aug 2014 21:01:33 GMT
Content-Length: 33115
Content-Type: text/html; charset=iso-8859-1

<!DOCTYPE html PUBLIC "-//W3C//DTD XHTML 1.0 Strict//EN" "http://www.w3.org/
     TR/xhtml1/DTD/xhtml1-strict.dtd"> <html xmlns='http://www.w3.org/1999/
     xhtml'> <head><title>Hypertext Transfer Protocol -- HTTP/1.1</title></
     head><body>…</body></html>
```

The first line of the HTTP response is the *status line*, which consists of the *status code* and a corresponding *reason phrase*, which is a short description of the code. In this case, the HTTP response has a message body, which is in HTML.

### 1.6.1 Response status code

As mentioned earlier, the status code in an HTTP response indicates what type of response it is. There are five classes of HTTP response status codes, depending on the first digit of the code (see table 1.2).

**Table 1.2 HTTP response status codes**

| Status code class | Description |
|---|---|
| 1XX | Informational. This tells the client that the server has already received the request and is processing it. |
| 2XX | Success. This is what clients want; the server has received the request and has processed it successfully. The standard response in this class is 200 OK. |
| 3XX | Redirection. This tells the client that the request is received and processed but the client needs to do more to complete the action. Most of the status codes in this class are for URL redirection. |
| 4XX | Client Error. This tells the client that there's something wrong with the request. The most widely known status in this class is 404 Not Found, where the server tells the client that the resource it's trying to get isn't found at that URL. |
| 5XX | Server Error. This tells the client that there's something wrong with the request but it's the server's fault. The generic status code in this class is 500 Internal Server Error. |

### 1.6.2 Response headers

Response headers are similar to that of request headers. They are both colon-separated name-value pairs in plain text, terminated by a CR and LF. Just as request headers tell the server more about the request and what the client wants, the response headers are the means for the server to tell the client more about the response and what the server wants (from the client). Some commonly used response headers are shown in table 1.3.

**Table 1.3 Common response headers**

| Header field | Description |
|---|---|
| Allow | Tells the client which request methods are supported by the server. |
| Content-Length | The length of the response body in octets (8-bit bytes). |
| Content-Type | The content type of the response body (when there is a response body). |
| Date | Tells the current time (formatted in GMT). |
| Location | This header is used with redirection, to tell the client where to request the next URL. |
| Server | Domain name of the server that's returning the response. |
| Set-Cookie | Sets a cookie at the client. Multiple Set-Cookie headers can be added to the same response. |
| WWW-Authenticate | Tells the client what type of authorization clients should supply in their Authorization request header. The server usually sends this along with a `401 Unauthorized` status line. This header also provides the challenge information to the authentication schemes that are accepted by the server (for example, the basic and digest access authentication schemes described in RFC 2617). |

## 1.7 URI

When Tim Berners-Lee introduced the World Wide Web to the world, he also introduced the idea of a location string representing a resource on the internet. In June 1994, Berners-Lee published RFC 1630, which defined the URI. In it he described the concepts of a string that represents the name of the resource (*uniform resource name*, or URN) and a string that represents the location of the resource (*uniform resource locator*, or URL). The URI is an umbrella term that includes both the URN and the URI, and they have similar syntax and format. This book uses only URLs, so for all purposes, both the URI and URL can be used interchangeably.

This is the general form of a URI: <scheme name> : <hierarchical part> [ ? <query> ] [ # <fragment> ]

The *scheme name* is the name of the URI scheme that defines the rest of the URI structure. A large number of URI schemes are in use, because URI is a popular way of identifying resources. But the one we'll be using mostly in this book is the HTTP scheme.

The *hierarchical part* contains the identification information and should be hierarchical in structure. If the hierarchical part starts with a double slash (//), then it'll contain optional user information that ends with an `@`, followed by the hierarchical path. Otherwise, it's just the path. The path is a sequence of segments, separated by a forward slash (/).

Only the scheme name and the hierarchical parts are mandatory. The *query*, which starts with a question mark (?), is optional and contains other information that's not hierarchical in nature. The query is often organized as a sequence of key-value pairs, separated by an ampersand (&).

Another optional part is the *fragment*, which is an identifier to a secondary resource that's part of the URI that's defined. The fragment starts after the hash (#). If a URI has a query, the fragment will follow the query. The fragment is meant to be processed by the client, so web browsers normally strip the fragment out before sending the URI to the server. But it doesn't mean that as a programmer you won't get the fragment; you can always include it in a GET request through JavaScript or some HTTP client libraries.

Let's look at an example of an HTTP scheme URI: http://sausheong:password@www.example.com/docs/file?name=sausheong&location=singapore#summary

The scheme is `http`, followed by the colon. The segment *sausheong:password* followed by the at sign (@) is the user and password information. This is followed by the rest of the hierarchical part, *www.example.com/docs/file*. The top level of the hierarchical part is the domain name of the server, *www.example.com*, followed on by *docs* and then *file*, each separated by a forward slash. Next is the query, which begins after the question mark (?). The query consists of two name-value pairs: *name=sausheong* and *location=singapore*, joined by a single ampersand (&). Finally, the fragment follows after the query, starting after the hash (#).

The URL is a single string, so spaces within the URL aren't permitted. Also, certain characters like the question mark (?) and the hash (#) have special meaning within the URL and so can't be permitted for other purposes. To get over this limitation, we use *URL encoding* (also called percent encoding) to convert those special characters into something else.

RFC 3986 defines a set of characters that are reserved or not reserved. Everything in the reserved list needs to be URL encoded. URL encoding encodes a character by converting the character to its corresponding byte value in ASCII, then representing that as a pair of hexadecimal digits and prepending it with a percent sign (%).

For example, a blank space's byte value in ASCII is 32, which is 20 in hexadecimal. Therefore, the URL encoding of a space is `%20`, and this is used in a URL instead of a space. This example shows the URL if I'd used my name with the space between sau and sheong: http://www.example.com/docs/file?name=sau%20sheong&location=singapore.

## 1.8 Introducing HTTP/2

HTTP/2, the new version of HTTP, focuses on performance. HTTP/2 is based on SPDY/2, an open networking protocol developed primarily at Google for transporting web content, though over time there have been a number of changes.

HTTP/2 is a binary protocol, unlike HTTP/1.x, which is text-based. This makes HTTP/2 more efficient to parse, and it is more compact and less prone for errors. But that means you can no longer send HTTP/2 messages directly through the network, through applications such as telnet, and so it is harder to debug if you're used to HTTP/1.x.

Unlike HTTP/1.x, which only allows a single request on a connection at a time, HTTP/2 is fully multiplexed. This means multiple requests and responses can be using the same connection at the same time. HTTP/2 also compresses the header to reduce overhead and allows the server to push responses to the client, generally improving performance.

As you can see, HTTP/2 generally improves the communications performance of the protocol. What is not changed, are the HTTP semantics; for example, the HTTP methods, status codes, and so on. This is because HTTP is so widely used, and any change to the semantics would break the existing web.

In Go 1.6, if you're using HTTPS, you'll be automatically using HTTP/2. For earlier versions of Go, the `golang.org/x/net/http2` package implements the HTTP/2 protocol. You will see how it can be used in chapter 3.

## 1.9 Parts of a web app

From the previous sections you've seen that a web application is a piece of program that does the following:

1. Takes input through HTTP from the client in the form of an HTTP request message
2. Processes the HTTP request message and performs necessary work
3. Generates HTML and returns it in an HTTP response message

As a result, there are two distinct parts of a web app: the *handlers* and the *template engine.*

### 1.9.1 Handler

A *handler* receives and processes the HTTP request sent from the client. It also calls the template engine to generate the HTML and finally bundles data into the HTTP response to be sent back to the client.

In the MVC pattern the handler is the controller, but also the model. In an ideal MVC pattern implementation, the controller would be thin, with only routing and HTTP message unpacking and packing logic. The models are fat, containing the application logic and data.

**Model-View-Controller pattern**

The Model-View-Controller (MVC) pattern is a popular pattern for writing web applications—so popular that it's sometimes mistaken as the web application development model itself.

MVC was introduced in Smalltalk in the late 1970s (more than 10 years before the World Wide Web and HTTP) at Xerox PARC. The MVC pattern divides a program into three parts: model, view, and controller. The model is a representation of the underlying data, the view is a visualization of the model for the user, and the controller uses input from the user to modify the model. When the model changes, the view updates automatically to show the latest visualization.

Although originally developed for the desktop, it became popular for writing web applications, and many web application frameworks—including Ruby on Rails, CodeIgniter, Play, and Spring MVC—use it as their foundation pattern. The model is often mapped to a database using structures or objects, the views are the returned HTML, and the controllers route the requests and manage access to the models.

Many novice programmers who build their web applications with MVC-based web application frameworks often mistake the MVC pattern as the only way to develop web applications. In fact, web applications are simply applications that interact with users over the HTTP protocol, and any pattern (or no pattern) that allows such applications to be written can be used.

Sometimes *service objects* or *functions* are used to manipulate the models, freeing the model from being too bloated and enabling reuse of code. In this case, service objects can be reused on different models and the same logic can be placed in single service object instead of being copied in different models. Service objects, though, are not strictly speaking part of the MVC pattern.

As you may realize by now, web applications don't necessarily need to follow the MVC pattern. It's perfectly fine to have the handler perform all the processing and simply return a response to the client. It's not necessary to split the work into controllers and models.

### 1.9.2 Template engine

A *template* is code that can be converted into HTML that's sent back to the client in an HTTP response message. Templates can be partly in HTML or not at all. A *template engine* generates the final HTML using templates and data. As you may recall, template engines evolved from an earlier technology, SSI.

There are two types of templates with different design philosophies:

- *Static templates* or *logic-less templates* are HTML interspersed with placeholder tokens. A static template engine will generate the HTML by replacing these tokens with the correct data. There's little to no logic in the template itself. As you can see, this is similar to the concepts from SSI. Examples of static template engines are CTemplate and Mustache.

- *Active templates* often contain HTML too, but in addition to placeholder tokens, they contain other programming language constructs like conditionals, iterators, and variables. Examples of active template engines are Java ServerPages (JSP), Active Server Pages (ASP), and Embedded Ruby (ERB). PHP started off as a kind of active template engine and has evolved into its own programming language.

We've covered a lot of the fundamentals and the theories behind web applications so far in this chapter. If it appears an excessive overload of technical minutiae to you, please hang in there! As we get to the chapters ahead, you'll start to realize why it's necessary to understand the fundamentals covered in this chapter. In the meantime, let's switch gears, hold our breath, and jump into the cold waters of Go programming—it's time to get some hands-on experience. In the next few sections, I'll start you on the road of developing web applications with Go.

## 1.10 Hello Go

Let's write our first Go web app. If you haven't installed Go, read appendix A and follow the installation instructions. Don't worry if you don't know the `net/http` package that is being used—you will learn it in the next few chapters. For now, just type out the code (listing 1.1), compile it, and then see how it works. If you're accustomed to a case-insensitive programming language, remember, Go code is case sensitive.

All source code in this book is in GitHub at https://github.com/sausheong/gwp.

**Listing 1.1 A Hello World Go web app**

```
package main

import (
    "fmt"
    "net/http"
)

func handler(writer http.ResponseWriter, request *http.Request) {
    fmt.Fprintf(writer, "Hello World, %s!", request.URL.Path[1:])
}

func main() {
    http.HandleFunc("/", handler)
    http.ListenAndServe(":8080", nil)
}
```

Create a subdirectory in your workspace src directory and name it first_webapp. Now go to that subdirectory and create a file named server.go. This will be your source file. Then from a console (or command-line interface or command prompt), execute this command:

```
$ go install first_webapp
```

You can do this in any directory. If your GOPATH is set up properly, this will create a binary executable file in your $GOPATH/bin directory named first_webapp. Run the executable file from the console. Because you have the $GOPATH/bin directory in your PATH you should be able to just run it from anywhere. This will start up your Go web application at port 8080. That's it!

Now fire up your browser and go to http://localhost:8080. Figure 1.3 shows what you should see.

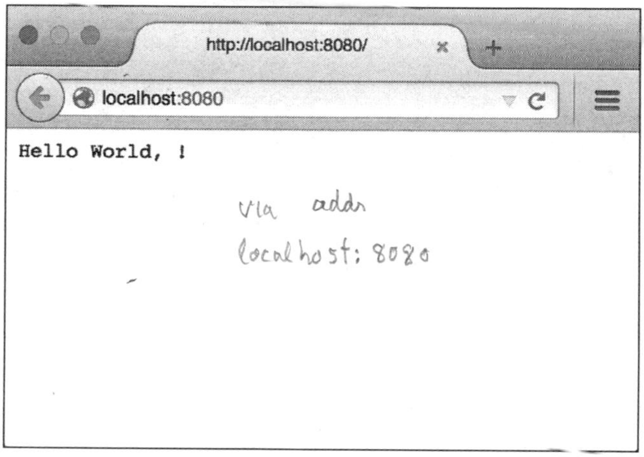


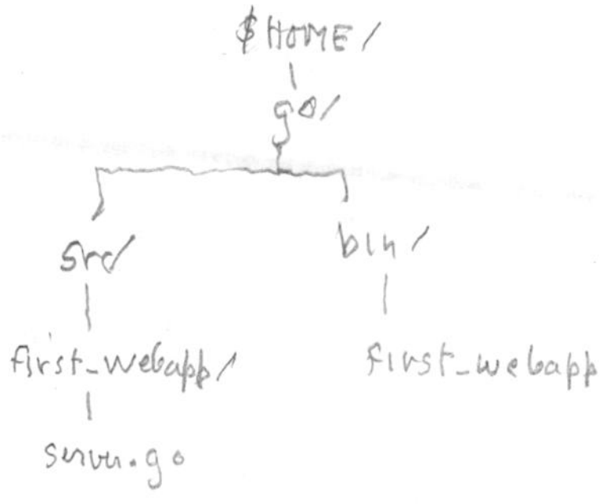

**Figure 1.3 First web application screenshot**

Take a closer look at the code. The first line declares what kind of program you're writing. The `package` keyword is followed by the name of the package. An executable program must always be in a package called `main`, and this is the same for a web app. If you have any experience with web application programming in some other languages (such as Ruby, Python, or Java) you might notice the difference right away. In those languages you often need to deploy the web application to an application server that provides an environment for your web applications to run. In Go, this environment is provided by the `net/http` package and is compiled together with the rest of your code to create a readily deployable standalone web app.

The next line imports the necessary libraries. You import standard Go libraries (packages) very much the same way you import other third-party libraries. Here you're importing two packages: `fmt`, which allows formatted I/O (allowing you to do stuff like `Fprintf`) and `http`, which is the main package for interacting with HTTP:

```
import (
    "fmt"
    "net/http"
)
```

This is followed by a function definition. You define a function named `handler`. The term *handler* is often used for callback functions triggered by an event, and that's what it's used for here (though technically, at least in Go, this isn't a handler but a handler function—we'll explore this in chapter 3).

```
func handler(writer http.ResponseWriter, request *http.Request) {
    fmt.Fprintf(writer, "Hello World, %s!", request.URL.Path[1:])
}
```

The handler function has two input parameters—a `ResponseWriter` interface and a pointer to a `Request` struct. It takes information from the `Request` to create an HTTP response, which is sent out through the `ResponseWriter`. The `Fprintf` function is called with the `ResponseWriter`, a format string with a single string *format specifier* (`%s`), followed by the path information extracted from the `Request`. Because you went to the address http://localhost:8080, there's no path information and so nothing is printed out. If you'd gone to the address http://localhost:8080/sausheong/was/here, figure 1.4 shows how it would've looked in the browser.

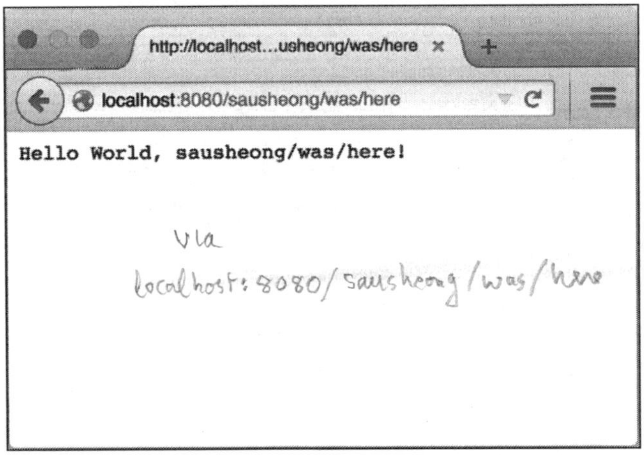


**Figure 1.4 Web application screenshot with path**

Every program that compiles into a binary executable file must have one function named `main`, where the execution of the program starts:

```
func main() {
    http.HandleFunc("/", handler)
    http.ListenAndServe(":8080", nil)
}
```

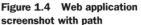

The `main` function in this program is straightforward. First, you set up the handler you defined earlier to trigger when the root URL (/) is called. Then you start the server to listen to port 8080. To stop the server, simply press Ctrl-C.

And there you have it: a working hello world web app, written in Go!

We started off with an explanation of concepts at the beginning of this chapter and ended up in a code rush where we wrote a simple (and useless) web application in Go.

In the next chapter, we'll jump into more code and show how a more realistic (though still not production-ready) web application can be written with Go and its standard libraries. Although chapter 2 might still be a bit of a code rush, you'll see how a typical Go web application can be structured.

## 1.11 Summary

- Go is a programming language that is well suited for web programming because it allows web applications that are scalable, modular, maintainable, and highly performant to be written relatively easily.
- Web applications are programs that return HTML to the calling client through HTTP, so understanding HTTP well is very important when learning how to write web applications.
- HTTP is a simple, stateless, text-based client-server protocol used in exchanging data between a client and a server.
- HTTP requests and responses are structured with similar formats—they start with a request (or response status) line, followed by one or more headers and an option body.
- Every HTTP request has a request line that contains an HTTP method that indicates the action asked of the server, the two most popular being GET and POST.
- Every HTTP response has a response status line that tells the calling client the status of the request.
- There are two major parts of any web application that correspond to requests and responses—handlers and the template engine.
- Handlers receive HTTP requests and process them.
- The template engine generates HTML that is sent back as part of the HTTP response.

# 2 Go ChitChat

> **This chapter covers**
> - Introducing Go web programming
> - Designing a typical Go web application
> - Writing a complete Go web application
> - Understanding the parts of a Go web application

Toward the end of chapter 1, we went through the simplest possible Go web application. That simple web application, I admit, is pretty useless and is nothing more than the equivalent of a Hello World application. In this chapter, we'll explore another basic but more useful web application. We'll be building a simple internet forum web application—one that allows users to log in and create conversations and respond to conversation topics.

By the end of the chapter, you might not have the skills to write a full-fledged web application but you'll be able to appreciate how one can be structured and developed. Throughout this chapter you'll see the bigger picture of how web applications can be written in Go.

If you find this chapter a bit too intimidating—especially with the rush of Go code—don't be too alarmed. Work through the next few chapters and then revisit this one and you'll find that things become a lot clearer!

## 2.1 Let's ChitChat

Internet forums are everywhere. They're one of the most popular uses of the internet, related to the older bulletin board systems (BBS), Usenet, and electronic mailing lists. Yahoo! and Google Groups are very popular (see figure 2.1), with Yahoo! reporting 10 million groups (each group is a forum on its own) and 115 million group members. One of the biggest internet forums around, Gaia Online, has 23 million registered users and a million posts made every day, with close to 2 billion posts and counting. Despite the introduction of social networks like Facebook, internet forums remain one of the most widely used means of communications on the internet.

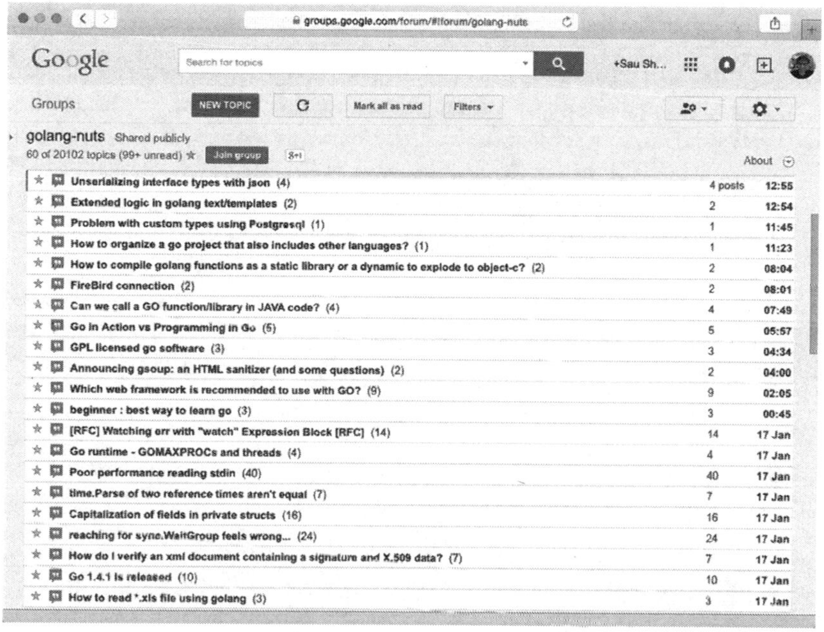


**Figure 2.1 Google Groups Go programming language forum, an example of an internet forum**

Essentially, internet forums are the equivalent of a giant bulletin board where anyone (either registered or anonymous users) can hold conversations by posting messages on the forum. These conversations, called *threads*, usually start off as a topic that a user wants to talk about, and other users add to the conversation by posting their replies to the original topic. More sophisticated forums are hierarchical, with forums having subforums with specific categories of topics that are being discussed. Most forums are moderated by one or more users, called *moderators*, who have special permissions.

In this chapter, we'll develop a simple internet forum called ChitChat. Because this is a simple example, we'll be implementing only the key features of an internet forum. Users will only be able to sign up for an account and log in to create a thread or post a reply to an existing thread. A nonregistered user will be able to read the threads but not add new threads or post to existing ones. Let's start off with the application design.

> **Code for this chapter**
>
> Unlike with the other chapters in this book, you won't see all the code that's written for ChitChat here (that would be too much!). But you can check out the entire application on GitHub at https://github.com/sausheong/gwp. If you're planning to run through the exercises while you read this chapter, you'll have an easier time if you get the code from the repository first.

## 2.2 Application design

ChitChat's application design is typical of any web application. As mentioned in chapter 1, web applications have the general flow of the client sending a request to a server, and a server responding to that request (figure 2.2).

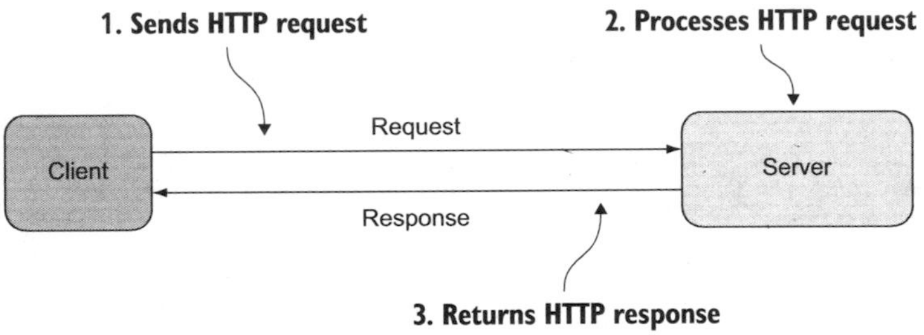

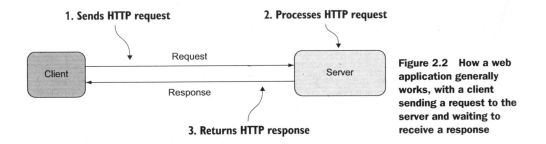

**Figure 2.2 How a web application generally works, with a client sending a request to the server and waiting to receive a response**

ChitChat's application logic is coded in the server. While the client triggers the requests and provides the data to the server, the format and the data requested are suggested by the server, provided in hyperlinks on the HTML pages that the server serves to the client (figure 2.3).

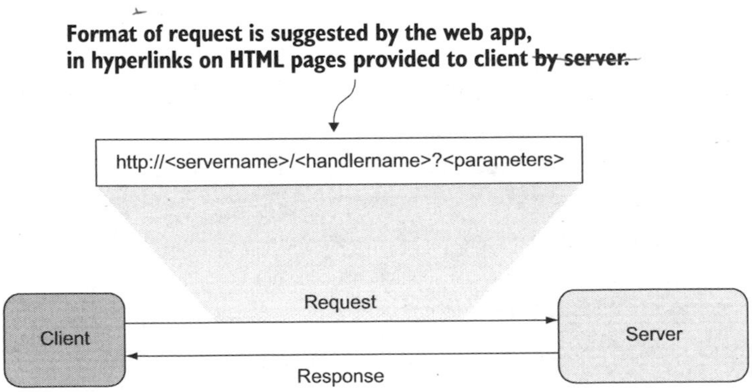


**Figure 2.3 The URL format of an HTTP request**

The format for the request is normally the prerogative of the application itself. For ChitChat, we'll be using the following format: http://<servername>/<handler-name>?<parameters>

The *server name* is the name of the ChitChat server; the *handler name* is the name of the handler that's being called. The handler name is hierarchical: the root of the handler name is the module that's being called, the second part the submodule, and so on, until it hits the leaf, which is the handler of the request within that submodule. If we have a module called `thread` and we need to have a handler to read the thread, the handler name is `/thread/read`.

The *parameters* of the application, which are URL queries, are whatever we need to pass to the handler to process the request. In this example, we need to provide the unique identifier (ID) of the thread to the handler, so the parameters will be `id=123`, where `123` is the unique ID.

Let's recap the request; this is how the URL being sent into the ChitChat server will look (assuming `chitchat` is the server name): http://chitchat/thread/read?id=123.

When the request reaches the server, a *multiplexer* will inspect the URL being requested and redirect the request to the correct handler. Once the request reaches a handler, the handler will retrieve information from the request and process it accordingly (figure 2.4). When the processing is complete, the handler passes the data to the template engine, which will use templates to generate HTML to be returned to the client.

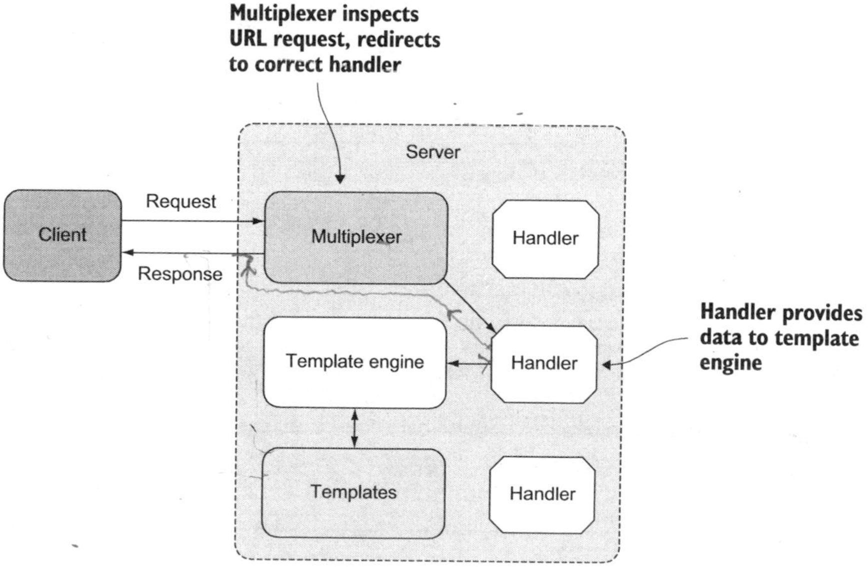


**Figure 2.4 How the server works in a typical web application**

## 2.3 Data model

Most applications need to work on data, in one form or another. In ChitChat, we store the data in a relational database (we use PostgreSQL in this book) and use SQL to interact with the database.

ChitChat's data model is simple and consists of only four data structures, which in turn map to a relational database. The four data structures are

- *User*—Representing the forum user's information
- *Session*—Representing a user's current login session
- *Thread*—Representing a forum thread (a conversation among forum users)
- *Post*—Representing a post (a message added by a forum user) within a thread

We'll have users who can log into the system to create and post to threads. Anonymous users can read but won't be able to create threads or posts. To simplify the application, we'll have only one type of user—there are no moderators to approve new threads or posts (figure 2.5).

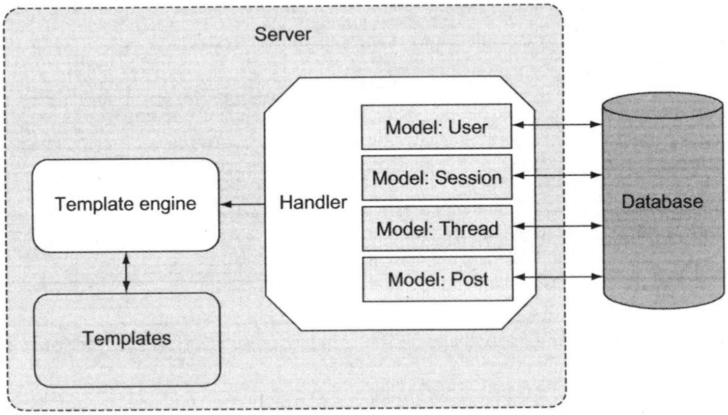


**Figure 2.5 How a web application can access the data store**

With our application design firmly in mind, let's move on to code. A bit of caution before we begin: there will be code in this chapter that might seem puzzling. If you're a new Go programmer, it might be worth your while to refresh your memory going through an introductory Go programming book like *Go in Action* by William Kennedy with Brian Ketelsen and Erik St. Martin (Manning, 2015).

Otherwise, please hang on; this chapter provides an overall picture of how a Go web application will look but is thin on details. The details will come in the later chapters. Where possible, I'll mention which chapters explore those details as we move along.

## 2.4 Receiving and processing requests

Receiving and processing requests is the heart of any web application. Let's recap what you've learned so far:

1. A client sends a request to a URL at the server.
2. The server has a multiplexer, which redirects the request to the correct handler to process the request.
3. The handler processes the request and performs the necessary work.
4. The handler calls the template engine to generate the correct HTML to send back to the client.

Let's begin at the beginning, which is the root URL (/). When you type http://localhost, this is where the application will take you. In the next few subsections, we'll discuss how to handle a request to this URL and respond with dynamically generated HTML.

### 2.4.1 The multiplexer

We start all Go applications with a main source code file, which is the file that contains the `main` function and is the starting point where the compiled binary executes. In ChitChat we call this file main.go.

**Listing 2.1 A simple `main` function in main.go**

```
package main

import (
  "net/http"
)

func main() {

  mux := http.NewServeMux()
  files := http.FileServer(http.Dir("/public"))
  mux.Handle("/static/", http.StripPrefix("/static/", files))

  mux.HandleFunc("/", index)

  server := &http.Server{
    Addr:     "0.0.0.0:8080",
    Handler:  mux,
  }
  server.ListenAndServe()
}
```

In main.go, you first create a *multiplexer*, the piece of code that redirects a request to a handler. The net/http standard library provides a default multiplexer that can be created by calling the `NewServeMux` function:

```
mux := http.NewServeMux()
```

To redirect the root URL to a handler function, you use the HandleFunc function:

```
mux.HandleFunc("/", index)
```

HandleFunc takes the URL as the first parameter, and the name of the handler function as the second parameter, so when a request comes for the root URL (/), it's redirected to a handler function named index. You don't need to provide the parameters to the handler function because all handler functions take ResponseWriter as the first parameter and a pointer to Request as the second parameter.

Notice that I've done some sleight-of-hand when talking about handlers. I started off talking about handlers and then switched to talking about handler functions. This is intentional; handlers and handler functions are *not* the same, though they provide the same results in the end. We'll talk more about them in chapter 3, but for now let's move on.

### 2.4.2 Serving static files

Besides redirecting to the appropriate handler, you can use the multiplexer to serve static files. To do this, you use the FileServer function to create a handler that will serve files from a given directory. Then you pass the handler to the Handle function of the multiplexer. You use the StripPrefix function to remove the given prefix from the request URL's path.

```
files := http.FileServer(http.Dir("/public"))
mux.Handle("/static/", http.StripPrefix("/static/", files))
```

In this code, you're telling the server that for all request URLs starting with /static/, strip off the string /static/ from the URL, and then look for a file with the name starting at the public directory. For example, if there's a request for the file http://localhost/static/css/bootstrap.min.css the server will look for the file

```
<application root>/css/bootstrap.min.css
```

When it's found, the server will serve it as it is, without processing it first.

### 2.4.3 Creating the handler function

In a previous section you used HandleFunc to redirect the request to a handler function. Handler functions are nothing more than Go functions that take a ResponseWriter as the first parameter and a pointer to a Request as the second, shown next.

**Listing 2.2 The index handler function in main.go**

```
func index(w http.ResponseWriter, r *http.Request) {
  files := []string{"templates/layout.html",
                    "templates/navbar.html",
                    "templates/index.html",}
  templates := template.Must(template.ParseFiles(files...))
  threads, err := data.Threads(); if err == nil {
```

```
    templates.ExecuteTemplate(w, "layout", threads)
  }
}
```

Notice that you're using the Template struct from the html/template standard library so you need to add that in the list of imported libraries. The index handler function doesn't do anything except generate the HTML and write it to the ResponseWriter. We'll cover generating HTML in the upcoming section.

We've talked about handler functions that handle requests for the root URL (/), but there are a number of other handler functions. Let's look at the rest of them in the following listing, also in the main.go file.

**Listing 2.3 ChitChat main.go source file**

```
package main

import (
  "net/http"
)

func main() {

  mux := http.NewServeMux()
  files := http.FileServer(http.Dir(config.Static))
  mux.Handle("/static/", http.StripPrefix("/static/", files))

  mux.HandleFunc("/", index)
  mux.HandleFunc("/err", err)

  mux.HandleFunc("/login", login)
  mux.HandleFunc("/logout", logout)
  mux.HandleFunc("/signup", signup)
  mux.HandleFunc("/signup_account", signupAccount)
  mux.HandleFunc("/authenticate", authenticate)

  mux.HandleFunc("/thread/new", newThread)
  mux.HandleFunc("/thread/create", createThread)
  mux.HandleFunc("/thread/post", postThread)
  mux.HandleFunc("/thread/read", readThread)

  server := &http.Server{
    Addr:          "0.0.0.0:8080",
    Handler:       mux,
  }
  server.ListenAndServe()
}
```

You might notice that the various handler functions aren't defined in the same main.go file. Instead, I split the definition of the handler functions in other files (please refer to the code in the GitHub repository). So how do you link these files? Do you write code to include the other files like in PHP, Ruby, or Python? Or do you run a special command to link them during compile time?

In Go, you simply make every file in the same directory part of the `main` package and they'll be included. Alternatively, you can place them in a separate package and import them. We'll use this strategy when connecting with the database, as you'll see later.

### 2.4.4 Access control using cookies

As in many web applications, ChitChat has public pages that are available to anyone browsing to those pages, as well as private pages that require users to log into their account first.

Once the user logs in, you need to indicate in subsequent requests that the user has already logged in. To do this, you write a cookie to the response header, which goes back to the client and is saved at the browser. Let's look at the `authenticate` handler function, which authenticates the user and returns a cookie to the client. The `authenticate` handler function is in the route_auth.go file, shown next.

**Listing 2.4 The `authenticate` handler function in route_auth.go**

```
func authenticate(w http.ResponseWriter, r *http.Request) {
  r.ParseForm()
  user, _ := data.UserByEmail(r.PostFormValue("email"))
  if user.Password == data.Encrypt(r.PostFormValue("password")) {
    session := user.CreateSession()
    cookie := http.Cookie{
      Name:      "_cookie",
      Value:     session.Uuid,
      HttpOnly:  true,
    }
    http.SetCookie(w, &cookie)
    http.Redirect(w, r, "/", 302)
  } else {
    http.Redirect(w, r, "/login", 302)
  }
}
```

Note that in the source code in the previous listing that we haven't yet discussed `data.Encrypt` and `data.UserbyEmail`. In order to keep with the flow, I won't explain these functions in detail; their names make them self-explanatory. For example, `data.UserByEmail` retrieves a `User` struct given the email; `data.Encrypt` encrypts a given string. We'll get into the `data` package later in this chapter. For now let's return to the authentication handler flow.

First, you need to authenticate the user. You must make sure the user exists and the user's encrypted password in the database is the same as the encrypted password posted to the handler. Once the user is authenticated, you create a `Session` struct using `user.CreateSession`, a method on the `User` struct. `Session` looks like this:

```
type Session struct {
  Id        int
  Uuid      string
  Email     string
```

```
  UserId    int
  CreatedAt time.Time
}
```

The `Email` named field stores the email of the user who is logged in; the `UserId` named field contains the ID of the user table row with the user information. The most important information is the `Uuid`, which is a randomly generated unique ID. `Uuid` is the value you want to store at the browser. The session record itself is stored in the database.

Once you have the session record created, you create the `Cookie` struct:

```
cookie := http.Cookie{
  Name:      "_cookie",
  Value:     session.Uuid,
  HttpOnly:  true,
}
```

The name is arbitrary and the value is the unique data that's stored at the browser. You don't set the expiry date so that the cookie becomes a session cookie and it's automatically removed when the browser shuts down. You set `HttpOnly` to only allow HTTP or HTTPS to access the cookie (and not other non-HTTP APIs like JavaScript).

To add the cookie to the response header, use this code:

```
http.SetCookie(writer, &cookie)
```

Now that we have the cookie in the browser, you want to be able to check in the handler function whether or not the user is logged in. You create a utility function called `session` that you'll be able to reuse in other handler functions. The `session` function, shown in the next listing, and all other utility functions are written to the util.go file. Note that even though you placed the function in a separate file, it's still part of the `main` package, so you can use it directly without mentioning the package name, unlike in `data.Encrypt`.

**Listing 2.5 `session` utility function in util.go**

```
func session(w http.ResponseWriter, r *http.Request)(sess data.Session, err
  error){
  cookie, err := r.Cookie("_cookie")
  if err == nil {
    sess = data.Session{Uuid: cookie.Value}
    if ok, _ := sess.Check(); !ok {
      err = errors.New("Invalid session")
    }
  }
  return
}
```

The `session` function retrieves the cookie from the request:

```
cookie, err := r.Cookie("_cookie")
```

If the cookie doesn't exist, then obviously the user hasn't logged in yet. If it exists, the session function performs a second check and checks the database to see if the session's unique ID exists. It does this by using the data.Session function (that you'll create in a bit) to retrieve the session and then calling the Check method on that session:

```
sess = data.Session{Uuid: cookie.Value}
if ok, _ := sess.Check(); !ok {
  err = errors.New("Invalid session")
}
```

Now that you're able to check and differentiate between a user who has logged in and a user who hasn't, let's revisit our index handler function, shown in the following listing, and see how you can use this session function (code shown in bold).

**Listing 2.6 The index handler function**

```
func index(w http.ResponseWriter, r *http.Request) {
  threads, err := data.Threads(); if err == nil {
    _, err := session(w, r)
    public_tmpl_files := []string{"templates/layout.html",
                                  "templates/public.navbar.html",
                                  "templates/index.html"}
    private_tmpl_files := []string{"templates/layout.html",
                                   "templates/private.navbar.html",
                                   "templates/index.html"}
    var templates *template.Template
    if err != nil {
      templates = template.Must(template.Parse-
  Files(private_tmpl_files...))
    } else {
      templates = template.Must(template.ParseFiles(public_tmpl_files...))
    }
    templates.ExecuteTemplate(w, "layout", threads)
  }
}
```

The session function returns a Session struct, which you can use to extract user information, but we aren't interested in that right now, so assign it to the *blank identifier* (_). What we are interested in is err, which you can use to determine whether the user is logged in and specify that the public navigation bar or the private navigation bar should be shown.

That's all there is to it. We're done with the quick overview of processing requests; we'll get on with generating HTML for the client next, and continue where we left off earlier.

## 2.5 Generating HTML responses with templates

The logic in the index handler function was mainly about generating HTML for the client. Let's start by defining a list of template files that you'll be using in a Go slice (I'll show private_tmpl_files here; public_tmpl_files is exactly the same).

```
private_tmpl_files := []string{"templates/layout.html",
                                "templates/private.navbar.html",
                                "templates/index.html"}
```

The three files are HTML files with certain embedded commands, called *actions*, very similar to other template engines like Mustache or CTemplate. Actions are annotations added to the HTML between {{ and }}.

You parse these template files and create a set of templates using the `ParseFiles` function. After parsing, you wrap the `Must` function around the results. This is to catch errors (the `Must` function panics when a `ParseFiles` returns an error).

```
templates := template.Must(template.ParseFiles(private_tmpl_files...))
```

We've talked a lot about these template files; let's look at them now.

Each template file defines a template (templates are described in detail in chapter 5). This is not mandatory—you don't need to define templates for every file—but doing so is useful, as you'll see later. In the layout.html template file, you begin with the `define` action, which indicates that the chunk of text starting with `{{ define "layout" }}` and ending with `{{ end }}` is part of the layout template, as shown next.

**Listing 2.7 layout.html template file**

```
{{ define "layout" }}

<!DOCTYPE html>
<html lang="en">
  <head>
    <meta charset="utf-8">
    <meta http-equiv="X-UA-Compatible" content="IE=9">
    <meta name="viewport" content="width=device-width, initial-scale=1">
    <title>ChitChat</title>
    <link href="/static/css/bootstrap.min.css" rel="stylesheet">
    <link href="/static/css/font-awesome.min.css" rel="stylesheet">
  </head>
  <body>
    {{ template "navbar" . }}

    <div class="container">

      {{ template "content" . }}

    </div> <!-- /container -->

    <script src="/static/js/jquery-2.1.1.min.js"></script>
    <script src="/static/js/bootstrap.min.js"></script>
  </body>
</html>

{{ end }}
```

Within the layout template, we have two other actions, both of which indicate positions where another template can be included. The dot (.) that follows the name of the template to be included is the data passed into the template. For example, listing 2.7 has `{{ template "navbar" . }}`, which indicates that the template named *navbar* should be included at that position, and the data passed into the layout template should be passed on to the navbar template too.

The navbar template in the public.navbar.html template file is shown next. The navbar template doesn't have any actions other than defining the template itself (actions aren't strictly necessary in template files).

**Listing 2.8 navbar.html template file**

```
{{ define "navbar" }}

<div class="navbar navbar-default navbar-static-top" role="navigation">
  <div class="container">
    <div class="navbar-header">
      <button type="button" class="navbar-toggle collapsed"
      ➥ data-toggle="collapse" data-target=".navbar-collapse">
        <span class="sr-only">Toggle navigation</span>
        <span class="icon-bar"></span>
        <span class="icon-bar"></span>
        <span class="icon-bar"></span>
      </button>
      <a class="navbar-brand" href="/">
        <i class="fa fa-comments-o"></i>
        ChitChat
      </a>
    </div>
    <div class="navbar-collapse collapse">
      <ul class="nav navbar-nav">
        <li><a href="/">Home</a></li>
      </ul>
      <ul class="nav navbar-nav navbar-right">
        <li><a href="/login">Login</a></li>
      </ul>
    </div>
  </div>
</div>

{{ end }}
```

Let's look at the content template in last template file, index.html, in the following listing. Notice that the name of the template doesn't necessary need to match the name of the template file, even though that has been the case for the past two files.

**Listing 2.9 index.html template**

```
{{ define "content" }}

<p class="lead">
  <a href="/thread/new">Start a thread</a> or join one below!
</p>
```

```
{{ range . }}
  <div class="panel panel-default">
    <div class="panel-heading">
      <span class="lead"> <i class="fa fa-comment-o"></i> {{ .Topic }}</span>
    </div>
    <div class="panel-body">
      Started by {{ .User.Name }} - {{ .CreatedAtDate }} - {{ .NumReplies }}
 posts.
      <div class="pull right">
        <a href="/thread/read?id={{.Uuid }}">Read more</a>
      </div>
    </div>
  </div>
{{ end }}

{{ end }}
```

The code in index.html is interesting. You'll notice a number of actions within the content template that start with a dot (.), such as `{{ .User.Name }}` and `{{ .CreatedAtDate }}`. To understand where this comes from, we need to go back to the index handler function.

```
threads, err := data.Threads(); if err == nil {
  templates.ExecuteTemplate(writer, "layout", threads)
}
```

Let's start off with this:

```
templates.ExecuteTemplate(writer, "layout", threads)
```

We take the set of templates we parsed earlier, and execute the layout template using `ExecuteTemplate`. Executing the template means we take the content from the template files, combine it with data from another source, and generate the final HTML content, shown in figure 2.6.

Why the layout template and not the other two templates? This should be obvious: the layout template includes the other two templates, so if we execute the layout template, the other two templates will also be executed and the intended HTML will be

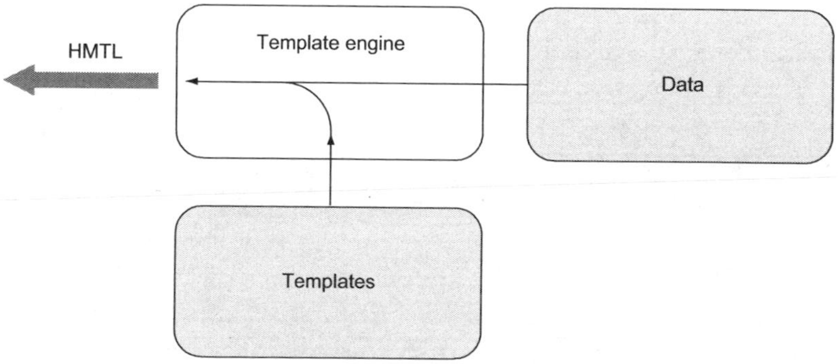


**Figure 2.6 The template engine combines the data and template to produce HTML.**

generated. If we executed either one of the other two templates, we would only get part of the HTML we want.

As you might realize by now, the dot (.) represents the data that's passed into the template (and a bit more, which is explained in the next section). Figure 2.7 shows what we end up with.

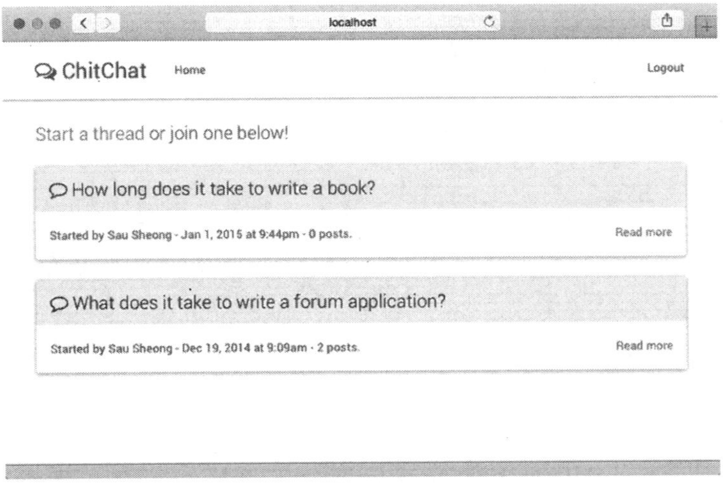


**Figure 2.7 The index page of the example ChitChat web application**

### 2.5.1 Tidying up

HTML generation will be used over and over again, so let's do some tidying up and move those steps into a function called generateHTML, shown next.

**Listing 2.10 The generateHTML function**

```
func generateHTML(w http.ResponseWriter, data interface{}, fn ...string) {
  var files []string
  for _, file := range fn {
    files = append(files, fmt.Sprintf("templates/%s.html", file))
  }
  templates := template.Must(template.ParseFiles(files...))
  templates.ExecuteTemplate(writer, "layout", data)
}
```

generateHTML takes a ResponseWriter, some data, and a list of template files to be parsed. The data parameter is the empty interface type, which means it can take in any type. This might come as a surprise if you're a new Go programmer; isn't Go a statically typed programming language? What's this about accepting any types in as a parameter?

As it turns out, Go has an interesting way of getting around being a statically typed programming language and it provides the flexibility of accepting different types, using interfaces. Interfaces in Go are constructs that are sets of methods and are also types. An empty interface is then an empty set, meaning any type can be an empty interface; you can pass any type into this function as the data.

The last parameter in the function starts with ... (three dots). This indicates that the `generateHTML` function is a *variadic* function, meaning it can take zero or more parameters in that last variadic parameter. This allows you to pass any number of template files to the function. Variadic parameters need to be the last parameter for the variadic function.

Now that we have the `generateHTML` function, let's go back and clean up the `index` handler function. The new `index` handler function, shown here, now looks a lot neater.

**Listing 2.11 The final `index` handler function**

```
func index(writer http.ResponseWriter, request *http.Request) {
  threads, err := data.Threads(); if err == nil {
    _, err := session(writer, request)
    if err != nil {
      generateHTML(writer, threads, "layout", "public.navbar", "index")
    } else {
      generateHTML(writer, threads, "layout", "private.navbar", "index")
    }
  }
}
```

We sort of glossed over the data source and what we used to combine with the templates to get the final HTML. Let's get to that now.

## 2.6 Installing PostgreSQL

In this chapter as well as for any remaining chapters in the book that require access to a relational database, we'll be using PostgreSQL. Before we start any code, I'll run through how to install and start up PostgreSQL, and also create the database that we need for this chapter.

### 2.6.1 Linux/FreeBSD

Prebuilt binaries are available for many variants of Linux and FreeBSD from www.postgresql.org/download. Download any one of them from the site and follow the instructions. For example, you can install Postgres on Ubuntu by executing this command on the console:

```
sudo apt-get install postgresql postgresql-contrib
```

This will install both the `postgres` package and an additional package of utilities, and also start it up.

By default Postgres creates a `postgres` user and that's the only user who can connect to the server. For convenience you can create another Postgres account with your username. First, you need to log in to the Postgres account:

```
sudo su postgres
```

Next, use createuser to create your postgreSQL account:

```
createuser -interactive
```

Finally, use createdb to create your database:

```
createdb  <YOUR ACCOUNT NAME>
```

### 2.6.2 Mac OS X

One of the easiest ways to install PostgreSQL on Mac OS X is to use the Postgres application. Download the zip file and unpack it. Then drag and drop the Postgres.app file into your Applications folder and you're done. You can start the application just like you start any Mac OS X application. The first time you start the application, Postgres will initialize a new database cluster and create a database for you. The command-line tool psql is part of the package, so you'll be able to access the database using psql once you set the correct path. Open up Terminal and add this line your ~/.profile or ~/.bashrc file:

```
export PATH=$PATH:/Applications/Postgres.app/Contents/Versions/9.4/bin
```

### 2.6.3 Windows

Installing PostgreSQL on Windows is fairly straightforward too. There are a number of graphical installers on Windows that do all the heavy lifting for you; you simply need to provide the settings accordingly. A popular installer is one from Enterprise DB at www.enterprisedb.com/products-services-training/pgdownload.

A number of tools, including pgAdmin III, are installed along with the package, which allows you to set up the rest of the configuration.

## 2.7 Interfacing with the database

In the design section earlier in this chapter, we talked about the four data structures used in ChitChat. Although you can place the data structures in the same main file, it's neater if you store all data-related code in another package, aptly named data.

To create a package, create a subdirectory called data and create a file named thread.go to store all thread-related code (you'll create a user.go file to store all user-related code). Then, whenever you need to use the data package (for example, in the handlers that need to access the database), you import the package:

```
import (
  "github.com/sausheong/gwp/Chapter_2_Go_ChitChat/chitchat/data"
)
```

Within the thread.go file, define a Thread struct, shown in the following listing, to contain the data.

**Listing 2.12 The Thread struct**

```
package data

import(
  "time"
)
```

```
type Thread struct {
  Id        int
  Uuid      string
  Topic     string
  UserId    int
  CreatedAt time.Time
}
```

Notice that the package name is no longer main but data (in bold). When you use anything in this package later (functions or structs or anything else), you need to provide the package name along with it. If you want to use the Thread struct you must use data.Thread instead of just Thread alone. This is the data package you used earlier in the chapter. Besides containing the structs and code that interact with the database, the package contains other functions that are closely associated.

The Thread struct should correspond to the DDL (Data Definition Language, the subset of SQL) that's used to create the relational database table called threads. You don't have these tables yet so let's create them first. Of course, before you create the database tables, you should create the database itself. Let's create a database called chitchat. Execute this command at the console:

```
createdb chitchat
```

Once you have the database, you can use setup.sql to create the database tables for ChitChat, shown next.

**Listing 2.13 setup.sql used to create database tables in PostgreSQL**

```
create table users (
  id         serial primary key,
  uuid       varchar(64) not null unique,
  name       varchar(255),
  email      varchar(255) not null unique,
  password   varchar(255) not null,
  created_at timestamp not null
);

create table sessions (
  id         serial primary key,
  uuid       varchar(64) not null unique,
  email      varchar(255),
  user_id    integer references users(id),
  created_at timestamp not null
);

create table threads (
  id         serial primary key,
  uuid       varchar(64) not null unique,
  topic      text,
  user_id    integer references users(id),
  created_at timestamp not null
);

create table posts (
  id         serial primary key,
```

```
  uuid       varchar(64) not null unique,
  body       text,
  user_id    integer references users(id),
  thread_id  integer references threads(id),
  created_at timestamp not null
);
```

To run the script, use the psql tool that's usually installed as part of your PostgreSQL installation (see the previous section). Go to the console and run this command:

```
psql -f setup.sql -d chitchat
```

This command should create the necessary database tables in your database. Once you have your database tables, you must be able to connect to the database and do stuff with the tables. So you'll create a global variable, `Db`, which is a pointer to `sql.DB`, a representation of a pool of database connections. You'll define `Db` in the data.go file, as shown in the following listing. Note that this listing also contains a function named `init` that initializes `Db` upon startup of your web application. You'll use `Db` to execute your queries.

**Listing 2.14 The `Db` global variable and the `init` function in data.go**

```
Var Db *sql.DB

func init() {
  var err error
  Db, err = sql.Open("postgres", "dbname=chitchat sslmode=disable")
  if err != nil {
    log.Fatal(err)
  }
  return
}
```

Now that you have the struct, the tables, and a database connection pool, how do you connect the `Thread` struct with the `threads` table? There's no particular magic to it. As with everything else in ChitChat, you simply create a function every time you want interaction between the struct and the database. To extract all threads in the database for the index handler function, create a `Threads` function in thread.go, as shown next.

**Listing 2.15 The `Threads` function in thread.go**

```
func Threads() (threads []Thread, err error){
  rows, err := Db.Query("SELECT id, uuid, topic, user_id, created_at FROM
   threads ORDER BY created_at DESC")
  if err != nil {
    return
  }
  for rows.Next() {
    th := Thread{}
    if err = rows.Scan(&th.Id, &th.Uuid, &th.Topic, &th.UserId,
    ➥ &th.CreatedAt); err != nil {
```

```
            return
        }
        threads = append(threads, th)
    }
    rows.Close()
    return
}
```

Without getting into the details (which will be covered in chapter 6), these are the general steps:

1. Connect to the database using the database connection pool.
2. Send an SQL query to the database, which will return one or more rows.
3. Create a struct.
4. Iterate through the rows and scan them into the struct.

In the `Threads` function, you return a slice of the `Thread` struct, so you need to create the slice and then continually append to it until you're done with all the rows.

Now that you can get the data from the database into the struct, how do you get the data in the struct to the templates? Let's return to the index.html template file (listing 2.9), where you find this code:

```
{{ range . }}
  <div class="panel panel-default">
    <div class="panel-heading">
      <span class="lead"> <i class="fa fa-comment-o"></i> {{ .Topic }}</span>
    </div>
    <div class="panel-body">
      Started by {{ .User.Name }} - {{ .CreatedAtDate }} - {{ .NumReplies }}
 posts.
      <div class="pull-right">
        <a href="/thread/read?id={{.Uuid }}">Read more</a>
      </div>
    </div>
  </div>
{{ end }}
```

As you'll recall, a dot (.) in an action represents the data that's passed into the template to be combined to generate the final output. The dot here, as part of `{{ range . }}`, is the `threads` variable extracted earlier using the `Threads` function, which is a slice of `Thread` structs.

The `range` action assumes that the data passed in is either a slice or an array of structs. The `range` action allows you to iterate through and access the structs using their named fields. For example, `{{ .Topic }}` allows you to access the `Topic` field of the `Thread` struct. Note that the field must start with a dot and the name of the field is capitalized.

What about `{{ .User.Name }}` and `{{ .CreatedAtDate }}` and `{{ .NumReplies }}`? The `Thread` struct doesn't have these as named fields, so where do they come from? Let's look at `{{ .NumReplies }}`. While using the name of a field after the dot accesses the data in the struct, you can do the same with a special type of function called *methods*.

Methods are functions that are attached to any named types (except a pointer or an interface), including structs. By attaching a function to a pointer to a `Thread` struct, you allow the function to access the thread. The `Thread` struct, also called the *receiver*, is normally changed after calling the method.

The `NumReplies` method is shown here.

**Listing 2.16 `NumReplies` method in thread.go**

```
func (thread *Thread) NumReplies() (count int) {
  rows, err := Db.Query("SELECT count(*) FROM posts where thread_id = $1",
  thread.Id)
  if err != nil {
    return
  }
  for rows.Next() {
    if err = rows.Scan(&count); err != nil {
      return
    }
  }
  rows.Close()
  return
}
```

The `NumReplies` method opens a connection to the database, gets the count of threads using an SQL query, and scans it into the `count` parameter passed into the method. The `NumReplies` method returns this count, which is then used to replace `.NumReplies` in the HTML, by the template engine, shown in figure 2.8.

By providing a combination of functions and methods on the data structs (`User`, `Session`, `Thread`, and `Post`), you create a data layer that shields you from directly accessing the database in the handler functions. Although there are plenty of libraries that provide this functionality, it's good to understand that the underlying basis of accessing the database is quite easy, with no magic involved. Just simple, straightforward code.

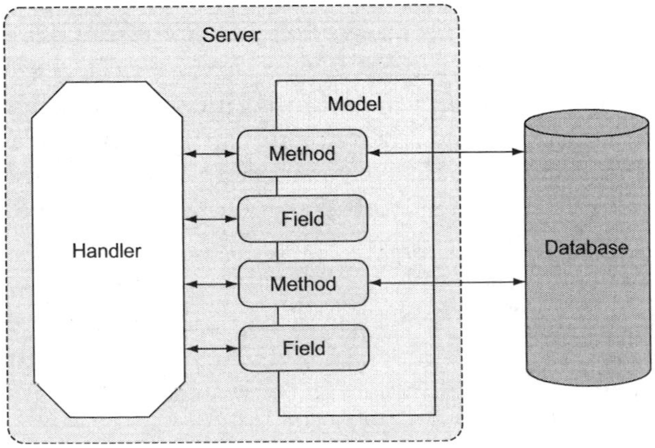


**Figure 2.8 Connecting the struct model with the database and the handler**

## 2.8 Starting the server

Let's round out this chapter by showing code that starts up the server and attaches the multiplexer to the server. This is part of the `main` function, so it will be in main.go.

```
server := &http.Server{
  Addr:      "0.0.0.0:8080",
  Handler:   mux,
}
server.ListenAndServe()
```

The code is simple; you create a `Server` struct and call the `ListenAndServe` function on it and you get your server.

Now let's get it up and running. Compile this from the console:

```
go build
```

This command will create a binary executable file named chitchat in the same directory (and also in in your $GOPATH/bin directory). This is our ChitChat server. Let's start the server:

```
./chitchat
```

This command will start the server. Assuming that you've created the necessary database tables, go to http://localhost:8080 and registered for an account; then log in and start creating your own forum threads.

## 2.9 Wrapping up

We went through a 20,000-foot overview of the various building blocks of a Go web application. Figure 2.9 shows a final recap of the entire flow. As illustrated,

1 The client sends a request to the server.
2 This is received by the multiplexer, which redirects it to the correct handler.

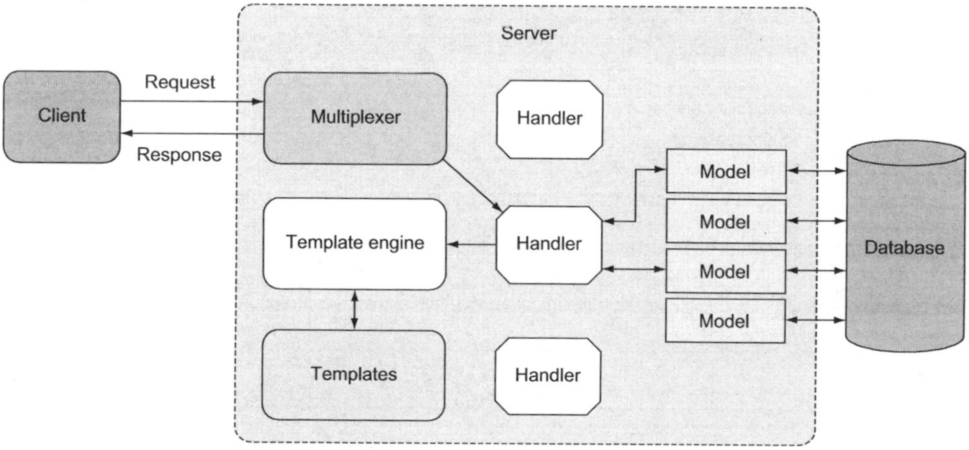


**Figure 2.9 The web application big picture**

3 The handler processes the request.
4 When data is needed, it will use one or more data structs that model the data in the database.
5 The model connects with the database, triggered by functions or methods on the data struct.
6 When processing is complete, the handler triggers the template engine, sometimes sending in data from the model.
7 The template engine parses template files to create templates, which in turn are combined with data to produce HTML.
8 The generated HTML is sent back to the client as part of the response.

And we're done! In the next few chapters, we will dive in deeper into this flow and get into the details of each component.

## 2.10 Summary

- Receiving and processing requests are the heart of any web application.
- The multiplexer redirects HTTP requests to the correct handler for processing, including static files.
- Handler functions are nothing more than Go functions that take a `ResponseWriter` as the first parameter and a pointer to a `Request` as the second.
- Cookies can be used as a mechanism for access control.
- HTML responses can be generated by parsing template files together with data to provide the final HTML data that is returned to the calling browser.
- Persisting data to a relational database can be done through direct SQL using the `sql` package.

# Part 2

# *Basic web applications*

Web applications follow a simple request-response model of programming. Every request from the client gets a response from the server. Every web application has a few basic components—the router that routes requests to different handlers, the handlers that process the requests, and the template engine that translates combines static content with dynamic data to produce the data that is sent back to the client.

In chapters 3-6, you will learn how to use Go to accept HTTP requests using a router, process them using handlers, and return responses with the template engine. In addition, most web applications store data in one way or another, so you will also learn how you can use Go to persist data.

# 3 Handling requests

***This chapter covers***

- Using the Go net/http library
- Serving out HTTP using the Go net/http library
- Understanding handlers and handler functions
- Working with multiplexers

Chapter 2 showed the steps for creating a simple internet forum web application. The chapter mapped out the various parts of a Go web application, and you saw the big picture of how a Go web application is structured. But there's little depth in each of those parts. In the next few chapters, we'll delve into the details of each of these parts and explore in depth how they can be put together.

In this and the next chapter, we'll focus on the brains of the web application: the handlers that receive and process requests from the client. In this chapter, you'll learn how to create a web server with Go, and then we'll move on to handling requests from the client.

## 3.1 The Go net/http library

Although using a mature and sophisticated web application framework to write web applications is usually easy and fast, the same frameworks often impose their own conventions and patterns. Many assume that these conventions and patterns are best practices, but best practices have a way of growing into *cargo cult programming* when they aren't understood properly. Programmers following these conventions without understanding why they're used often follow them blindly and reuse them when it's unnecessary or even harmful.

**Cargo cult programming**

During World War II, the Allied forces set up air bases on islands in the Pacific to help with the war efforts. Large amounts of supplies and military equipment were air-dropped to troops and islanders supporting the troops, drastically changing their lives. For the first time, the islanders saw manufactured clothes, canned food, and other goods. When the war ended, the bases were abandoned and the cargo stopped arriving. So the islanders did a very natural thing—they dressed themselves up as air traffic controllers, soldiers, and sailors, waved landing signals using sticks on the airfields, and performed parade ground drills in an attempt to get cargo to continue falling by parachute from planes.

These cargo cultists gave their names to the practice of cargo cult programming. While not exactly waving landing signals, cargo cult programmers copy and paste code they either inherit or find on the internet (often, StackOverflow) without understanding why it works, only that it works. As a result, they're often unable to extend or make changes to code. Similarly, cargo cult programmers often use web frameworks without understanding why the framework uses certain patterns or conventions, as well as the trade-offs that are being made.

The reason data is persisted as cookies in the client and sessions in the server is because HTTP is a connection-less protocol, and each call to the server has no stored knowledge of the previous call. Without this understanding, using cookies and sessions seems a convoluted way of persisting information between connections. Using a framework to get around this complexity is smart because a framework normally hides the complexity and presents a uniform interface for persistence between connections. As a result, a new programmer would simply assume all it takes to persist data between connections is to use this interface. This uniform interface is based on the conventions of a specific framework, though, and such practices might or might not be consistent across all frameworks. What's worse, the same interface name might be used in different frameworks, with different implementations and different names, adding to the confusion. This means that the web application that's developed is now tied to the framework; moving it to another framework or even extending the application or adding new features requires deep knowledge of the framework (or customized versions of the framework).

This book isn't about rejecting frameworks or conventions or patterns. A good web application framework is often the best way to build scalable and robust web applications quickly. But it's important to understand the underlying concepts infrastructure that these frameworks are built on. In the case of the Go programming language, using the standard libraries typically means using the net/http and html/template libraries. With proper understanding, it becomes easier to see why certain conventions and patterns are what they are. This helps us to avoid pitfalls, gives clarity, and stops us from following patterns blindly.

In this and the next chapter, we'll be focusing on net/http; chapter 5 covers html/template.

The net/http library is divided into two parts, with various structs and functions supporting either one or both (see figure 3.1):

- *Client*—Client, Response, Header, Request, Cookie
- *Server*—Server, ServeMux, Handler/HandleFunc, ResponseWriter, Header, Request, Cookie

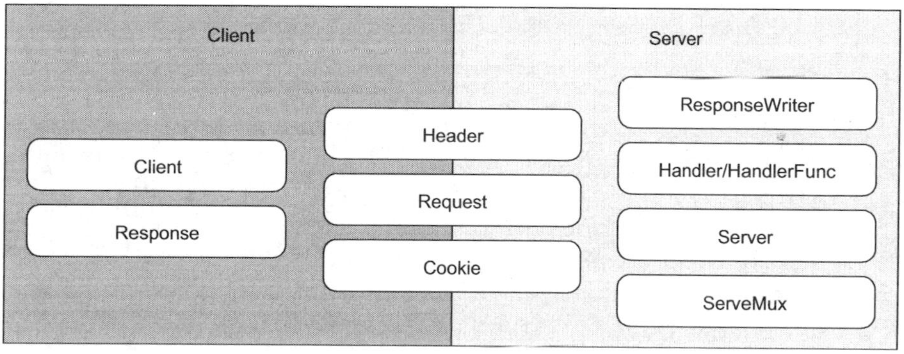


**Figure 3.1 Chaining handlers**

We'll start by using the net/http library as the server, and in this chapter we'll talk about how Go handles requests from the client. In the next chapter, we'll continue with the net/http library but focus on using it to process the request.

In this book, we'll focus on using the net/http library's server capabilities and not its client capabilities.

## 3.2 Serving Go

The net/http library provides capabilities for starting up an HTTP server that handles requests and sends responses to those requests (see figure 3.2). It also provides an interface for a multiplexer and a default multiplexer.

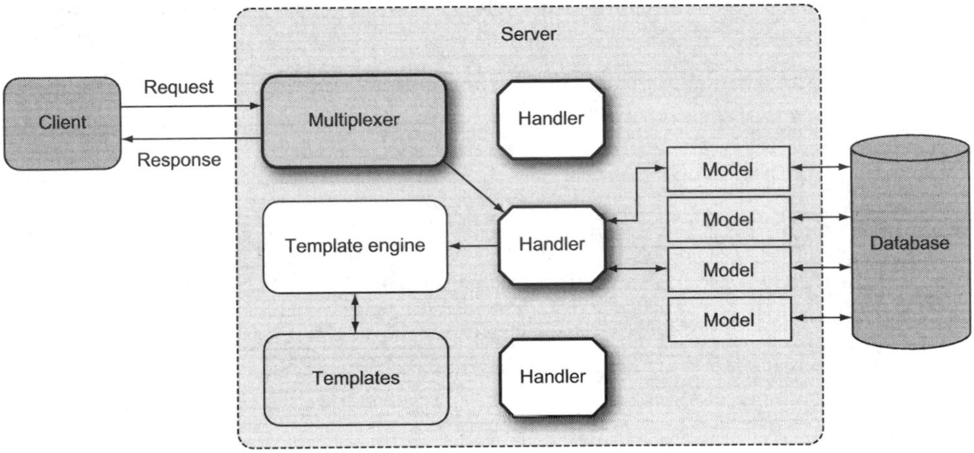


**Figure 3.2 Handling requests with the Go server**

### 3.2.1 The Go web server

Unlike most standard libraries in other programming languages, Go provides a set of libraries to create a web server. Creating a server is trivial and can be done with a call to `ListenAndServe`, with the network address as the first parameter and the handler that takes care of the requests the second parameter, as shown in the following listing. If the network address is an empty string, the default is all network interfaces at port 80. If the handler parameter is `nil`, the default multiplexer, `DefaultServeMux`, is used.

**Listing 3.1 The simplest web server**

```
package main

import (
	"net/http"
)

func main() {
	http.ListenAndServe("", nil)
}
```

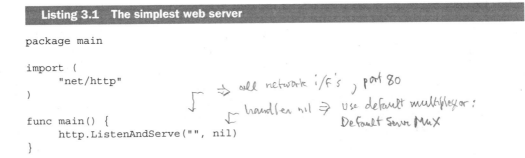

This simple server doesn't allow much configuration, but Go also provides a `Server` struct that's essentially a server configuration.

**Listing 3.2 Web server with additional configuration**

```
package main

import (
    "net/http"
)

func main() {
    server := http.Server{
        Addr:    "127.0.0.1:8080",
        Handler: nil,
    }
    server.ListenAndServe()
}
```

The following listing does almost the same thing as the previous code but now allows more configurations. Configurations include setting the timeout for reading the request and writing the response and setting an error logger for the `Server` struct.

**Listing 3.3 The `Server` struct configuration**

```
type Server struct {
    Addr           string
    Handler        Handler
    ReadTimeout    time.Duration
    WriteTimeout   time.Duration
    MaxHeaderBytes int
    TLSConfig      *tls.Config
    TLSNextProto   map[string]func(*Server, *tls.Conn, Handler)
    ConnState      func(net.Conn, ConnState)
    ErrorLog       *log.Logger
}
```

### 3.2.2 Serving through HTTPS

Most major websites use HTTPS to encrypt and protect the communications between the client and the server when confidential information like passwords and credit card information is shared. In some cases, this protection is mandated. If you accept credit card payments, you need to be compliant with the Payment Card Industry (PCI) Data Security Standard, and to be compliant you need to encrypt the communications between the client and the server. Some sites like Gmail and Facebook use HTTPS throughout their entire site. If you're planning to run a site that requires the user to log in, you'll need to use HTTPS.

HTTPS is nothing more than layering HTTP on top of SSL (actually, Transport Security Layer [TLS]). To serve our simple web application through HTTPS, we'll use the `ListenAndServeTLS` function, shown in listing 3.4.

> **SSL, TLS, and HTTPS**
>
> SSL (Secure Socket Layer) is a protocol that provides data encryption and authentication between two parties, usually a client and a server, using Public Key Infrastructure (PKI). SSL was originally developed by Netscape and was later taken over by the Internet Engineering Task Force (IETF), which renamed it TLS. HTTPS, or HTTP over SSL, is essentially just that—HTTP layered over an SSL/TLS connection.
>
> An SSL/TLS certificate (I'll use the term SSL certificate as it's more widely known) is used to provide data encryption and authentication. An SSL certificate is an X.509-formatted piece of data that contains some information, as well as a public key, stored at a web server. SSL certificates are usually signed by a certificate authority (CA), which assures the authenticity of the certificate. When the client makes a request to the server, it returns with the certificate. If the client is satisfied that the certificate is authentic, it will generate a random key and use the certificate (or more specifically the public key in the certificate) to encrypt it. This symmetric key is the actual key used to encrypt the data between the client and the server.

**Listing 3.4 Serving through HTTPS**

```
package main

import (
    "net/http"
)

func main() {
    server := http.Server{
        Addr:     "127.0.0.1:8080",
        Handler: nil,
    }
    server.ListenAndServeTLS("cert.pem", "key.pem")
}
```

In the previous listing, the cert.pem file is the *SSL certificate* whereas key.pem is the *private key* for the server. In a production scenario you'll need to get the SSL certificate from a CA like VeriSign, Thawte, or Comodo SSL. But if you need a certificate and private key only to try things out, you can generate your own certificates. There are many ways of generating them, including using Go standard libraries, mostly under the crypto library group.

Although you won't use them (the certificate and private key created here) in a production server, it's useful to understand how an SSL certificate and private key can be generated for development and testing purposes. This listing shows how we can do this.

**Listing 3.5 Generating your own SSL certificate and server private key**

```
package main

import (
    "crypto/rand"
    "crypto/rsa"
    "crypto/x509"
    "crypto/x509/pkix"
    "encoding/pem"
    "math/big"
    "net"
    "os"
    "time"
)

func main() {
    max := new(big.Int).Lsh(big.NewInt(1), 128)
    serialNumber, _ := rand.Int(rand.Reader, max)
    subject := pkix.Name{
        Organization:       []string{"Manning Publications Co."},
        OrganizationalUnit: []string{"Books"},
        CommonName:         "Go Web Programming",
    }

    template := x509.Certificate{
        SerialNumber: serialNumber,
        Subject:      subject,
        NotBefore:    time.Now(),
        NotAfter:     time.Now().Add(365 * 24 * time.Hour),
        KeyUsage:     x509.KeyUsageKeyEncipherment | x509.KeyUsageDigitalSig-
  nature,
        ExtKeyUsage:  []x509.ExtKeyUsage{x509.ExtKeyUsageServerAuth},
        IPAddresses:  []net.IP{net.ParseIP("127.0.0.1")},
    }

    pk, _ := rsa.GenerateKey(rand.Reader, 2048)

    derBytes, _ := x509.CreateCertificate(rand.Reader, &template,
    ➥ &template, &pk.PublicKey, pk)
    certOut, _ := os.Create("cert.pem")
    pem.Encode(certOut, &pem.Block{Type: "CERTIFICATE", Bytes: derBytes})
    certOut.Close()

    keyOut, _ := os.Create("key.pem")
    pem.Encode(keyOut, &pem.Block{Type: "RSA PRIVATE KEY", Bytes:
    ➥ x509.MarshalPKCS1PrivateKey(pk)})
    keyOut.Close()
}
```

Generating the SSL certificate and private key is relatively easy. An SSL certificate is essentially an X.509 certificate with the extended key usage set to server authentication, so we'll be using the crypto/x509 library to create the certificate. The private key is required to create the certificate, so we simply take the private key we created for the certificate and save it into a file for the server private key file.

Let's go through the code. First, we need to have a `Certificate` struct, which allows us to set the configuration for our certificate:

```
template := x509.Certificate{
  SerialNumber: serialNumber,
  Subject: subject,
  NotBefore: time.Now(),
  NotAfter:  time.Now().Add(365*24*time.Hour),
  KeyUsage: x509.KeyUsageKeyEncipherment | x509.KeyUsageDigitalSignature,
  ExtKeyUsage: []x509.ExtKeyUsage{x509.ExtKeyUsageServerAuth},
  IPAddresses: []net.IP{net.ParseIP("127.0.0.1")},
}
```

We need a certificate serial number, which is a unique number issued by the CA. For our purposes, it's good enough to use a very large integer that's randomly generated. Next, we create the distinguished name and set it up as the subject for the certificate, and we also set up the validity period to last for one year from the day the certificate is created. The KeyUsage and ExtKeyUsage fields are used to indicate that this X.509 certificate is used for server authentication. Finally, we set up the certificate to run from the IP 127.0.0.1 only.

### SSL certificates

X.509 is an ITU-T (International Telecommunication Union Telecommunication Standardization Sector) standard for a Public Key Infrastructure (PKI). X.509 includes standard formats for public key certificates.

An X.509 certificate (also colloquially called an SSL certificate) is a digital document expressed in ASN.1 (Abstract Syntax Notation One) that has been encoded. ASN.1 is a standard and notation that describes rules and structures for representing data in telecommunications and computer networking.

X.509 certificates can be encoded in various formats, including BER (Basic Encoding Rules). The BER format specifies a self-describing and self-delimiting format for encoding ASN.1 data structures. DER is a subset of BER, providing for exactly one way to encode an ASN.1 value, and is widely used in cryptography, especially X.509 certificates.

In SSL, the certificates can be saved in files of different formats. One of them is PEM (Privacy Enhanced Email, which doesn't have much relevance here except as the name of the file format used), which is a Base64-encoded DER X.509 certificate enclosed between "—BEGIN CERTIFICATE—" and "—END CERTIFICATE—".

Next, we need to generate a private key. We use the crypto/rsa library and call the `GenerateKey` function to create an RSA private key:

```
pk, _ := rsa.GenerateKey(rand.Reader, 2048)
```

The RSA private key struct that's created has a public key that we can access, useful when we use the `x509.CreateCertificate` function to create our SSL certificate:

```
derBytes, _ := x509.CreateCertificate(rand.Reader, &template, &template,
➥ &pk.PublicKey, pk)
```

The `CreateCertificate` function takes a number of parameters, including the `Certificate` struct and the public and private keys, to create a slice of DER-formatted bytes. The rest is relatively straightforward: we use the encoding/pem library to encode the certificate into the cert.pem file:

```
certOut, _ := os.Create("cert.pem")
pem.Encode(certOut, &pem.Block{Type: "CERTIFICATE", Bytes: derBytes})
certOut.Close()
```

We also PEM encode and save the key we generated earlier into the key.pem file:

```
keyOut, _ := os.Create("key.pem")
pem.Encode(keyOut, &pem.Block{Type: "RSA PRIVATE KEY", Bytes:
➥ x509.MarshalPKCS1PrivateKey(pk)})
keyOut.Close()
```

Note that if the certificate is signed by a CA, the certificate file should be the concatenation of the server's certificate followed by the CA's certificate.

## 3.3 Handlers and handler functions

Starting up a server is easy, but it doesn't do anything. If you access the server, you'll get only a 404 HTTP response code. The default multiplexer that will be used if the handler parameter is nil can't find any handlers (because we haven't written any) and will respond with the 404. To do any work, we need to have handlers.

### 3.3.1 Handling requests

So what exactly is a handler? We talked briefly about handlers and handler functions in chapters 1 and 2, so let's elaborate here. In Go, a handler is an interface that has a method named `ServeHTTP` with two parameters: an `HTTPResponseWriter` interface and a pointer to a `Request` struct. In other words, anything that has a method called `ServeHTTP` with this method signature is a handler:

```
ServeHTTP(http.ResponseWriter, *http.Request)
```

Let me digress and answer a question that might have occurred to you as you're reading this chapter. If the second parameter for `ListenAndServe` is a handler, then why is the default value a multiplexer, `DefaultServeMux`?

That's because `ServeMux` (which is what `DefaultServeMux` is an instance of) has a method named `ServeHTTP` with the same signature! In other words, a `ServeMux` is also an instance of the `Handler` struct. `DefaultServeMux` is an instance of `ServeMux`, so it is also an instance of the `Handler` struct. It's a special type of handler, though, because the only thing it does is redirect your requests to different handlers depending on the URL that's provided. If we use a handler instead of the default multiplexer, we'll be able to respond, as shown in this listing.

**Listing 3.6 Handling requests**

```
package main

import (
    "fmt"
    "net/http"
)

type MyHandler struct{}

func (h *MyHandler) ServeHTTP(w http.ResponseWriter, r *http.Request) {
    fmt.Fprintf(w, "Hello World!")
}

func main() {
    handler := MyHandler{}
    server := http.Server{
        Addr:     "127.0.0.1:8080",
        Handler: &handler,
    }
    server.ListenAndServe()
}
```

Now let's start the server (if you're a bit hazy on how to do this, please flip to section 2.7). If you go to http://localhost:8080 in your browser you'll see Hello World!

Here's the tricky bit: if you go to http://localhost:8080/anything/at/all you'll still get the same response! Why this is so should be quite obvious. We just created a handler and attached it to our server, so we're no longer using any multiplexers. This means there's no longer any URL matching to route the request to a particular handler, so all requests going into the server will go to this handler.

In our handler, the `ServeHTTP` method does all the processing. It doesn't do anything except return Hello World!, so that's what it does for all requests into the server.

This is the reason why we'd normally use a multiplexer. Most of the time we want the server to respond to more than one request, depending on the request URL. Naturally if you're writing a very specialized server for a very specialized purpose, simply creating one handler will do the job marvelously.

### 3.3.2 More handlers

Most of the time, we don't want to have a single handler to handle all the requests like in listing 3.6; instead we want to use different handlers instead for different URLs. To do this, we don't specify the Handler field in the `Server` struct (which means it will use the `DefaultServeMux` as the handler); we use the `http.Handle` function to attach a handler to `DefaultServeMux`. Notice that some of the functions like `Handle` are functions for the `http` package and also methods for `ServeMux`. These functions are actually convenience functions; calling them simply calls `DefaultServeMux`'s corresponding functions. If you call `http.Handle` you're actually calling `DefaultServeMux`'s `Handle` method.

In the following listing, we create two handlers and then attach the handler to the respective URL. If you now go to http://localhost:8080/hello you'll get Hello! whereas if you go to http://localhost:8080/world, you'll get World!.

**Listing 3.7 Handling requests with multiple handlers**

```
package main

import (
    "fmt"
    "net/http"
)

type HelloHandler struct{}

func (h *HelloHandler) ServeHTTP (w http.ResponseWriter, r *http.Request) {
    fmt.Fprintf(w, "Hello!")
}

type WorldHandler struct{}

func (h *WorldHandler) ServeHTTP (w http.ResponseWriter, r *http.Request) {
    fmt.Fprintf(w, "World!")
}

func main() {
    hello := HelloHandler{}
    world := WorldHandler{}

    server := http.Server{
        Addr: "127.0.0.1:8080",
    }

    http.Handle("/hello", &hello)
    http.Handle("/world", &world)

    server.ListenAndServe()
}
```

### 3.3.3 Handler functions

We talked about handlers, but what are handler functions? Handler functions are functions that behave like handlers. Handler functions have the same signature as the `ServeHTTP` method; that is, they accept a `ResponseWriter` and a pointer to a `Request`. The following listing shows how this works with our server.

**Listing 3.8 Handling requests with handler functions**

```
package main

import (
    "fmt"
    "net/http"
)

func hello(w http.ResponseWriter, r *http.Request) {
    fmt.Fprintf(w, "Hello!")
}

func world(w http.ResponseWriter, r *http.Request) {
    fmt.Fprintf(w, "World!")
}

func main() {
    server := http.Server{
        Addr: "127.0.0.1:8080",
    }
    http.HandleFunc("/hello", hello)
    http.HandleFunc("/world", world)

    server.ListenAndServe()
}
```

How does this work? Go has a function type named `HandlerFunc`, which will adapt a function `f` with the appropriate signature into a `Handler` with a method `f`. For example, take the `hello` function:

```
func hello(w http.ResponseWriter, r *http.Request) {
    fmt.Fprintf(w, "Hello!")
}
```

If we do this:

```
helloHandler := HandlerFunc(hello)
```

then `helloHandler` becomes a `Handler`. Confused? Let's go back to our earlier server, which accepts handlers.

```
type MyHandler struct{}

func (h *MyHandler) ServeHTTP (w http.ResponseWriter, r *http.Request) {
    fmt.Fprintf(w, "Hello World!")
}

func main() {
    handler := MyHandler{}
    server := http.Server{
        Addr:     "127.0.0.1:8080",
        Handler: &handler,
    }
    server.ListenAndServe()
}
```

The line that registers the `hello` function to the URL */hello* is

```
http.Handle("/hello", &hello)
```

This shows us how the `Handle` function registers a pointer to a `Handler` to a URL. To simplify things, the `HandleFunc` function converts the `hello` function into a `Handler` and registers it to `DefaultServeMux`. In other words, handler functions are merely convenient ways of creating handlers. The following listing shows the code for the `http.HandleFunc` function.

**Listing 3.9 `http.HandleFunc` source code**

```
func HandleFunc(pattern string, handler func(ResponseWriter, *Request)) {
    DefaultServeMux.HandleFunc(pattern, handler)
}
```

Here's the source code for the `HandleFunc` function:

```
func (mux *ServeMux) HandleFunc(pattern string, handler func(ResponseWriter,
    *Request)) {
    mux.Handle(pattern, HandlerFunc(handler))
}
```

Notice that `handler`, a function, is converted into an actual handler by `HandlerFunc`.

Because using handler functions is cleaner and it does the job just as well, why use handlers at all? It all boils down to design. If you have an existing interface or if you want a type that can also be used as a handler, simply add a `ServeHTTP` method to that interface and you'll get a handler that you can assign to a URL. It can also allow you to build web applications that are more modular.

### 3.3.4 Chaining handlers and handler functions

Although Go isn't considered a functional language, it has some features that are common to functional languages, including function types, anonymous functions, and closures. As you noticed earlier, we passed a function into another function and we referred to a named function by its identifier. This means we can pass a function f1 into another function f2 for f2 to do its processing, and then call f1 (see figure 3.3).

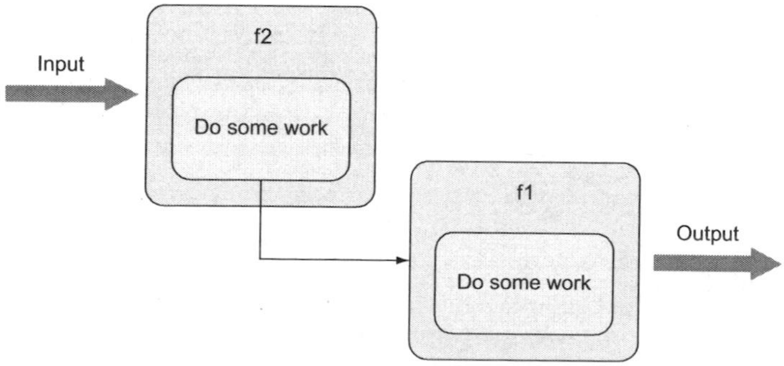


**Figure 3.3 Chaining handlers**

Let's work through an example. Say every time we call a handler we want to log it down somewhere that it was called. We can always add this code into the handler, or we can refactor a utility function (as we did in chapter 2) that can be called by every function. Doing this can be intrusive, though; we usually want our handler to contain logic for processing the request only.

Logging, along with a number of similar functions like security and error handling, is what's commonly known as a *cross-cutting concern*. These functions are common and we want to avoid adding them everywhere, which causes code duplication and dependencies. A common way of cleanly separating cross-cutting concerns away from your other logic is *chaining*. This listing shows how we can chain handlers.

**Listing 3.10 Chaining two handler functions**

```
package main

import (
    "fmt"
    "net/http"
    "reflect"
    "runtime"
)

func hello(w http.ResponseWriter, r *http.Request) {
    fmt.Fprintf(w, "Hello!")
}

func log(h http.HandlerFunc) http.HandlerFunc {
    return func(w http.ResponseWriter, r *http.Request) {
        name := runtime.FuncForPC(reflect.ValueOf(h).Pointer()).Name()
        fmt.Println("Handler function called - " + name)
        h(w, r)
    }
}

func main() {
    server := http.Server{
        Addr: "127.0.0.1:8080",
    }
    http.HandleFunc("/hello", log(hello))
    server.ListenAndServe()
}
```

We have our usual `hello` handler function. We also have a `log` function, which takes in a `HandlerFunc` and returns a `HandlerFunc`. Remember that `hello` is a `HandlerFunc`, so this sends the `hello` function into the `log` function; in other words it chains the `log` and the `hello` functions.

```
log(hello)
```

The `log` function returns an anonymous function that takes a `ResponseWriter` and a pointer to a `Request`, which means that the anonymous function is a `HandlerFunc`. Inside the anonymous function, we print out the name of the `HandlerFunc` (in this case it's `main.hello`), and then call it. As a result, we'll get hello! in the browser and a printed statement on the console that says this:

```
Handler function called - main.hello
```

Naturally if we can chain together two handler functions, we can chain more. The same principle allows us to stack handlers to perform multiple actions, like Lego bricks. This is sometimes called *pipeline processing* (see figure 3.4).

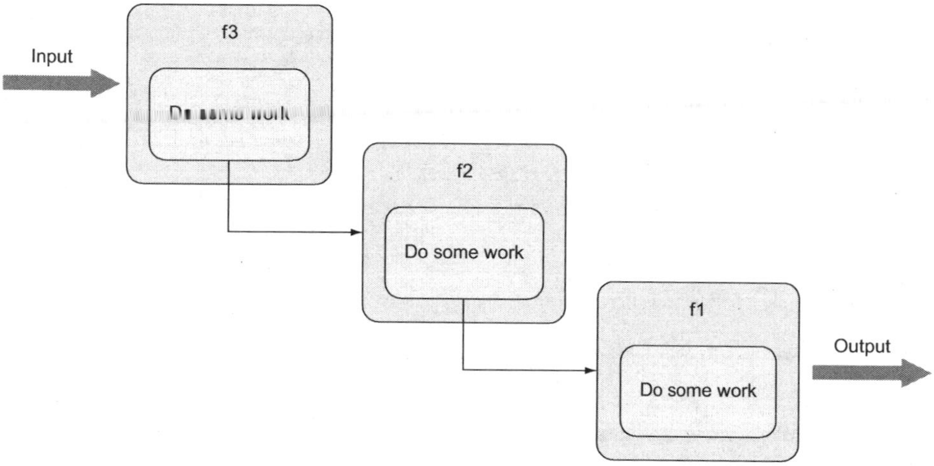


**Figure 3.4 Chaining more handlers**

Say we have another function named `protect`, which checks for the user's authorization before executing the handler:

```
func protect(h http.HandlerFunc) http.HandlerFunc {
    return func(w http.ResponseWriter, r *http.Request) {
        . . .
        h(w, r)
    }
}
```

**Code, omitted for brevity, to make sure the user is authorized.**

Then to use `protect`, we simply chain them together:

```
http.HandleFunc("/hello", protect(log(hello)))
```

You might have noticed that while I mentioned earlier that we're chaining handlers, the code in listing 3.10 actually shows chaining handler functions. The mechanisms for both chaining handlers and handler functions are very similar, as shown next.

**Listing 3.11 Chaining handlers**

```
package main

import (
    "fmt"
```

chain handlers

satisfies handler i/f

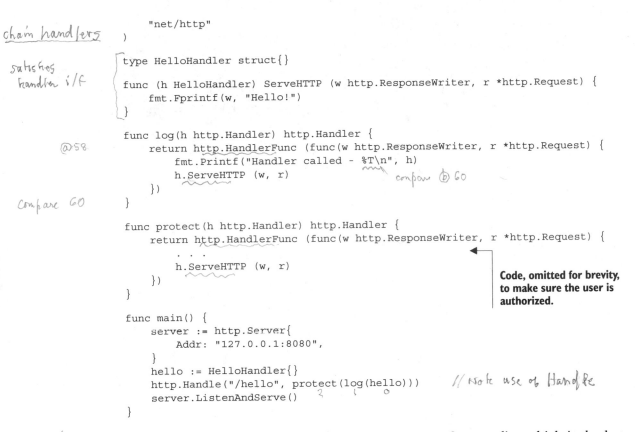

@58

compare 60

```
    "net/http"
)

type HelloHandler struct{}

func (h HelloHandler) ServeHTTP (w http.ResponseWriter, r *http.Request) {
    fmt.Fprintf(w, "Hello!")
}

func log(h http.Handler) http.Handler {
    return http.HandlerFunc (func(w http.ResponseWriter, r *http.Request) {
        fmt.Printf("Handler called - %T\n", h)
        h.ServeHTTP (w, r)
    })
}

func protect(h http.Handler) http.Handler {
    return http.HandlerFunc (func(w http.ResponseWriter, r *http.Request) {
        . . .
        h.ServeHTTP (w, r)
    })
}

func main() {
    server := http.Server{
        Addr: "127.0.0.1:8080",
    }
    hello := HelloHandler{}
    http.Handle("/hello", protect(log(hello)))
    server.ListenAndServe()
}
```

**Code, omitted for brevity, to make sure the user is authorized.**

compare (b) 60

// Note use of Handle

Let's see what's different. We have our HelloHandler from earlier, which is the last handler in the chain, as before. The log function, instead of taking in a HandlerFunc and returning a HandlerFunc, takes in a Handler and returns a Handler:

```
func log(h http.Handler) http.Handler {
    return http.HandlerFunc (func(w http.ResponseWriter, r *http.Request) {
        fmt.Printf("Handler called - %T\n", h)
        h.ServeHTTP (w, r)
    })
}
```

Instead of returning an anonymous function, now we adapt that anonymous function using HandlerFunc, which, if you remember from earlier, returns a Handler. Also, instead of executing the handler function, we now take the handler and call its ServeHTTP function. Everything else remains mostly the same, except that instead of registering a handler function, we register the handler:

```
hello := HelloHandler{}
http.Handle("/hello", protect(log(hello)))
```

Chaining handlers or handler functions is a common idiom you'll find in many web application frameworks.

### 3.3.5 ServeMux and DefaultServeMux

We discussed `ServeMux` and `DefaultServeMux` earlier in this chapter and in the previous chapter. `ServeMux` is an HTTP request multiplexer. It accepts an HTTP request and redirects it to the correct handler according to the URL in the request, illustrated in figure 3.5.

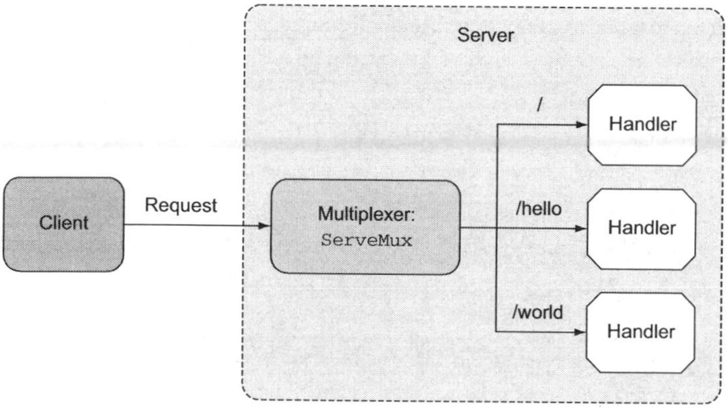


**Figure 3.5 Multiplexing requests to handlers**

`ServeMux` is a struct with a map of entries that map a URL to a handler. It's also a handler because it has a `ServeHTTP` method. `ServeMux`'s `ServeHTTP` method finds the URL most closely matching the requested one and calls the corresponding handler's `ServeHTTP` (see figure 3.6).

So what is `DefaultServeMux`? `ServeMux` isn't an interface, so `DefaultServeMux` isn't an implementation of `ServeMux`. `DefaultServeMux` is an instance of `ServeMux` that's

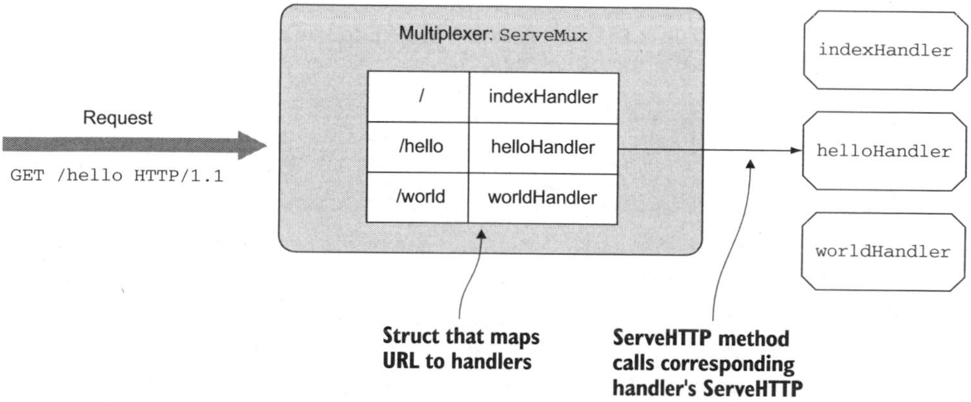


**Figure 3.6 Inside a multiplexer**

publicly available to the application that imports the net/http library. It's also the instance of `ServeMux` that's used when no handler is provided to the `Server` struct.

Stepping back a bit, you'll also come to a realization that `ServeMux` is also another take on chaining handlers, because `ServeMux` is a handler.

In these examples the requested URL /hello matches nicely with the registered URL in the multiplexer. What happens if we call the URL /random? Or if we call the URL /hello/there?

It all depends on how we register the URLs. If we register the root URL (/) as in figure 3.6, any URLs that don't match will fall through the hierarchy and land on the root URL. If we now call /random and don't have the handler for this URL, the root URL's handler (in this case indexHandler) will be called.

How about /hello/there then? The *Principle of Least Surprise* would dictate that because we have the URL /hello registered we should default to that URL and `helloHandler` should be called. But in figure 3.6, `indexHandler` is called instead. Why is that so?

**The Principle of Least Surprise**

The Principle of Least Surprise, also known as the Principle of Least Astonishment, is a general principle in the design of all things (including software) that says that when designing, we should do the least surprising thing. The results of doing something should be obvious, consistent, and predictable.

If we place a button next to a door, we'd expect the button to do something with the door (ring the doorbell or open the door). If the button turns off the corridor lights instead, that would be against the Principle of Least Surprise because it's doing something that a user of that button wouldn't be expecting.

The reason is because we registered the `helloHandler` to the URL /hello instead of /hello/. For any registered URLs that don't end with a slash (/), `ServeMux` will try to match the exact URL pattern. If the URL ends with a slash (/), `ServeMux` will see if the requested URL starts with any registered URL.

If we'd registered the URL /hello/ instead, then when /hello/there is requested, if `ServeMux` can't find an exact match, it'll start looking for URLs that start with /hello/. There's a match, so `helloHandler` will be called.

### 3.3.6 Other multiplexers

Because what it takes to be a handler or even a multiplexer is to implement the `ServeHTTP`, it's possible to create alternative multiplexers to net/http's `ServeMux`. Sure enough, a number of third-party multiplexers are available, including the excellent Gorilla Toolkit (www.gorillatoolkit.org). The Gorilla Toolkit has two different multiplexers that work quite differently: mux and pat. In this section, we'll go through a lightweight but effective third-party multiplexer called HttpRouter.

One of the main complaints about `ServeMux` is that it doesn't support variables in its pattern matching against the URL. `ServeMux` handles /threads pretty well to retrieve and display all threads in the forum, but it's difficult to handle /thread/123 for retrieving and displaying the thread with id 123. To process such URLs, your handler will need to parse the request path and extract the relevant sections. Also, because of the way `ServeMux` does pattern matching for the URLs, you can't use something like /thread/123/post/456 if you want to retrieve the post with id 456 from the thread with id 123 (at least not with a lot of unnecessary parsing complexity).

The HttpRouter library overcomes some of these limitations. In this section, we'll explore some of the more important features of this library, but you can always look up the rest of the documentation at https://github.com/julienschmidt/httprouter. This listing shows an implementation using HttpRouter.

**Listing 3.12 Using HttpRouter**

```
package main

import (
    "fmt"
    "github.com/julienschmidt/httprouter"
    "net/http"
)

func hello(w http.ResponseWriter, r *http.Request, p httprouter.Params) {
    fmt.Fprintf(w, "hello, %s!\n", p.ByName("name"))
}

func main() {
    mux := httprouter.New()
    mux.GET("/hello/:name", hello)

    server := http.Server{
        Addr:     "127.0.0.1:8080",
        Handler: mux,
    }
    server.ListenAndServe()
}
```

Most of the code should look familiar to you now. We create the multiplexer by calling the `New` function.

```
mux := httprouter.New()
```

Instead of using `HandleFunc` to register the handler functions, we use the method names:

```
mux.GET("/hello/:name", hello)
```

In this case we're registering a URL for the GET method to the `hello` function. If we send a GET request, the `hello` function will be called; if we send any other HTTP requests it won't. Notice that the URL now has something called a *named parameter*. These named parameters can be replaced by any values and can be retrieved later by the handler.

```
func hello(w http.ResponseWriter, r *http.Request, p httprouter.Params) {
    fmt.Fprintf(w, "hello, %s!\n", p.ByName("name"))
}
```

The handler function has changed too; instead of taking two parameters, we now take a third, a `Params` type. `Params` contain the named parameters, which we can retrieve using the `ByName` method.

Finally, instead of using `DefaultServeMux`, we pass our multiplexer into the `Server` struct and let Go use that instead:

```
server := http.Server{
    Addr:    "127.0.0.1:8080",
    Handler: mux,
}
server.ListenAndServe()
```

But wait. How exactly do we include the third-party library? If we do what we did for the other examples and run `go build` at the console, we'll get something like this:

```
$ go build
server.go:5:5: cannot find package "github.com/julienschmidt/httprouter" in
  any of:
   /usr/local/go/src/github.com/julienschmidt/httprouter (from $GOROOT)
   /Users/sausheong/gws/src/github.com/julienschmidt/httprouter (from $GOPATH)
```

A simple package management system is one of the strengths of Go. We simply need to run

```
$ go get github.com/julienschmidt/httprouter
```

at the console and if we're connected to the internet, it'll download the code from the HttpRouter repository (in GitHub) and store it in the $GOPATH/src directory. Then when we run `go build`, it'll import the code and compile our server.

## 3.4 Using HTTP/2

Before leaving this chapter, let me show you how you can use HTTP/2 in Go with what you have learned in this chapter.

In chapter 1, you learned about HTTP/2 and how Go 1.6 includes HTTP/2 by default when you start up a server with HTTPS. For older versions of Go, you can enable this manually through the `golang.org/x/net/http2` package.

If you're using a Go version prior to 1.6, the http2 package is not installed by default, so you need to get it using go get:

```
go get "golang.org/x/net/http2"
```

Modify the code from listing 3.6 by importing the http2 package and also adding a line to set up the server to use HTTP/2.

In the following listing you can see by calling the `ConfigureServer` method in the `http2` package, and passing it the server configuration, you have set up the server to run in HTTP/2.

**Listing 3.13 Using HTTP/2**

```
package main

import (
    "fmt"
    "golang.org/x/net/http2"
    "net/http"
)

type MyHandler struct{}

func (h *MyHandler) ServeHTTP (w http.ResponseWriter, r *http.Request) {
    fmt.Fprintf(w, "Hello World!")
}

func main() {
    handler := MyHandler{}
    server := http.Server{
        Addr:    "127.0.0.1:8080",
        Handler: &handler,
    }
    http2.ConfigureServer(&server, &http2.Server{})
    server.ListenAndServeTLS("cert.pem", "key.pem")
}
```

Now, run the server:

```
go run server.go
```

To check whether the server is running in HTTP/2, you can use cURL. You will be using cURL quite a bit in this book, because it's widely available on most platforms, so it's a good time to get familiar with it.

> **cURL**
>
> cURL is a command-line tool that allows users to get or send files through a URL. It supports a large number of common internet protocols, including HTTP and HTTPS. cURL is installed by default in many variants of Unix, including OS X, but is also available in Windows. To download and install cURL manually, go to http://curl.haxx.se/download.html.

Starting from version 7.43.0, cURL supports HTTP/2. You can perform a request using the HTTP/2 protocol passing the `--http2` flag. To use cURL with HTTP/2, you need to link it to nghttp2, a C library that provides support for HTTP/2. As of this writing, many default cURL implementations don't yet support HTTP/2 (including the one shipped with OS X), so if you need to recompile cURL, link it with nghttp2 and replace the previous cURL version with the one you just built.

Once you have done that, you can use cURL to check your HTTP/2 web application:

```
curl -I --http2 --insecure https://localhost:8080/
```

Remember, you need to run it against HTTPS. Because you created your own certificate and private key, by default cURL will not proceed as it will try to verify the certificate. To force cURL to accept your certificate, you need to set the insecure flag.

You should get an output similar to this:

```
HTTP/2.0 200
content-type:text/plain; charset=utf-8
content-length:12
date:Mon, 15 Feb 2016 05:33:01 GMT
```

We've discussed how to handle requests, but we mostly glossed over how to process the incoming request and send responses to the client. Handlers and handler functions are the key to writing web applications in Go, but processing requests and sending responses is the real reason why web applications exist. In the next chapter, we'll turn to the details on requests and responses and you'll see how to extract information from requests and pass on information through responses.

## 3.5 Summary

- Go has full-fledged standard libraries for building web applications, with net/http and html/template.
- Although using good web frameworks is often easier and saves time, it is important to learn the basics of web programming before using them.
- Go's `net/http` package allows HTTP to be layered on top of SSL to be more secured, creating HTTPS.
- Go handlers can be any struct that has a method named `ServeHTTP` with two parameters: an `HTTPResponseWriter` interface and a pointer to a `Request` struct.
- Handler functions are functions that behave like handlers. Handler functions have the same signature as the `ServeHTTP` method and are used to process requests.
- Handlers and handler functions can be chained to allow modular processing of requests through separation of concerns.
- Multiplexers are also handlers. `ServeMux` is an HTTP request multiplexer. It accepts an HTTP request and redirects it to the correct handler according to the URL in the request. `DefaultServeMux` is a publicly available instance of `ServeMux` that is used as the default multiplexer.
- In Go 1.6 and later, `net/http` supports HTTP/2 by default. Before 1.6, HTTP/2 support can be added manually by using the `http2` package.

# 4 Processing requests

***This chapter covers***

- Using Go requests and responses
- Processing HTML forms with Go
- Sending responses back to the client with `ResponseWriter`
- Working with cookies
- Implementing flash messages with cookies

In the previous chapter we explored serving web applications with the built-in net/http library. You also learned about handlers, handler functions, and multiplexers. Now that you know about receiving and handing off the request to the correct set of functions, in this chapter we'll investigate the tools that Go provides to programmers to process requests and send responses back to the client.

## 4.1 Requests and responses

In chapter 1 we went through quite a bit of information about HTTP messages. If that chapter was a blur to you, now would be a great time to revisit it. HTTP messages are messages sent between the client and the server. There are two types of HTTP messages: HTTP request and HTTP response.

Both requests and responses have basically the same structure:

1. Request or response line
2. Zero or more headers
3. An empty line, followed by …
4. … an optional message body

Here's an example of a GET request:

```
GET /Protocols/rfc2616/rfc2616.html HTTP/1.1
Host: www.w3.org
User-Agent: Mozilla/5.0
(empty line)
```

The net/http library provides structures for HTTP messages, and you need to know these structures to understand how to process requests and send responses. Let's start with the request.

### 4.1.1 Request

The `Request` struct represents an HTTP request message sent from the client. The representation isn't literal because HTTP requests are only lines of text. The struct contains the parsed information that's considered to be important, as well as a number of useful methods. Some important parts of `Request` are

- URL
- Header
- Body
- Form, PostForm, and MultipartForm

You can also get access to the cookies in the request and the referring URL and the user agent from methods in `Request`. `Request` can either be requests sent to the server, or requests sent from the client, when the net/http library is used as an HTTP client.

### 4.1.2 Request URL

The URL field of a `Request` is a representation of the URL that's sent as part of the request line (the first line of the HTTP request). The URL field is a pointer to the `url.URL` type, which is a struct with a number of fields, as shown here.

**Listing 4.1 The URL struct**

```
type URL struct {
    Scheme   string
    Opaque   string
    User     *Userinfo
    Host     string
    Path     string
    RawQuery string
    Fragment string
}
```

The general form is

```
scheme://[userinfo@]host/path[?query][#fragment]
```

URLs that don't start with a slash after the scheme are interpreted as

```
scheme:opaque[?query][#fragment]
```

When programming web applications, we often pass information from the client to the server using the URL query. The RawQuery field provides the actual query string that's passed through. For example, if we send a request to the URL http://www.example.com/post?id=123&thread_id=456 RawQuery will contain `id=123&thread_id=456` and we'll need to parse it to get the key-value pairs. There's a convenient way of getting these key-value pairs through the Form field in the `Request`. We'll get to the Form, PostForm, and MultipartForm fields in a bit.

It's interesting to note that you can't extract the Fragment field out of a `URL` struct if you're getting a request from the browser. Recall from chapter 1 that fragments are stripped by the browser before being sent to the server, so it's not the Go libraries being annoying—it's because the fragment you see on the browser never gets sent to the server. So why have it at all? It's because not all requests come from browsers; you can get requests from HTTP client libraries or other tools, or even client frameworks like Angular. Also, `Request` isn't used only at the server—it can also be used as part of the client library.

### 4.1.3 Request header

Request and response headers are described in the `Header` type, which is a map representing the key-value pairs in an HTTP header. There are four basic methods on `Header`, which allow you to add, delete, get, and set values, given a key. Both the key and the value are strings.

The difference between adding and setting a value is straightforward but tells us quite a lot about the structure of the `Header` type. A header is a map with keys that are strings and values that are slices of strings. Setting a key creates a blank slice of strings as the value, with the first element in the slice being the new header value. To add a new header value to a given key, you append the new element to the existing slice of string (see figure 4.1).

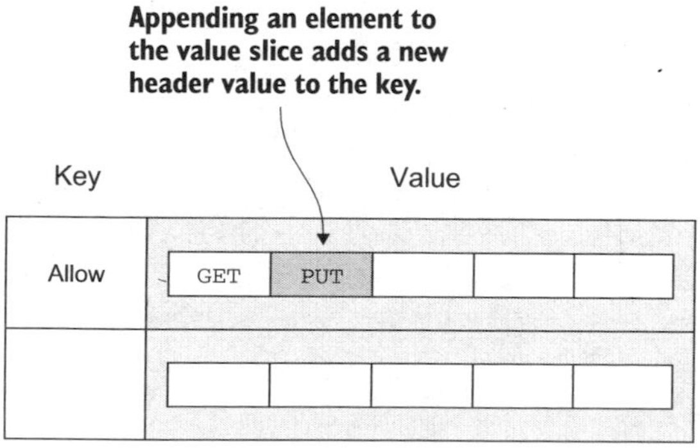
Appending an element to the value slice adds a new header value to the key.
Key
Value
Allow
GET
PUT

**Figure 4.1 A header is a map, with the key a string and the value a slice of strings.**

This listing shows how you'd read headers from a request.

**Listing 4.2 Reading headers from a request**

```
package main

import (
    "fmt"
    "net/http"
)

func headers(w http.ResponseWriter, r *http.Request) {
    h := r.Header
    fmt.Fprintln(w, h)
}

func main() {
    server := http.Server{
        Addr: "127.0.0.1:8080",
    }
    http.HandleFunc("/headers", headers)
    server.ListenAndServe()
}
```

The previous listing shows the simple server from chapter 3, but this time the handler prints out the header. Figure 4.2 shows what you'll see in your browser (I used Safari on my OS X machine).

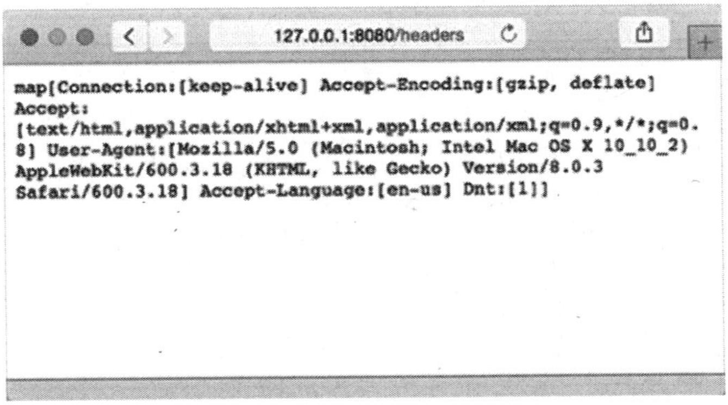
127.0.0.1:8080/headers
map[Connection:[keep-alive] Accept-Encoding:[gzip, deflate]
Accept:
[text/html,application/xhtml+xml,application/xml;q=0.9,*/*;q=0.
8] User-Agent:[Mozilla/5.0 (Macintosh; Intel Mac OS X 10_10_2)
AppleWebKit/600.3.18 (KHTML, like Gecko) Version/8.0.3
Safari/600.3.18] Accept-Language:[en-us] Dnt:[1]]

**Figure 4.2 Header output as viewed in the browser**

To get just one particular header, instead of using

```
h := r.Header
```

you'd use

```
h := r.Header["Accept-Encoding"]
```

and you'd get

```
[gzip, deflate]
```

You can also use

```
h := r.Header.Get("Accept-Encoding")
```

which will give you

```
gzip, deflate
```

Notice the difference. If you refer to the `Header` directly, you'll get a map of strings; if you use the `Get` method on the `Header`, then you'll get the comma-delimited list of values (which is the actual string in the header).

### 4.1.4 Request body

Both request and response bodies are represented by the Body field, which is an `io.ReadCloser` interface. In turn the Body field consists of a `Reader` interface and a `Closer` interface. A `Reader` is an interface that has a `Read` method that takes in a slice of bytes and returns the number of bytes read and an optional error. A `Closer` is an interface that has a `Close` method, which takes in nothing and returns an optional error. What this really means is that you can call on the `Read` and `Close` methods of the Body field. To read the contents of a request body, you can call the Body field's `Read` method, as shown in this listing.

**Listing 4.3 Reading data from a request body**

```
package main

import (
    "fmt"
    "net/http"
)

func body(w http.ResponseWriter, r *http.Request) {
    len := r.ContentLength
    body := make([]byte, len)
    r.Body.Read(body)
    fmt.Fprintln(w, string(body))
}

func main() {
    server := http.Server{
        Addr: "127.0.0.1:8080",
    }
    http.HandleFunc("/body", body)
    server.ListenAndServe()
}
```

Notice that you first need to determine how much to read; then you create a byte array of the content length, and call the `Read` method to read into the byte array.

If you want to test this, you'll need to send a POST request to the server with the appropriate message body, because GET requests don't have message bodies. Remember that you can't normally send POST requests through a browser—you need an HTTP client. There are plenty of choices. You can use a desktop graphical HTTP client, a browser plug-in or extension, or even cURL from the command line.

Type this on your console:

```
$ curl -id "first_name=sausheong&last_name=chang" 127.0.0.1:8080/body
```

cURL will display the full, raw HTTP response, with the HTTP body after the blank line. This is what you should be getting:

```
HTTP/1.1 200 OK
Date: Tue, 13 Jan 2015 16:11:58 GMT
Content-Length: 37
Content-Type: text/plain; charset=utf-8

first_name=sausheong&last_name=chang
```

Normally you wouldn't need to read the raw form of the body, though, because Go provides methods such as `FormValue` and `FormFile` to extract the values from a POST form.

## 4.2 HTML forms and Go

Before we delve into getting form data from a POST request, let's take a deeper look at HTML forms. Most often, POST requests come in the form (pun intended) of an HTML form and often look like this:

```
<form action="/process" method="post">
  <input type="text" name="first_name"/>
  <input type="text" name="last_name"/>
  <input type="submit"/>
</form>
```

Within the `<form>` tag, we place a number of HTML form elements including text input, text area, radio buttons, checkboxes, and file uploads. These elements allow users to enter data to be submitted to the server. Data is submitted to the server when the user clicks a button or somehow triggers the form submission.

We know the data is sent to the server through an HTTP POST request and is placed in the body of the request. But how is the data formatted? The HTML form data is always sent as name-value pairs, but how are these name-value pairs formatted in the POST body? It's important for us to know this because as we receive the POST request from the browser, we need to be able to parse the data and extract the name-value pairs.

The format of the name-value pairs sent through a POST request is specified by the content type of the HTML form. This is defined using the `enctype` attribute like this:

```
<form action="/process" method="post" enctype="application/x-www-
➥ form-urlencoded">
  <input type="text" name="first_name"/>
  <input type="text" name="last_name"/>
  <input type="submit"/>
</form>
```

The default value for `enctype` is `application/x-www-form-urlencoded`. Browsers are required to support at least `application/x-www-form-urlencoded` and `multipart/form-data` (HTML5 also supports a `text/plain` value).

If we set `enctype` to `application/x-www-form-urlencoded`, the browser will encode in the HTML form data a long query string, with the name-value pairs separated by an ampersand (&) and the name separated from the values by an equal sign (=). That's the same as URL encoding, hence the name (see chapter 1). In other words, the HTTP body will look something like this:

```
first_name=sau%20sheong&last_name=chang
```

If you set `enctype` to `multipart/form-data`, each name-value pair will be converted into a MIME message part, each with its own content type and content disposition. Our form data will now look something like this:

```
------WebKitFormBoundaryMPNjKpeO9cLiocMw
Content-Disposition: form-data; name="first_name"

sau sheong
------WebKitFormBoundaryMPNjKpeO9cLiocMw
Content-Disposition: form-data; name="last_name"

chang
------WebKitFormBoundaryMPNjKpeO9cLiocMw--
```

When would you use one or the other? If you're sending simple text data, the URL encoded form is better—it's simpler and more efficient and less processing is needed. If you're sending large amounts of data, such as uploading files, the multipart-MIME form is better. You can even specify that you want to do Base64 encoding to send binary data as text.

So far we've only talked about POST requests—what about GET requests in an HTML form? HTML allows the `method` attribute to be either POST or GET, so this is also a valid format:

```
<form action="/process" method="get">
  <input type="text" name="first_name"/>
  <input type="text" name="last_name"/>
  <input type="submit"/>
</form>
```

In this case, there's no request body (GET requests have no request body), and all the data is set in the URL as name-value pairs.

Now that you know how data is sent from an HTML form to the server, let's go back to the server and see how you can use `net/http` to process the request.

### 4.2.1 Form

In the previous sections, we talked about extracting data from the URL and the body in the raw form, which requires us to parse the data ourselves. In fact, we normally don't need to, because the net/http library includes a rather comprehensive set of functions that normally provides us with all we need. Let's talk about each in turn.

The functions in `Request` that allow us to extract data from the URL and/or the body revolve around the Form, PostForm, and MultipartForm fields. The data is in the form of key-value pairs (which is what we normally get from a POST request anyway). The general algorithm is:

1. Call `ParseForm` or `ParseMultipartForm` to parse the request.
2. Access the Form, PostForm, or MultipartForm field accordingly.

This listing shows parsing forms.

**Listing 4.4 Parsing forms**

```
package main

import (
    "fmt"
    "net/http"
)

func process(w http.ResponseWriter, r *http.Request) {
    r.ParseForm()
    fmt.Fprintln(w, r.Form)
}

func main() {
    server := http.Server{
        Addr: "127.0.0.1:8080",
    }
    http.HandleFunc("/process", process)
    server.ListenAndServe()
}
```

The focus of the server in listing 4.4 is on these two lines:

```
r.ParseForm()
fmt.Fprintln(w, r.Form)
```

As mentioned earlier, you need to first parse the request using `ParseForm`, and then access the Form field.

Let's look at the client that's going to call this server. You'll create a simple, minimal HTML form to send the request to the server. Place the code in a file named client.html.

```
<html>
  <head>
    <meta http-equiv="Content-Type" content="text/html; charset=utf-8" />
    <title>Go Web Programming</title>
  </head>
  <body>
    <form action=http://127.0.0.1:8080/process?hello=world&thread=123
    ➥ method="post" enctype="application/x-www-form-urlencoded">
```

```
      <input type="text" name="hello" value="sau sheong"/>
      <input type="text" name="post" value="456"/>
      <input type="submit"/>
    </form>
  </body>
</html>
```

In this form, you are

- Sending the URL http://localhost:8080/process?hello=world&thread=123 to the server using the POST method
- Specifying the content type (in the enctype field) to be `application/x-www-form-urlencoded`
- Sending two HTML form key-value pairs—`hello=sau sheong` and `post=456`—to the server

Note that you have two values for the key `hello`. One of them is `world` in the URL and the other is `sau sheong` in the HTML form.

Open the client.html file directly in your browser (you don't need to serve it out from a web server—just running it locally on your browser is fine) and click the submit button. You'll see the following in the browser:

```
map[thread:[123] hello:[sau sheong world] post:[456]]
```

This is the raw string version of the `Form` struct in the POST request, after the request has been parsed. The `Form` struct is a map, whose keys are strings and values are a slice of strings. Notice that the map isn't sorted, so you might get a different sorting of the returned values. Nonetheless, what we get is the combination of the query values `hello=world` and `thread=123` as well as the form values `hello=sau sheong` and `post=456`. As you can see, the values are URL decoded (there's a space between `sau` and `sheong`).

### 4.2.2 PostForm

Of course, if you only want to get the value to the key `post`, you can use `r.Form["post"]`, which will give you a map with one element: `[456]`. If the form and the URL have the same key, both of them will be placed in a slice, with the form value always prioritized before the URL value.

What if you need just the form key-value pairs and want to totally ignore the URL key-value pairs? For that you can use the PostForm field, which provides key-value pairs only for the form and not the URL. If you change from using `r.Form` to using `r.PostForm` in the code, this is what you get:

```
map[post:[456] hello:[sau sheong]]
```

This example used `application/x-www-form-urlencoded` for the content type. What happens if you use `multipart/form-data`? Make the change to the client HTML form, switch back to using `r.Form`, and let's find out:

```
map[hello:[world] thread:[123]]
```

What happened here? You only get the URL query key-value pairs this time and not the form key-value pairs, because the PostForm field only supports `application/x-www-form-urlencoded`. To get multipart key-value pairs from the body, you must use the `MultipartForm` field.

### 4.2.3 *MultipartForm*

Instead of using the `ParseForm` method on the `Request` struct and then using the Form field on the request, you have to use the `ParseMultipartForm` method and then use the MultipartForm field on the request. The `ParseMultipartForm` method also calls the `ParseForm` method when necessary.

```
r.ParseMultipartForm(1024)
fmt.Fprintln(w, r.MultipartForm)
```

You need to tell the `ParseMultipartForm` method how much data you want to extract from the multipart form, in bytes. Now let's see what happens:

```
&{map[hello:[sau sheong] post:[456]] map[]}
```

This time you see the form key-value pairs but not the URL key-value pairs. This is because the MultipartForm field contains only the form key-value pairs. Notice that the returned value is no longer a map but a struct that contains two maps. The first map has keys that are strings and values that are slices of string; the second map is empty. It's empty because it's a map with keys that are strings but values that are files, which we're going to talk about in the next section.

There's one last set of methods on `Request` that allows you to access the key-value pairs even more easily. The `FormValue` method lets you access the key-value pairs just like in the Form field, except that it's for a specific key and you don't need to call the `ParseForm` or `ParseMultipartForm` methods beforehand—the `FormValue` method does that for you.

Taking our previous example, this means if you do this in your handler function:

```
fmt.Fprintln(w, r.FormValue("hello"))
```

and set the client's form `enctype` attribute to `application/x-www-form-urlencoded`, you'll get this:

```
sau sheong
```

That's because the `FormValue` method retrieves only the first value, even though you actually have both values in the `Form` struct. To prove this, let's add another line below the earlier line of code, like this:

```
fmt.Fprintln(w, r.FormValue("hello"))
fmt.Fprintln(w, r.Form)
```

This time you'll see

```
sau sheong
map[post:[456] hello:[sau sheong world] thread:[123]]
```

r. PostFormValue

The `PostFormValue` method does the same thing, except that it's for the PostForm field instead of the Form field. Let's make some changes to the code to use the `PostFormValue` method:

```
fmt.Fprintln(w, r.PostFormValue("hello"))
fmt.Fprintln(w, r.PostForm)
```

This time you get this instead:

```
sau sheong
map[hello:[sau sheong] post:[456]]
```

As you can see, you get only the form key-value pairs.

Both the `FormValue` and `PostFormValue` methods call the `ParseMultipartForm` method for you so you don't need to call it yourself, but there's a slightly confusing gotcha that you should be careful with (at least as of Go 1.4). If you set the client form's `enctype` to `multipart/form-data` and try to get the value using either the `FormValue` or the `PostFormValue` method, you won't be able to get it even though the `MultipartForm` method has been called!

To help clarify, let's make changes to the server's handler function again:

```
fmt.Fprintln(w, "(1)", r.FormValue("hello"))
fmt.Fprintln(w, "(2)", r.PostFormValue("hello"))
fmt.Fprintln(w, "(3)", r.PostForm)
fmt.Fprintln(w, "(4)", r.MultipartForm)
```

Here's the result from using our form with enctype set to `multipart/form-data`:

```
(1) world
(2)
(3) map[]
(4) &{map[hello:[sau sheong] post:[456]] map[]}
```

The first line in the results gives you the value for hello that's found in the URL and not the form. The second and third lines tell you why, because if you just take the form key-value pairs, you get nothing. That's because the `FormValue` and `PostFormValue` methods correspond to the Form and PostForm fields, and not the MultipartForm field. The last line in the results proves that the `ParseMultipartForm` method was actually called—that's why if you try to access the MultipartForm field you'll get the data there.

We covered quite a bit in these sections, so let's recap, in table 4.1, how these functions are different. The table shows the methods that should be called if you're looking for values in the corresponding fields. The table also shows where the data comes from and what type of data you'll get. For example, in the first row, if you're looking for data in the Form field, you should be calling the `ParseForm` method (either directly or indirectly). You'll then get both the URL data and the form data from the request and the data will be URL-encoded. Undoubtedly the naming convention leaves much to be desired!

**Table 4.1 Comparing Form, PostForm, and MultipartForm fields**

| | | Key-value pairs from | | Content type | |
|---|---|---|---|---|---|
| **Field** | **Should call method** | **URL** | **Form** | **URL encoded** | **Multipart** |
| Form | `ParseForm` | ✓ | ✓ | ✓ | - |
| PostForm | Form | - | ✓ | ✓ | - |
| MultipartForm | `ParseMultipartForm` | - | ✓ | - | ✓ |
| FormValue | NA | ✓ | ✓ | ✓ | - |
| PostFormValue | NA | - | ✓ | ✓ | - |

### 4.2.4 Files

Probably the most common use for `multipart/form-data` is for uploading files. This mostly means the file HTML tag, so let's make some changes, shown in bold in the following listing, to our client form.

**Listing 4.5 Uploading files**

```
<html>
  <head>
    <meta http-equiv="Content-Type" content="text/html; charset=utf-8" />
    <title>Go Web Programming</title>
  </head>
  <body>
    <form action="http://localhost:8080/process?hello=world&thread=123"
   method="post" enctype="multipart/form-data">
      <input type="text" name="hello" value="sau sheong"/>
      <input type="text" name="post" value="456"/>
      <input type="file" name="uploaded">
      <input type="submit">
    </form>
  </body>
</html>
```

To receive files, we'll make changes, shown next, in our handler function.

**Listing 4.6 Receiving uploaded files using the MultipartForm field**

```
package main

import (
    "fmt"
    "io/ioutil"
    "net/http"
)

func process(w http.ResponseWriter, r *http.Request) {
    r.ParseMultipartForm(1024)
```

```
    fileHeader := r.MultipartForm.File["uploaded"][0]
    file, err := fileHeader.Open()
    if err == nil {
        data, err := ioutil.ReadAll(file)
        if err == nil {
            fmt.Fprintln(w, string(data))
        }
    }
}

func main() {
    server := http.Server{
        Addr: "127.0.0.1:8080",
    }
    http.HandleFunc("/process", process)
    server.ListenAndServe()
}
```

As mentioned earlier, you need to call the `ParseMultipartForm` method first. After that you get a FileHeader from the File field of the MultipartForm field and call its `Open` method to get the file. If you upload a text file and send it across to the server, the handler will get the file, read it into a byte array, and then print it out to the browser.

As with the `FormValue` and `PostFormValue` methods, there's a shorter way of getting an uploaded file using the `FormFile` method, shown in the following listing. The `FormFile` method returns the first value given the key, so this approach is normally faster if you have only one file to be uploaded.

**Listing 4.7 Retrieving uploaded files using FormFile**

```
func process(w http.ResponseWriter, r *http.Request) {
    file, _, err := r.FormFile("uploaded")
    if err == nil {
        data, err := ioutil.ReadAll(file)
        if err == nil {
            fmt.Fprintln(w, string(data))
        }
    }
}
```

As you can see, you no longer have to call the `ParseMultipartForm` method, and the `FormFile` method returns both the file and the file header at the same time. You simply need to process the file that's returned.

### 4.2.5 Processing POST requests with JSON body

So far in our discussion we've focused on name-value pairs in the request body. This is because we've been focusing on HTML forms only. But not all POST requests will come from HTML forms. Sending POST requests is increasingly common with client libraries such as JQuery as well as client-side frameworks such as Angular or Ember, or even the older Adobe Flash or Microsoft Silverlight technologies.

If you're trying to get the JSON data from a POST request sent by an Angular client and you're calling the `ParseForm` method to get the data, you won't be able to. At the same time, other JavaScript libraries like JQuery allow you to do so. What gives?

Client frameworks encode their POST requests differently. JQuery encodes POST requests like an HTML form with `application/x-www-form-urlencoded` (that is, it sets the request header `Content-Type` to `application/x-www-form-urlencoded`); Angular encodes POST requests with `application/json`. Go's `ParseForm` method only parses forms and so doesn't accept `application/json`. If you call the `ParseForm` method, you won't get any data at all!

The problem doesn't lie with the implementation of any of the libraries. It lies in the lack of sufficient documentation (although there will arguably never be enough documentation) and the programmer making certain assumptions based on their dependency on frameworks.

Frameworks help programmers by hiding the underlying complexities and implementation details. As a programmer you should be using frameworks. But it's also important to understand how things work and what the framework simplifies for you because eventually there will be cases where the framework's seams show at the joints.

We've covered quite a lot on processing requests. Now let's look at sending responses to the user.

## 4.3 ResponseWriter

If you were thinking that sending a response to the client would involve creating a `Response` struct, setting up the data in it, and sending it out, then you'd be wrong. The correct interface to use when sending a response from the server to the client is `ResponseWriter`.

`ResponseWriter` is an interface that a handler uses to create an HTTP response. The actual struct backing up `ResponseWriter` is the nonexported struct `http.response`. Because it's nonexported, you can't use it directly; you can only use it through the `ResponseWriter` interface.

> **Why do we pass ResponseWriter into ServeHTTP by value?**
>
> Having read the earlier part of this chapter, you might wonder why the ServeHTTP function takes two parameters—the `ResponseWriter` interface and a pointer to a `Request` struct. The reason why it's a pointer to `Request` is simple: changes to `Request` by the handler need to be visible to the server, so we're only passing it by reference instead of by value. But why are we passing in a `ResponseWriter` by value? The server needs to know the changes to `ResponseWriter` too, doesn't it?
>
> If you dig into the net/http library code, you'll find that `ResponseWriter` is an interface to a nonexported struct response, and we're passing the struct by reference (we're passing in a pointer to response) and not by value.
>
> In other words, both the parameters are passed in by reference; it's just that the method signature takes a `ResponseWriter` that's an interface to a pointer to a struct, so it looks as if it's passed in by value.

The ResponseWriter interface has three methods:

- Write
- WriteHeader
- Header

### 4.3.1 Writing to the ResponseWriter

The Write method takes in an array of bytes, and this gets written into the body of the HTTP response. If the header doesn't have a content type by the time Write is called, the first 512 bytes of the data are used to detect the content type. This listing shows how to use the Write method.

**Listing 4.8 Write to send responses to the client**

```
package main

import (
    "net/http"
)

func writeExample(w http.ResponseWriter, r *http.Request) {
    str := `<html>
<head><title>Go Web Programming</title></head>
<body><h1>Hello World</h1></body>
</html>`
    w.Write([]byte(str))
}

func main() {
    server := http.Server{
        Addr: "127.0.0.1:8080",
    }
    http.HandleFunc("/write", writeExample)
    server.ListenAndServe()
}
```

In listing 4.8 you're writing an HTML string to the HTTP response body using ResponseWriter. You send this command through cURL:

```
curl -i 127.0.0.1:8080/write
HTTP/1.1 200 OK
Date: Tue, 13 Jan 2015 16:16:13 GMT
Content-Length: 95
Content-Type: text/html; charset=utf-8

<html>
<head><title>Go Web Programming</title></head>
<body><h1>Hello World</h1></body>
</html>
```

Notice that you didn't set the content type, but it was detected and set correctly.

The WriteHeader method's name is a bit misleading. It doesn't allow you to write any headers (you use Header for that), but it takes an integer that represents the status code of the HTTP response and writes it as the return status code for the HTTP response. After calling this method, you can still write to the `ResponseWriter`, though you can no longer write to the header. If you don't call this method, by default when you call the `Write` method, 200 OK will be sent as the response code.

The `WriteHeader` method is pretty useful if you want to return error codes. Let's say you're writing an API and though you defined the interface, you haven't fleshed it out, so you want to return a 501 Not Implemented status code. Let's see how this works by adding a new handler function to our existing server, shown in the following listing. Remember to register this to DefaultServeMux by calling the `HandleFunc` function!

**Listing 4.9 Writing headers to responses using `WriteHeader`**

```
package main

import (
    "fmt"
    "net/http"
)

func writeExample(w http.ResponseWriter, r *http.Request) {
    str := `<html>
<head><title>Go Web Programming</title></head>
<body><h1>Hello World</h1></body>
</html>`
    w.Write([]byte(str))
}

func writeHeaderExample(w http.ResponseWriter, r *http.Request) {
    w.WriteHeader(501)
    fmt.Fprintln(w, "No such service, try next door")
}

func main() {
    server := http.Server{
        Addr: "127.0.0.1:8080",
    }
    http.HandleFunc("/write", writeExample)
    http.HandleFunc("/writeheader", writeHeaderExample)
    server.ListenAndServe()
}
```

Call the URL through cURL:

```
curl -i 127.0.0.1:8080/writeheader
HTTP/1.1 501 Not Implemented
Date: Tue, 13 Jan 2015 16:20:29 GMT
Content-Length: 31
Content-Type: text/plain; charset=utf-8

No such service, try next door
```

Finally the `Header` method returns a map of headers that you can modify (refer to section 4.1.3). The modified headers will be in the HTTP response that's sent to the client.

**Listing 4.10 Writing headers to redirect the client**

```
package main

import (
    "fmt"
    "net/http"
)

func writeExample(w http.ResponseWriter, r *http.Request) {
    str := `<html>
<head><title>Go Web Programming</title></head>
<body><h1>Hello World</h1></body>
</html>`
    w.Write([]byte(str))
}

func writeHeaderExample(w http.ResponseWriter, r *http.Request) {
    w.WriteHeader(501)
    fmt.Fprintln(w, "No such service, try next door")
}

func headerExample(w http.ResponseWriter, r *http.Request) {
    w.Header().Set("Location", "http://google.com")
    w.WriteHeader(302)
}

func main() {
    server := http.Server{
        Addr: "127.0.0.1:8080",
    }
    http.HandleFunc("/write", writeExample)
    http.HandleFunc("/writeheader", writeHeaderExample)
    http.HandleFunc("/redirect", headerExample)
    server.ListenAndServe()
}
```

The previous listing shows how a redirect works—it's simple to set the status code to 302 and then add a header named `Location` with the value of the location you want the user to be redirected to. Note that you must add the `Location` header before writing the status code because `WriteHeader` prevents the header from being modified after it's called. When you call the URL from the browser, you'll be redirected to Google.

If you use cURL, you will see this:

```
curl -i 127.0.0.1:8080/redirect
HTTP/1.1 302 Found
Location: http://google.com
Date: Tue, 13 Jan 2015 16:22:16 GMT
Content-Length: 0
Content-Type: text/plain; charset=utf-8
```

Let's look at one last example of how to use `ResponseWriter` directly. This time, you want to return JSON to the client. Assuming that you have a struct named `Post`, the following listing shows the handler function.

**Listing 4.11 Writing JSON output**

```
package main

import (
    "fmt"
    "encoding/json"
    "net/http"
)

type Post struct {
    User    string
    Threads []string
}

func writeExample(w http.ResponseWriter, r *http.Request) {
    str := `<html>
<head><title>Go Web Programming</title></head>
<body><h1>Hello World</h1></body>
</html>`
    w.Write([]byte(str))
}

func writeHeaderExample(w http.ResponseWriter, r *http.Request) {
    w.WriteHeader(501)
    fmt.Fprintln(w, "No such service, try next door")
}

func headerExample(w http.ResponseWriter, r *http.Request) {
    w.Header().Set("Location", "http://google.com")
    w.WriteHeader(302)
}

func jsonExample(w http.ResponseWriter, r *http.Request) {
    w.Header().Set("Content-Type", "application/json")
    post := &Post{
        User:    "Sau Sheong",
        Threads: []string{"first", "second", "third"},
    }
    json, _ := json.Marshal(post)
    w.Write(json)
}

func main() {
    server := http.Server{
        Addr: "127.0.0.1:8080",
    }
    http.HandleFunc("/write", writeExample)
    http.HandleFunc("/writeheader", writeHeaderExample)
    http.HandleFunc("/redirect", headerExample)
    http.HandleFunc("/json", headerExample)
    server.ListenAndServe()
}
```

Focus only on the `ResponseWriter`. It's okay if you don't understand the JSON bits yet—we'll be covering JSON in chapter 7. Just know that the variable `json` is a JSON string that's marshaled from a `Post` struct.

First you set the content type to `application/json` using `Header`; then you write the JSON string to the `ResponseWriter`. If you call this using cURL, you will see:

```
curl -i 127.0.0.1:8080/json
HTTP/1.1 200 OK
Content-Type: application/json
Date: Tue, 13 Jan 2015 16:27:01 GMT
Content-Length: 58

{"User":"Sau Sheong","Threads":["first","second","third"]}
```

## 4.4 Cookies

In chapter 2, you saw how to use cookies to create sessions for authentication. In this section, we'll delve into the details of using cookies not just for sessions but for persistence at the client in general.

A cookie is a small piece of information that's stored at the client, originally sent from the server through an HTTP response message. Every time the client sends an HTTP request to the server, the cookie is sent along with it. Cookies are designed to overcome the stateless-ness of HTTP. Although it's not the only mechanism that can be used, it's one of the most common and popular methods. Entire industries' revenues depend on it, especially in the internet advertising domain.

There are a number of types of cookies, including interestingly named ones like super cookies, third-party cookies, and zombie cookies. But generally there are only two classes of cookies: session cookies and persistent cookies. Most other types of cookies are variants of the persistent cookies.

### 4.4.1 Cookies with Go

The `Cookie` struct, shown in this listing, is the representation of a cookie in Go.

**Listing 4.12 The `Cookie` struct**

```
type Cookie struct {
  Name       string
  Value      string
  Path       string
  Domain     string
  Expires    time.Time
  RawExpires string
  MaxAge     int
  Secure     bool
  HttpOnly   bool
  Raw        string
  Unparsed   []string
}
```

If the Expires field isn't set, then the cookie is a session or temporary cookie. Session cookies are removed from the browser when the browser is closed. Otherwise, the cookie is a persistent cookie that'll last as long as it isn't expired or removed.

There are two ways of specifying the expiry time: the Expires field and the MaxAge field. Expires tells us exactly when the cookie will expire, and MaxAge tells us how long the cookie should last (in seconds), starting from the time it's created in the browser. This isn't a design issue with Go, but rather results from the inconsistent implementation differences of cookies in various browsers. Expires was deprecated in favor of MaxAge in HTTP 1.1, but almost all browsers still support it. MaxAge isn't supported by Microsoft Internet Explorer 6, 7, and 8. The pragmatic solution is to use only Expires or to use both in order to support all browsers.

### 4.4.2 Sending cookies to the browser

Cookie has a `String` method that returns a serialized version of the cookie for use in a `Set-Cookie` response header. Let's take a closer look.

**Listing 4.13 Sending cookies to the browser**

```
package main

import (
    "net/http"
)

func setCookie(w http.ResponseWriter, r *http.Request) {
    c1 := http.Cookie{
        Name:     "first_cookie",
        Value:    "Go Web Programming",
        HttpOnly: true,
    }
    c2 := http.Cookie{
        Name:     "second_cookie",
        Value:    "Manning Publications Co",
        HttpOnly: true,
    }
    w.Header().Set("Set-Cookie", c1.String())
    w.Header().Add("Set-Cookie", c2.String())
}

func main() {
    server := http.Server{
        Addr: "127.0.0.1:8080",
    }
    http.HandleFunc("/set_cookie", setCookie)
    server.ListenAndServe()
}
```

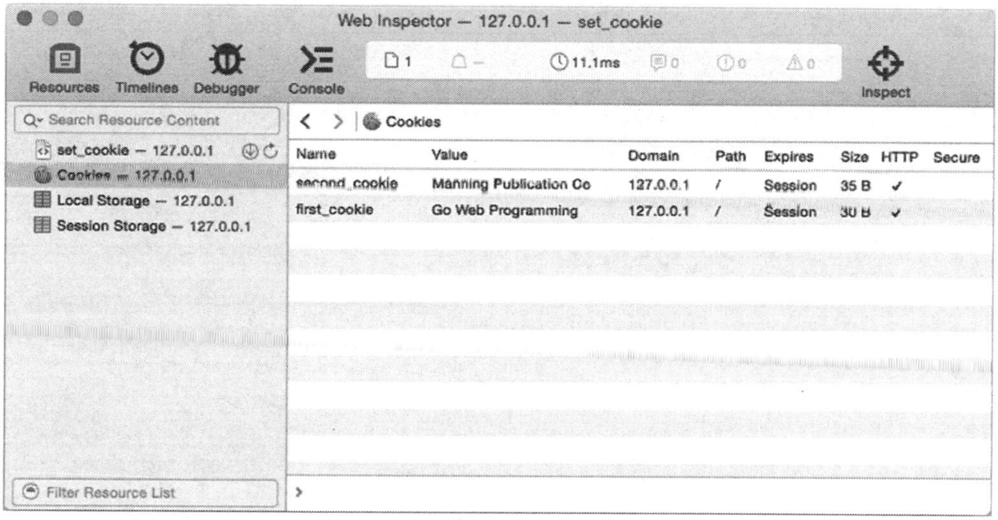

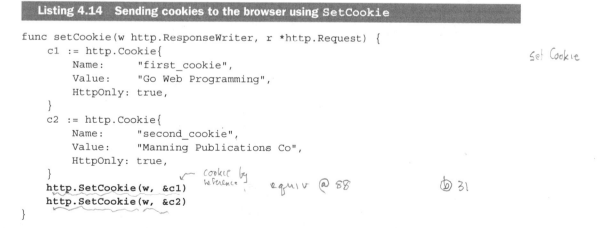

**Figure 4.3 Viewing cookies on Web Inspector (Safari)**

You use the `Set` method to add the first cookie and then the `Add` method to add a second cookie. Go to http://127.0.0.1:8080/set_cookie in your browser, and then inspect the list of cookies set on the browser. (In figure 4.3 I'm using Web Inspector in Safari, but any corresponding tool on other browsers should show the same thing.)

Go provides a simpler shortcut to setting the cookie: using the `SetCookie` function in the net/http library. Taking the example from listing 4.13, let's make a change (shown in bold in the following listing) to the response header.

**Listing 4.14 Sending cookies to the browser using `SetCookie`**

```
func setCookie(w http.ResponseWriter, r *http.Request) {
    c1 := http.Cookie{
        Name:     "first_cookie",
        Value:    "Go Web Programming",
        HttpOnly: true,
    }
    c2 := http.Cookie{
        Name:     "second_cookie",
        Value:    "Manning Publications Co",
        HttpOnly: true,
    }
    http.SetCookie(w, &c1)
    http.SetCookie(w, &c2)
}
```

It doesn't make too much of a difference, though you should take note that you need to pass in the cookies by reference instead.

### 4.4.3 *Getting cookies from the browser*

Now that you can set a cookie, you want to also retrieve that cookie from the client. This listing demonstrates how.

**Listing 4.15 Getting cookies from the header**

```
package main

import (
    "fmt"
    "net/http"
)

func setCookie(w http.ResponseWriter, r *http.Request) {
    c1 := http.Cookie{
        Name:     "first_cookie",
        Value:    "Go Web Programming",
        HttpOnly: true,
    }
    c2 := http.Cookie{
        Name:     "second_cookie",
        Value:    "Manning Publications Co",
        HttpOnly: true,
    }
    http.SetCookie(w, &c1)
    http.SetCookie(w, &c2)
}

func getCookie(w http.ResponseWriter, r *http.Request) {
    h := r.Header["Cookie"]
    fmt.Fprintln(w, h)
}

func main() {
    server := http.Server{
        Addr: "127.0.0.1:8080",
    }
    http.HandleFunc("/set_cookie", setCookie)
    http.HandleFunc("/get_cookie", getCookie)
    server.ListenAndServe()
}
```

After you recompile and start the server, when you go to http://127.0.0.1:8080/get_cookie you'll see this in the browser:

```
[first_cookie=Go Web Programming; second_cookie=Manning Publications Co]
```

This is a slice, with a single string. If you want to get the individual name-value pairs you'll have to parse the string yourself. But as you can see in the following listing, Go provides a couple of easy ways to get cookies.

**Listing 4.16 Using the `Cookie` and `Cookies` methods**

```
package main

import (
    "fmt"
    "net/http"
)

func setCookie(w http.ResponseWriter, r *http.Request) {
    c1 := http.Cookie{
        Name:     "first_cookie",
        Value:    "Go Web Programming",
        HttpOnly: true,
    }
    c2 := http.Cookie{
        Name:     "second_cookie",
        Value:    "Manning Publications Co",
        HttpOnly: true,
    }
    http.SetCookie(w, &c1)
    http.SetCookie(w, &c2)
}

func getCookie(w http.ResponseWriter, r *http.Request) {
    c1, err := r.Cookie("first_cookie")
    if err != nil {
        fmt.Fprintln(w, "Cannot get the first cookie")
    }
    cs := r.Cookies()
    fmt.Fprintln(w, c1)
    fmt.Fprintln(w, cs)
}

func main() {
    server := http.Server{
        Addr: "127.0.0.1:8080",
    }
    http.HandleFunc("/set_cookie", setCookie)
    http.HandleFunc("/get_cookie", getCookie)
    server.ListenAndServe()
}
```

Go provides a `Cookie` method on `Request` (shown in bold text in listing 4.16) that allows you to retrieve a named cookie. If the cookie doesn't exist, it'll throw an error. This is a single value, though, so if you want to get multiple cookies you can use the `Cookies` method on `Request`. That way, you retrieve all cookies into a Go slice; in fact, it's the same as getting it through the `Header` yourself. If you recompile, restart the server, and go to http://127.0.0.1:8080/get_cookie now, you'll see this in your browser:

```
first_cookie=Go Web Programming
[first_cookie=Go Web Programming second_cookie=Manning Publications Co]
```

We didn't set the Expires or the MaxAge fields when we set the cookie, so what was returned are session cookies. To prove the point, quit your browser (don't just close the tab or window; completely quit your browser). Then go to http://127.0.0.1:8080/get_cookie again and you'll see that the cookies are gone.

### 4.4.4 Using cookies for flash messages

In chapter 2 we looked at using cookies for managing sessions, so let's try out our new-found cookie skills on something else.

Sometimes it's necessary to show users a short informational message telling them whether or not they've successfully completed an action. If the user submits a post to a forum and his posting fails, you'll want to show him a message that tells him that the post didn't go through. Following the Principle of Least Surprise from the previous chapter, you want to show the message on the same page. But this page doesn't normally show any messages, so you want the message to show on certain conditions and it must be *transient* (which means it doesn't show again when the page is refreshed). These transient messages are commonly known as *flash messages*.

There are many ways to implement flash messages, but one of the most common is to store them in session cookies that are removed when the page is refreshed. This listing shows how you can do this in Go.

**Listing 4.17 Implementing flash messaging using Go cookies**

```
package main

import (
    "encoding/base64"
    "fmt"
    "net/http"
    "time"
)

func setMessage(w http.ResponseWriter, r *http.Request) {
    msg := []byte("Hello World!")
    c := http.Cookie{
        Name:  "flash",
        Value: base64.URLEncoding.EncodeToString(msg),
    }
    http.SetCookie(w, &c)
}

func showMessage(w http.ResponseWriter, r *http.Request) {
    c, err := r.Cookie("flash")
    if err != nil {
        if err == http.ErrNoCookie {
            fmt.Fprintln(w, "No message found")
        }
    } else {
        rc := http.Cookie{
            Name:    "flash",
```

```
            MaxAge:  -1,
            Expires: time.Unix(1, 0),
        }
        http.SetCookie(w, &rc)
        val, _ := base64.URLEncoding.DecodeString(c.Value)
        fmt.Fprintln(w, string(val))
    }
}

func main() {
    server := http.Server{
        Addr: "127.0.0.1:8080",
    }
    http.HandleFunc("/set_message", setMessage)
    http.HandleFunc("/show_message", showMessage)
    server.ListenAndServe()
}
```

You create two handler functions, `setMessage` and `showMessage`, and attach them to `/set_message` and `/show_message`, respectively. Let's start with `setMessage`, which is straightforward.

**Listing 4.18 Setting the message**

```
func setMessage(w http.ResponseWriter, r *http.Request) {
    msg := []byte("Hello World!")
    c := http.Cookie{
        Name:  "flash",
        Value: base64.URLEncoding.EncodeToString(msg),
    }
    http.SetCookie(w, &c)
}
```

This isn't much different from the `setCookie` handler function from earlier, except this time you do a Base64 URL encoding of the message. You do so because the cookie values need to be URL encoded in the header. You managed to get away with it earlier because you didn't have any special characters like a space or the percentage sign, but you can't get away with here because messages will eventually need to have them.

Now let's look at the `showMessage` function:

```
func showMessage(w http.ResponseWriter, r *http.Request) {
    c, err := r.Cookie("flash")
    if err != nil {
        if err == http.ErrNoCookie {
            fmt.Fprintln(w, "No message found")
        }
    } else {
        rc := http.Cookie{
            Name:    "flash",
            MaxAge:  -1,
            Expires: time.Unix(1, 0),
        }
```

```
        http.SetCookie(w, &rc)
        val, _ := base64.URLEncoding.DecodeString(c.Value)
        fmt.Fprintln(w, string(val))
    }
}
```

First, you get the cookie. If you can't find the cookie (`err` will have a value of `http.ErrNoCookie`), you'll show the message "No message found."

If you find the message, you have to do two things:

1. Create a cookie with the same name, but with MaxAge set to a negative number and an Expires value that's in the past.
2. Send the cookie to the browser with `SetCookie`.

Here you're replacing the existing cookie, essentially removing it altogether because the MaxAge field is a negative number and the Expires field is in the past. Once you do that, you can decode your string and show the value.

Now let's see that in action. Start up your browser and go to http://localhost:8080/set_message. Figure 4.4 shows what you'll see in Web Inspector.

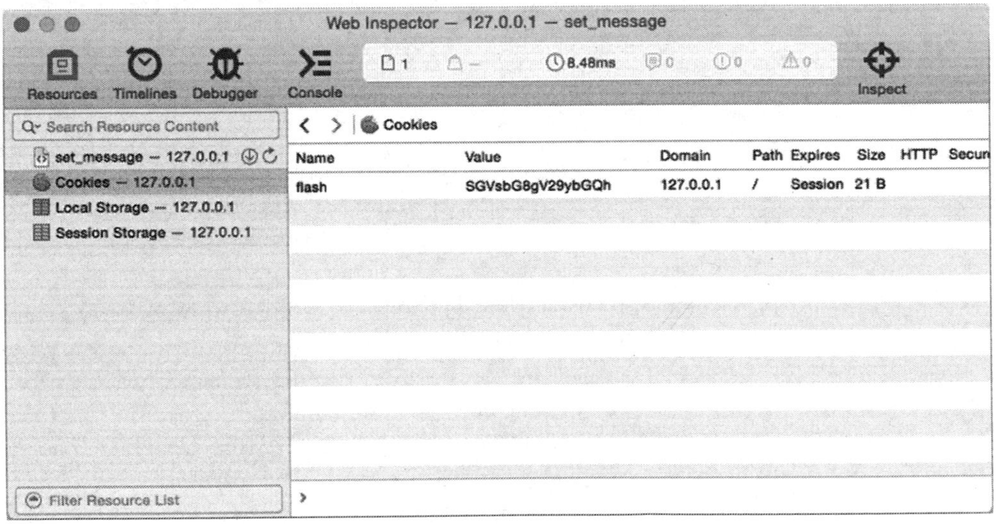


**Figure 4.4 The flash message cookie in Web Inspector (Safari)**

Notice that the value is Base64 URL encoded. Now, using the same browser window, go to http://localhost:8080/show_message. This is what you should see in the browser:

```
Hello World!
```

Go back to the Web Inspector and look at the cookies. Your cookie is gone! Setting a cookie with the same name to the browser will replace the old cookie with the new cookie of the same name. Because the new cookie has a negative number for MaxAge and expires in some time in the past, this tells the browser to remove the cookie, which means the earlier cookie you set is removed.

This is what you'll see in the browser:

```
No message found
```

This chapter wraps up our two-part tour of what net/http offers for web application development on the server. In the next chapter, we move on to the next big component in a web application: templates. I will cover template engines and templates in Go and show you how they can be used to generate responses to the client.

## 4.5 Summary

- Go provides a representation of the HTTP requests through various structs, which can be used to extract data from the requests.
- The Go `Request` struct has three fields, Form, PostForm, and MultipartForm, that allow easy extraction of different data from a request. To get data from these fields, call `ParseForm` or `ParseMultipartForm` to parse the request and then access the Form, PostForm, or MultipartForm field accordingly.
- Form is used for URL-encoded data from the URL and HTML form, PostForm is used for URL-encoded data from the HTML form only, and MultipartForm is used for multi-part data from the URL and HTML form.
- To send data back to the client, write header and body data to `ResponseWriter`.
- To persist data at the client, send cookies in the `ResponseWriter`.
- Cookies can be used for implementing flash messages.

# 5 Displaying content

***This chapter covers***

- Templates and template engines
- The Go template libraries text/template and html/template
- Actions, pipelines, and functions in templates
- Nesting of templates and layouts

A *web template* is a predesigned HTML page that's used repeatedly by a software program, called a template engine, to generate one or more HTML pages. Web template engines are an important part of any web application framework, and most if not all full-fledged frameworks have one. Although a number of frameworks have embedded template engines, many frameworks use a mix-and-match strategy that allows programmers to choose the template engine they prefer.

Go is no exception. Although Go is a relatively new programming language, there are already a few template engines built on it. However the Go's standard library provides strong template support through the text/template and html/template libraries, and unsurprisingly, most Go frameworks support these libraries as the default template engine.

In this chapter we'll focus on these two libraries and show how they can be used to generate HTML responses.

## 5.1 Templates and template engines

Template engines often combine data with templates to produce the final HTML (see figure 5.1). Handlers usually call template engines to combine data with the templates and return the resultant HTML to the client.

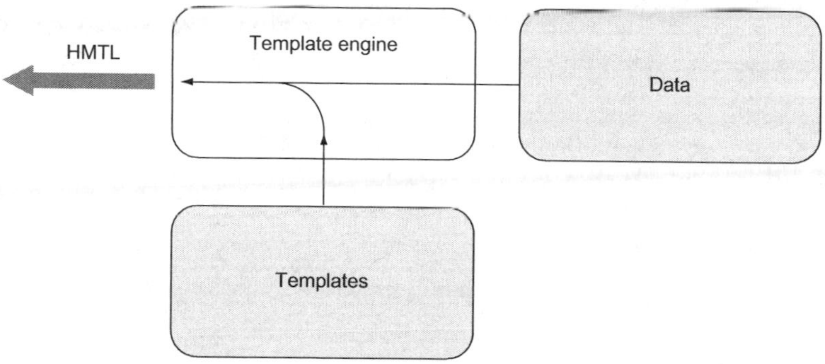


**Figure 5.1 Template engines combine data and templates to produce the final displayed HTML.**

Web template engines evolved from server-side includes (SSIs), which eventually branched out into web programming languages like PHP, ColdFusion, and JSP. As a result, no standards exist for template engines and the features of existing template engines vary widely, depending on why they were created. But there are roughly two ideal types of template engines, at opposite ends of the spectrum:

- *Logic-less template engines*—Dynamic data is substituted into the templates at specified placeholders. The template engine doesn't do any logic processing; it only does string substitutions. The idea behind having logic-less template engines is to have a clean separation between presentation and logic, where the processing is done by the handlers only.
- *Embedded logic template engines*—Programming language code is embedded into the template and executed during runtime by the template engine, including substitutions. This makes these types of template engines very powerful. Because the logic is embedded in the template itself, though, we often get the logic distributed between the handlers, making the code harder to maintain.

Logic-less template engines are usually faster to render because less processing is involved. Some template engines claim to be logic-less (such as Mustache), but the ideal of substitution-only is impossible to achieve. Mustache claims to be logic-less but has tags that behave like conditionals and loops.

Embedded logic template engines that are completely at the other end of the spectrum are indistinguishable from a computer program itself. We can see this with PHP.

PHP originated as a standalone web template engine, but today many PHP pages are written without a single line of HTML. It's difficult to even say that PHP is still a template engine. In fact, plenty of template engines, like Smarty and Blade, are built for PHP.

The biggest argument against embedded logic template engines is that presentation and logic are mixed up together and logic is distributed in multiple places, resulting in code that's hard to maintain. The counter-argument against logic-less template engines is that the ideal logic-less template engine would be impractical and that placing more logic into the handlers, especially for presentation, would add unnecessary complexity to the handlers.

In reality, most useful template engines would lie somewhere between these two ideal types, with some closer to being logic-less and others closer to having embedded logic. Go's template engine, mostly in text/template and the HTML-specific bits in html/template, is such a hybrid. It can be used as a logic-less template engine, but there's enough embedded features that make Go's template engine an interesting and powerful one.

## 5.2 The Go template engine

The Go template engine, like most template engines, lies somewhere along the spectrum between logic-less and embedded logic. In a web app, the handler normally triggers the template engine. Figure 5.2 shows how Go's template engine is called from a handler. The handler calls the template engine, passing it the template(s) to be used, usually as a list of template files and the dynamic data. The template engine then generates the HTML and writes it to the `ResponseWriter`, which adds it to the HTTP response sent back to the client.

Go templates are text documents (for web apps, these would normally be HTML files), with certain commands embedded in them, called *actions*. In the Go template

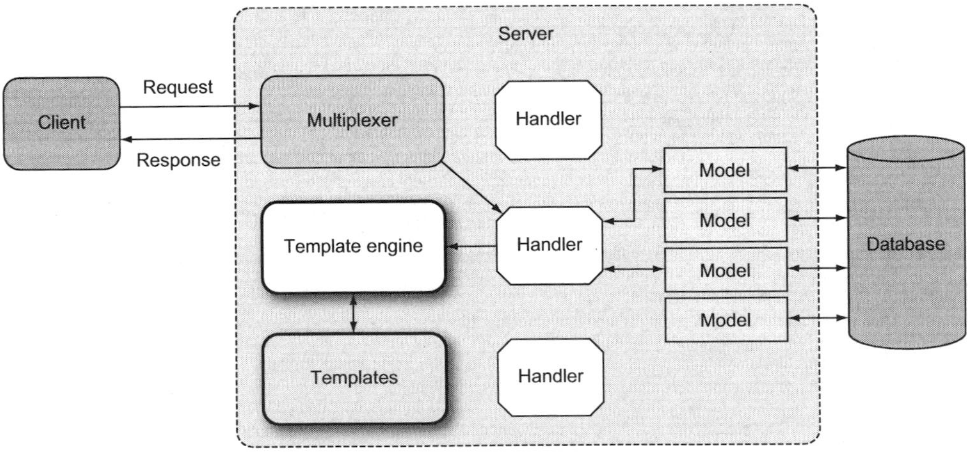


**Figure 5.2 The Go template engine as part of a web application**

engine, a template is text (usually in a template file) that has embedded actions. The text is parsed and executed by the template engine to produce another piece of text. Go has a text/template standard library that's a generic template engine for any type of text format, as well as an html/template library that's a specific template engine for HTML. Actions are added between two double braces, {{ and }} (although these delimiters can be changed programmatically). We'll get into actions later in this chapter. This listing shows an example of a very simple template.

**Listing 5.1 A simple template**

```
<!DOCTYPE html>
<html>
  <head>
    <meta http-equiv="Content-Type" content="text/html; charset=utf-8">
    <title>Go Web Programming</title>
  </head>
  <body>
    {{ . }}
  </body>
</html>
```

This template is placed in a template file named tmpl.html. Naturally we can have as many template files as we like. Template files must be in a readable text format but can have any extension. In this case because it generates HTML output, I used the .html extension.

Notice the dot (.) between the double braces. The dot is an action, and it's a command for the template engine to replace it with a value when the template is executed.

Using the Go web template engine requires two steps:

1. Parse the text-formatted template source, which can be a string or from a template file, to create a parsed template struct.
2. Execute the parsed template, passing a `ResponseWriter` and some data to it. This triggers the template engine to combine the parsed template with the data to generate the final HTML that's passed to the `ResponseWriter`.

This listing provides a concrete, simple example.

**Listing 5.2 Triggering a template engine from a handler function**

```
package main

import (
    "net/http"
    "html/template"
)

func process(w http.ResponseWriter, r *http.Request) {
    t, _ := template.ParseFiles("tmpl.html")
    t.Execute(w, "Hello World!")
}
```

```
func main() {
    server := http.Server{
        Addr: "127.0.0.1:8080",
    }
    http.HandleFunc("/process", process)
    server.ListenAndServe()
}
```

We're back to our server again. This time we have a handler function named `process`, which triggers the template engine. First, we parse the template file tmpl.html using the `ParseFiles` function which returns a parsed template of type `Template` and an error, which we conveniently ignore for brevity.

```
t, _ := template.ParseFiles("tmpl.html")
```

Then we call the `Execute` method to apply data (in this case, the string `Hello World!`) to the template:

```
t.Execute(w, "Hello World!")
```

We pass in the `ResponseWriter` along with the data so that the generated HTML can be passed into it. When you're running this example, the template file should be in the same directory as the binary (remember that we didn't specify the absolute path to the file).

This is the simplest way to use the template engine, and as expected, there are variations, which I'll describe later in the chapter.

### 5.2.1 Parsing templates

`ParseFiles` is a standalone function that parses template files and creates a parsed template struct that you can execute later. The `ParseFiles` function is actually a convenience function to the `ParseFiles` method on the `Template` struct. When you call the `ParseFiles` function, Go creates a new template, with the name of the file as the name of the template:

```
t, _ := template.ParseFiles("tmpl.html")
```

Then it calls the `ParseFiles` method on that template:

```
t := template.New("tmpl.html")
t, _ := t.ParseFiles("tmpl.html")
```

`ParseFiles` (both the function and the method) can take in one or more filenames as parameters (making it a *variadic* function—that is, a function that can take in a variable number of parameters). But it still returns just one template, regardless of the number of files it's passed. What's up with that?

When we pass in more than one file, the returned parsed template has the name and content of the first file. The rest of the files are parsed as a map of templates, which can be referred to later on during the execution. You can think of this as `ParseFiles` returning a template when you provide a single file and a template set when you provide more than one file. This fact is important when we look at including a template within a template, or nesting templates, later in this chapter.

Another way to parse files is to use the ParseGlob function, which uses pattern matching instead of specific files. Using the same example:

```
t, _ := template.ParseFiles("tmpl.html")
```

and

```
t, _ := template.ParseGlob("*.html")
```

would be the same, if tmpl.html were the only file in the same path.

Parsing files is probably the most common use, but you can also parse templates using strings. In fact, all other ways of parsing templates ultimately call the Parse method to parse the template. Using the same example again:

```
t, _ := template.ParseFiles("tmpl.html")
```

and

```
tmpl := `<!DOCTYPE html>
<html>
  <head>
    <meta http-equiv="Content-Type" content="text/html; charset=utf-8">
    <title>Go Web Programming</title>
  </head>
  <body>
    {{ . }}
  </body>
</html>
`
t := template.New("tmpl.html")
t, _ = t.Parse(tmpl)
t.Execute(w, "Hello World!")
```

are the same, assuming tmpl.html contains the same HTML.

So far we've been ignoring the error that's returned along with the parsed template. The usual Go practice is to handle the error, but Go provides another mechanism to handle errors returned by parsing templates:

```
t  := template.Must(template.ParseFiles("tmpl.html"))
```

The Must function wraps around a function that returns a pointer to a template and an error, and panics if the error is not a nil. (In Go, *panicking* refers to a situation where the normal flow of execution is stopped, and if it's within a function, the function returns to its caller. The process continues up the stack until it reaches the main program, which then crashes.)

### 5.2.2 Executing templates

The usual way to execute a template is to call the Execute function on a template, passing it the ResponseWriter and the data. This works well when the parsed template is a single template instead of a template set. If you call the Execute method on a template set, it'll take the first template in the set. But if you want to execute a different template in the template set and not the first one, you need to use the `ExecuteTemplate` method. For example:

```
t, _ := template.ParseFiles("t1.html", "t2.html")
```

The argument `t` is a template set containing two templates, the first named t1.html and the second t2.html (the name of the template is the name of the file, extension and all, unless you change it). If you call the `Execute` method on it:

```
t.Execute(w, "Hello World!")
```

it'll result in t1.html being executed. If you want to execute t2.html, you need to do this instead:

```
t.ExecuteTemplate(w, "t2.html", "Hello World!")
```

We've discussed how to trigger the template engine to parse and execute templates. Let's look at the templates next.

## 5.3 Actions

As mentioned earlier, *actions* are embedded commands in Go templates, placed between a set of double braces, {{ and }}. Go has an extensive set of actions, which are quite powerful and flexible. In this section, we'll discuss some of the important ones:

- Conditional actions
- Iterator actions
- Set actions
- Include actions

We'll discuss another important action, the define action, later in this chapter. You can look up the other actions in the text/template library documentation.

It might come as a surprise, but the dot (.) is an action, and it's the most important one. The dot is the evaluation of the data that's passed to the template. The other actions and functions mostly manipulate the dot for formatting and display.

### 5.3.1 Conditional actions

The conditional actions are ones that select one of many data evaluations depending on value of the argument. The simplest action is one with this format:

```
{{ if arg }}
  some content
{{ end }}
```

The other variant is

```
{{ if arg }}
  some content
{{ else }}
  other content
{{ end }}
```

The arg in both formats is the argument to the action. We'll examine arguments in detail later in this chapter. For now, consider arguments to be values like a string constant, a variable, a function, or a method that returns a value. Let's see how it can be used in a template. First, you need to create a handler that generates a random integer between 0 and 10, shown in the next listing. Then you check if it's larger than 5 and return it as a Boolean to the template.

**Listing 5.3 Generating a random number in the handler**

```
package main

import (
    "net/http"
    "html/template"
    "math/rand"
    "time"
)

func process(w http.ResponseWriter, r *http.Request) {
    t, _ := template.ParseFiles("tmpl.html")
    rand.Seed(time.Now().Unix())
    t.Execute(w, rand.Intn(10) > 5)
}

func main() {
    server := http.Server{
        Addr: "127.0.0.1:8080",
    }
    http.HandleFunc("/process", process)
    server.ListenAndServe()
}
```

Next, in the template file tmpl.html, you test the argument (which happens to be the dot, which is the value passed from the handler) and display either *Number is greater than 5!* or *Number is 5 or less!*

**Listing 5.4 Template file tmpl.html for conditional action**

```
<!DOCTYPE html>
<html>
  <head>
    <meta http-equiv="Content-Type" content="text/html; charset=utf-8">
    <title>Go Web Programming</title>
  </head>
  <body>
    {{ if . }}
      Number is greater than 5!
    {{ else }}
      Number is 5 or less!
    {{ end }}
  </body>
</html>
```

### 5.3.2 Iterator actions

Iterator actions are those that iterate through an array, slice, map, or channel. Within the iteration loop, the dot (.) is set to the successive elements of the array, slice, map, or channel. This is how it looks:

```
{{ range array }}
  Dot is set to the element {{ . }}
{{ end }}
```

The example in this listing shows the template file tmpl.html.

**Listing 5.5 Iterator action**

```
<!DOCTYPE html>
<html>
  <head>
    <meta http-equiv="Content-Type" content="text/html; charset=utf-8">
    <title>Go Web Programming</title>
  </head>
  <body>
    <ul>
    {{ range . }}
      <li>{{ . }}</li>
    {{ end}}
    </ul>
  </body>
</html>
```

Let's look at the triggering handler:

```
func process(w http.ResponseWriter, r *http.Request) {
    t, _ := template.ParseFiles("tmpl.html")
    daysOfWeek := []string{"Mon", "Tue", "Wed", "Thu", "Fri", "Sat", "Sun"}
    t.Execute(w, daysOfWeek)
}
```

You're simply passing a slice of strings with the short names of the days in a week. This slice is then passed on to the dot (.) in the {{ range . }}, which loops through the elements of this slice.

The {{ . }} within the iterator loop is an element in the slice, so figure 5.3 shows what you'll see in the browser.

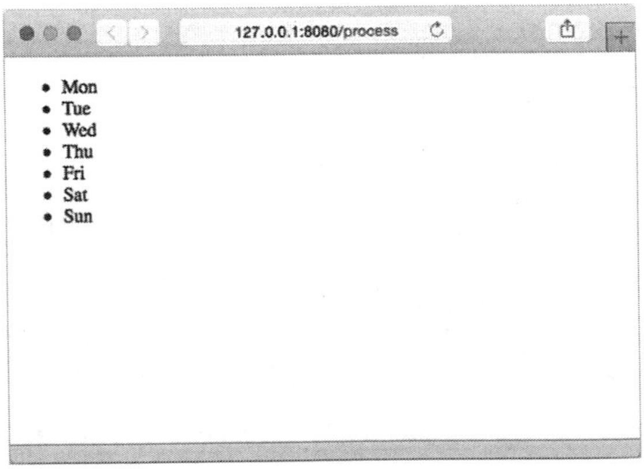


**Figure 5.3 Iterating with the iterator action**

The following listing shows a variant of the iterator action that allows you to display a fallback in case the iterator is empty.

**Listing 5.6 Iterator action with fallback**

```
<html>
  <head>
    <meta http-equiv="Content-Type" content="text/html; charset=utf-8">
    <title>Go Web Programming</title>
  </head>
  <body>
    <ul>
    {{ range . }}
      <li>{{ . }}</li>
    {{ else }}
      <li> Nothing to show </li>
    {{ end}}
    </ul>
  </body>
</html>
```

// iterator action w. fallback

In the listing the content after `{{ else }}` and before `{{ end }}` will be displayed if the dot (.) is `nil`. In this case, we're displaying the text *Nothing to show.*

### 5.3.3 Set actions

The set actions allow us to set the value of dot (.) for use within the enclosed section. This is how it looks:

```
{{ with arg }}
  Dot is set to arg
{{ end }}
```

The dot (.) between `{{ with arg }}` and `{{ end }}` is now pointing to `arg`. In the next listing, let's look at something more concrete and make changes to tmpl.html again.

**Listing 5.7 Setting the dot**

```
<html>
  <head>
    <meta http-equiv="Content-Type" content="text/html; charset=utf-8">
    <title>Go Web Programming</title>
  </head>
  <body>
    <div>The dot is {{ . }}</div>
    <div>
    {{ with "world"}}
      Now the dot is set to {{ . }}
    {{ end }}
    </div>
    <div>The dot is {{ . }} again</div>
  </body>
</html>
```

For the handler, we'll pass a string `hello` to the template:

```
func process(w http.ResponseWriter, r *http.Request) {
    t, _ := template.ParseFiles("tmpl.html")
    t.Execute(w,"hello")
}
```

The dot before `{{ with "world"}}` is set to `hello`. The value is from the handler, but between `{{ with "world"}}` and `{{ end }}` it's set to `world`. After `{{ end }}` it'll revert to `hello` again, as shown in figure 5.4.

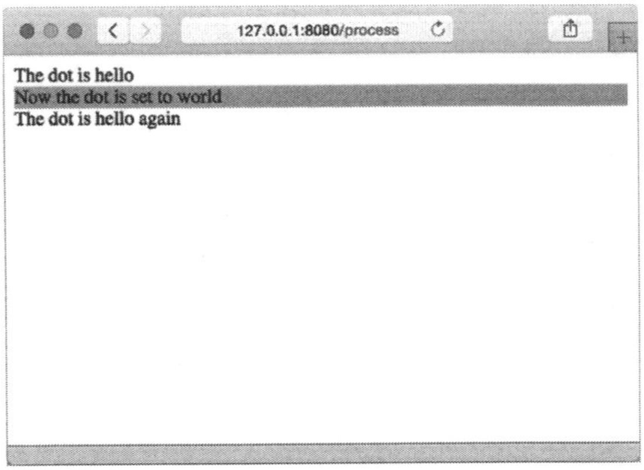


**Figure 5.4 Setting the dot with the set action**

As with the iterator action, there's a variant of the set action that allows a fallback:

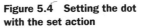

```
{{ with arg }}
  Dot is set to arg
{{ else }}
  Fallback if arg is empty
{{ end }}
```

This listing takes another look at how this is used in tmpl.html.

**Listing 5.8 Setting the dot with fallback**

```
<html>
  <head>
    <meta http-equiv="Content-Type" content="text/html; charset=utf-8">
    <title>Go Web Programming</title>
  </head>
  <body>
    <div>The dot is {{ . }}</div>
    <div>
    {{ with "" }}
      Now the dot is set to {{ . }}
    {{ else }}
      The dot is still {{ . }}
    {{ end }}
```

```
    </div>
    <div>The dot is {{ . }} again</div>
  </body>
</html>
```

The argument next to the `with` action is an empty string, which means the content after `{{ else }}` will be displayed. The dot in the content is still `hello` because it's not affected. If you run the server again (you don't need to make any changes to the handler—in fact, you don't even need to stop the server), you'll see figure 5.5.

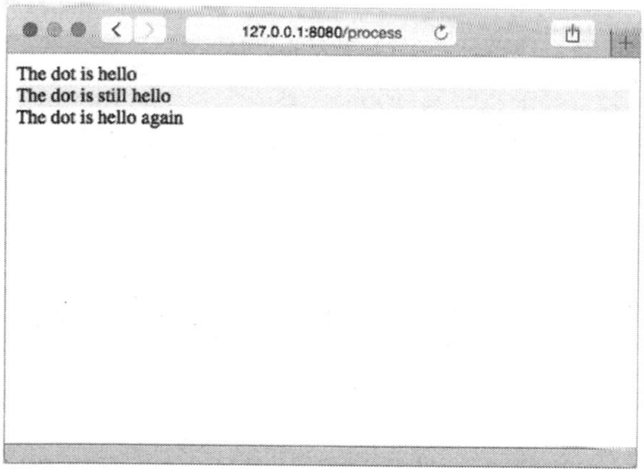

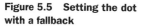

**Figure 5.5 Setting the dot with a fallback**

### 5.3.4 *Include actions*

Next, we have the include actions, which allow us to include a template in another template. As you might realize, these actions let us nest templates. The format of the include action is `{{ template "name" }}`, where `name` is the name of the template to be included.

In our example, we have two templates: t1.html and t2.html. The template t1.html includes t2.html. Let's look at t1.html first.

**Listing 5.9 t1.html**

```
<!DOCTYPE html>
<html lang="en">
  <head>
    <meta charset="utf-8">
    <meta http-equiv="X-UA-Compatible" content="IE=9">
    <title>Go Web Programming</title>
  </head>
  <body>
    <div> This is t1.html before</div>
    <div>This is the value of the dot in t1.html - [{{ . }}]</div>
    <hr/>
    {{ template "t2.html" }}
    <hr/>
```

```
    <div> This is t1.html after</div>
  </body>
</html>
```

As you can see, the name of the file is used as the name of the template. Remember that if we don't set the name of the template when it's created, Go will set the name of the file, including its extension, as the name of the template.

Let's look at t2.html now.

**Listing 5.10 t2.html**

```
<div style="background-color: yellow;">
  This is t2.html<br/>
  This is the value of the dot in t2.html - [{{ . }}]
</div>
```

The template t2.html is a snippet of HTML. The next listing shows the handler, which is just as short.

**Listing 5.11 Handler that includes templates**

```
func process(w http.ResponseWriter, r *http.Request) {
    t, _ := template.ParseFiles("t1.html", "t2.html")
    t.Execute(w, "Hello World!")
}
```

Unlike with the previous handlers, we need to parse both the template files that we're going to use. This is extremely important because if we forget to parse our template files, we'll get nothing.

Because we didn't set the name of the templates, the templates in the template set use the name of the files. As mentioned earlier, the parameters for the `ParseFiles` function are position-sensitive for the first parameter. The first template file that's parsed is the main template, and when we call the `Execute` method on the template set, this is the template that'll be called.

Figure 5.6 shows what happens in the browser when you run the server.

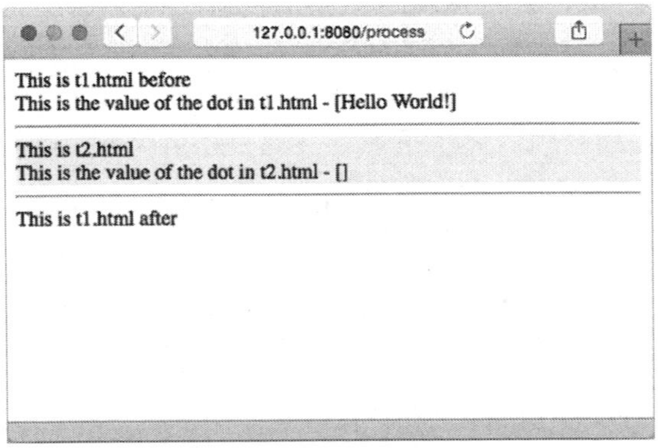


**Figure 5.6 Including a template within a template**

You can see that in t1.html the dot is replaced correctly with `Hello World!` And the contents of t2.html are inserted where `{{ template "t2.html" }}` appears. You can also see that the dot in t2.html is empty because the string `Hello World!` isn't passed to included templates. But there's a variant of the include action that allows this: `{{ template "name" arg }}`, where `arg` is the argument you want to pass on to the included template. This listing shows how this works in our example.

**Listing 5.12 t1.html with an argument passed to t2.html**

```
<html>
  <head>
    <meta charset="utf-8">
    <meta http-equiv="X-UA-Compatible" content="IE=9">
    <title>Go Web Programming</title>
  </head>
  <body>
    <div> This is t1.html before</div>
    <div>This is the value of the dot in t1.html - [{{ . }}]</div>
    <hr/>
    {{ template "t2.html" . }}
    <hr/>
    <div> This is t1.html after</div>
  </body>
</html>
```

The change isn't obvious, but what we did here in t1.html is pass the dot to t2.html. If we go back to the browser now, we'll see figure 5.7.

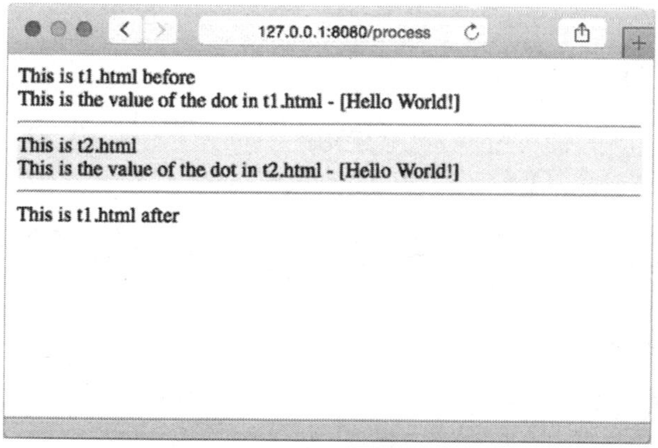

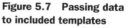

**Figure 5.7 Passing data to included templates**

Actions provide flexibility for programmers, but so far we've only seen the simpler and more straightforward use of templates. We'll get back into nested templates later in this chapter, and also talk about another action that we didn't cover in this section: the define action. But first, we need to talk about arguments, variables, and pipelines.

## 5.4 Arguments, variables, and pipelines

An *argument* is a value that's used in a template. It can be a Boolean, integer, string, and so on. It can also be a struct, or a field of a struct, or the key of an array. Arguments can be a variable, a method (which must return either one value, or a value and an error) or a function. An argument can also be a dot (.), which is the value passed from the template engine.

In the example

```
{{ if arg }}
  some content
{{ end }}
```

the argument is `arg`.

We can also set variables in the action. Variables start with the dollar sign (`$`) and look like this:

```
$variable := value
```

Variables don't look too useful at first glance, but they can be quite invaluable in actions. Here's one way to use a variable as a variant of the iterator action:

```
{{ range $key, $value := . }}
  The key is {{ $key }} and the value is {{ $value }}
{{ end }}
```

In this snippet, the dot (.) is a map and `range` initializes the `$key` and `$value` variables with the key and value of the successive elements in the map.

*Pipelines* are arguments, functions, and methods chained together in a sequence. This works much like the Unix pipeline. In fact, the syntax looks very similar

```
{{ p1 | p2 | p3 }}
```

where `p1`, `p2`, and `p3` are either arguments or functions. Pipelining allows us to send the output of an argument into the next one, which is separated by the pipeline (|). The next listing shows how this looks in a template.

**Listing 5.13 Pipelining in a template**

```
<!DOCTYPE html>
<html>
  <head>
    <meta http-equiv="Content-Type" content="text/html; charset=utf-8">
    <title>Go Web Programming</title>
  </head>
  <body>
    {{ 12.3456 | printf "%.2f" }}
  </body>
</html>
```

We often need to reformat data for display in our templates, and in the previous listing we want to display a floating point number with two decimal points accuracy. To do so, we can use the `fmt.Sprintf` function or the built-in `printf` function that wraps around `fmt.Sprintf`.

In listing 5.13, we pipe the number 12.3456 to the `printf` function, with the format specifier as the first parameter (we'll talk about functions later in this chapter). This will result in *12.35* being displayed in the browser.

Pipelining doesn't look terribly exciting, but when we talk about functions you'll understand why it can be a very powerful feature.

## 5.5 Functions

As mentioned earlier, an argument can be a Go function. The Go template engine has a set of built-in functions that are pretty basic, including a number of aliases for variants of `fmt.Sprint`.(Refer to the `fmt` package documentation to see the list.) What's more useful is the capability for programmers to define their own functions.

Go template engine functions are limited. Although a function can take any number of input parameters, it must only return either one value, or two values only if the second value is an error.

To define custom functions, you need to:

1. Create a `FuncMap` map, which has the name of the function as the key and the actual function as the value.
2. Attach the `FuncMap` to the template.

Let's look at how you can create your own custom function. When writing web applications, you may need to convert a time or date object to an ISO8601 formatted time or date string, respectively. Unfortunately, this formatter isn't a built-in function, which gives you a nice excuse for creating it as a custom function, shown next.

**Listing 5.14 Custom function for templates**

```
package main

import (
    "net/http"
    "html/template"
    "time"
)

func formatDate(t time.Time) string {
    layout := "2006-01-02"
    return t.Format(layout)
}

func process(w http.ResponseWriter, r *http.Request) {
    funcMap := template.FuncMap { "fdate": formatDate }
    t := template.New("tmpl.html").Funcs(funcMap)
    t, _ = t.ParseFiles("tmpl.html")
```

```
    t.Execute(w, time.Now())
}

func main() {
    server := http.Server{
        Addr: "127.0.0.1:8080",
    }
    http.HandleFunc("/process", process)
    server.ListenAndServe()
}
```

The previous listing defines a function named `formatDate` that takes in a `Time` struct and returns an ISO8601 formatted string in the Year-Month-Day format. This is the function that we'll be using later.

In the handler, you first create a `FuncMap` struct named `funcMap`, mapping the name `fdate` to the `formatDate` function. Next, you create a template with the name tmpl.html using the `template.New` function. This function returns a template, so you can chain it with the `Funcs` function, passing it `funcMap`. This attaches `funcMap` to the template, which you can then use to parse your template file tmpl.html. Finally, you call `Execute` on the template, passing it the `ResponseWriter` as well as the current time.

There are potentially a few minor gotchas here. First you need to attach the `FuncMap` before you parse the template. This is because when you parse the template you must already know the functions used within the template, which you won't unless the template has the `FuncMap`.

Second, remember that when you call `ParseFiles` if no templates are defined in the template files, it'll take the name of the file as the template name. When you create a new template using the `New` function, you'll have to pass in the template name. If this template name and the template name derived from the filename don't match, you'll get an error.

Now that you have the handler done, the following listing shows you how you can use it in tmpl.html.

**Listing 5.15 Using a custom function by pipelining**

```
<html>
  <head>
    <meta http-equiv="Content-Type" content="text/html; charset=utf-8">
    <title>Go Web Programming</title>
  </head>
  <body>
    <div>The date/time is {{ . | fdate }}</div>
  </body>
</html>
```

You can use your function in a couple of ways. You can use it in a pipeline, piping the current time into the `fdate` function, which will produce figure 5.8.

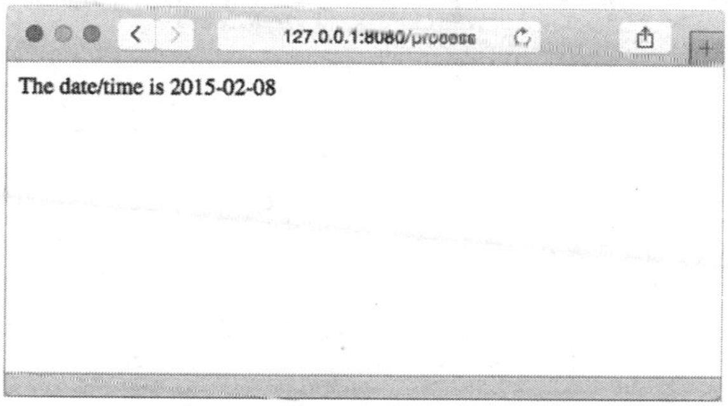

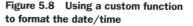

**Figure 5.8 Using a custom function to format the date/time**

An alternative is to use it as with a normal function, passing the dot as a parameter to the `fdate` function, as illustrated in this listing.

**Listing 5.16 Using a custom function by passing parameters**

```
<html>
  <head>
    <meta http-equiv="Content-Type" content="text/html; charset=utf-8">
    <title>Go Web Programming</title>
  </head>
  <body>
    <div>The date/time is {{ fdate . }}</div>
  </body>
</html>
```

Both produce the same results, but you can see that pipelining is more powerful and flexible. If you define a number of custom functions, you can pipeline the output of one function to the input of another, as well as mix and match them. Although you can also do this with normal function calls, this approach is a lot more readable and creates simpler code.

## 5.6 Context awareness

One of the most interesting features of the Go template engine is that the content it displays can be changed according to its context. Yes, you read this correctly. The content that's displayed changes depending on where you place it within the document; that is, the display of the content is *context-aware.* Why would anyone want that and how is it useful?

One obvious use of this is to escape the displayed content properly. This means if the content is HTML, it will be HTML escaped; if it is JavaScript, it will be JavaScript escaped; and so on. The Go template engine also recognizes content that's part of a URL or is a CSS style. This listing demonstrates how this works.

**Listing 5.17 Handler for context awareness in templates**

```
package main

import (
    "net/http"
  "html/template"
)

func process(w http.ResponseWriter, r *http.Request) {
    t, _ := template.ParseFiles("tmpl.html")
    content := `I asked: <i>"What's up?"</i>`
    t.Execute(w, content)
}

func main() {
    server := http.Server{
        Addr: "127.0.0.1:8080",
    }
    http.HandleFunc("/process", process)
    server.ListenAndServe()
}
```

For the handler, we're going to send a text string I asked: <i>"What's up?"</i>. This string has a number of special characters that normally should be escaped beforehand. This listing contains the template file tmpl.html.

**Listing 5.18 Context-aware template**

```
<html>
  <head>
    <meta http-equiv="Content-Type" content="text/html; charset=utf-8">
    <title>Go Web Programming</title>
  </head>
  <body>
    <div>{{ . }}</div>
    <div><a href="/{{ . }}">Path</a></div>
    <div><a href="/?q={{ . }}">Query</a></div>
    <div><a onclick="f('{{ . }}')">Onclick</a></div>
  </body>
</html>
```

As you can see, we're placing it in various places within the HTML. The "control" text is within a normal <div> tag. When we run cURL to get the raw HTML (please refer to section 4.1.4), we get this:

```
curl -i 127.0.0.1:8080/process
HTTP/1.1 200 OK
Date: Sat, 07 Feb 2015 05:42:41 GMT
```

```
Content-Length: 505
Content-Type: text/html; charset=utf-8

<html>
  <head>
    <meta http-equiv="Content-Type" content="text/html; charset=utf-8">
    <title>Go Web Programming</title>
  </head>
  <body>
    <div>I asked: &lt;i&gt;&#34;What&#39;s up?&#34;&lt;/i&gt;</div>
    <div>
      <a href="/I%20asked:%20%3ci%3e%22What%27s%20up?%22%3c/i%3e">
        Path
      </a>
    </div>
    <div>
      <a href="/?q=I%20asked%3a%20%3ci%3e%22What%27s%20up%3f%22%3c%2fi%3e">
        Query
      </a>
    </div>
    <div>
      <a onclick="f('I asked: \x3ci\x3e\x22What\x27s up?\x22\x3c\/i\x3e')">
        Onclick
        </a>
    </div>
  </body>
</html>
```

which looks a bit messy. Let's explore the differences in table 5.1.

**Table 5.1 Context awareness in Go templates: different content is produced according to the location of the actions**

| Context | Content |
|---|---|
| Original text | I asked: <i>"What's up?"</i> |
| {{ . }} | I asked: <i>"What's up?"</i> |
| <a href="/{{ . }}"> | I%20asked:%20%3ci%3e%22What%27s%20up?%22%3c/i%3e |
| <a href="/?q={{ . }}"> | I%20asked%3a%20%3ci%3e%22What%27s%20up%3f%22%3c%2fi%3e |
| <a onclick="{{ . }}"> | I asked: \x3ci\x3e\x22What\x27s up?\x22\x3c\/i\x3e |

This feature is pretty convenient, but its critical use is for automating defensive programming. By changing the content according to the context, we eliminate certain obvious and newbie programmer mistakes. Let's see how this feature can be used to defend against XSS (cross-site scripting) attacks.

### 5.6.1 Defending against XSS attacks

A common XSS attack is the persistent XSS vulnerability. This happens when data provided by an attacker is saved to the server and then displayed to other users as it is. Say there's a vulnerable forum site that allows its users to create posts or comments to be saved and read by other users. An attacker can post a comment that includes malicious JavaScript code within the `<script>` tag. Because the forum displays the comment as is and whatever is within the `<script>` tag isn't shown to the user, the malicious code is executed with the user's permissions but without the user's knowledge. The normal way to prevent this is to escape whatever is passed into the system before displaying or storing it. But as with most exploits and bugs, the biggest culprit is the human factor.

Rather than hardcoding data at the handler, you can put your newly acquired knowledge from chapter 4 to good use and create an HTML form, shown in the following listing, that allows you to submit data to your web application and place it in a form.html file.

**Listing 5.19 Form for submitting XSS attack**

```
<html>
  <head>
    <meta http-equiv="Content-Type" content="text/html; charset=utf-8">
    <title>Go Web Programming</title>
  </head>
  <body>
    <form action="/process" method="post">
      Comment: <input name="comment" type="text">
      <hr/>
      <button id="submit">Submit</button>
    </form>
  </body>
</html>
```

Next, change your handler accordingly to process the data from the form shown in this listing.

**Listing 5.20 Testing an XSS attack**

```
package main

import (
    "net/http"
    "html/template"
)

func process(w http.ResponseWriter, r *http.Request) {
    t, _ := template.ParseFiles("tmpl.html")
    t.Execute(w, r.FormValue("comment"))
}
```

```
func form(w http.ResponseWriter, r *http.Request) {
    t, _ := template.ParseFiles("form.html")
    t.Execute(w, nil)
}

func main() {
    server := http.Server{
        Addr: "127.0.0.1:8080",
    }
    http.HandleFunc("/process", process)
    http.HandleFunc("/form", form)
    server.ListenAndServe()
}
```

In your tmpl.html, clean up the output a bit to better see the results.

**Listing 5.21 Cleaned-up tmpl.html**

```
<html>
  <head>
    <meta http-equiv="Content-Type" content="text/html; charset=utf-8">
    <title>Go Web Programming</title>
  </head>
  <body>
    <div>{{ . }}</div>
  </body>
</html>
```

Now compile the server and start it up, then go to http://127.0.0.1:8080/form. Enter the following into the text field and click the submit button, shown in figure 5.9:

```
<script>alert('Pwnd!');</script>
```

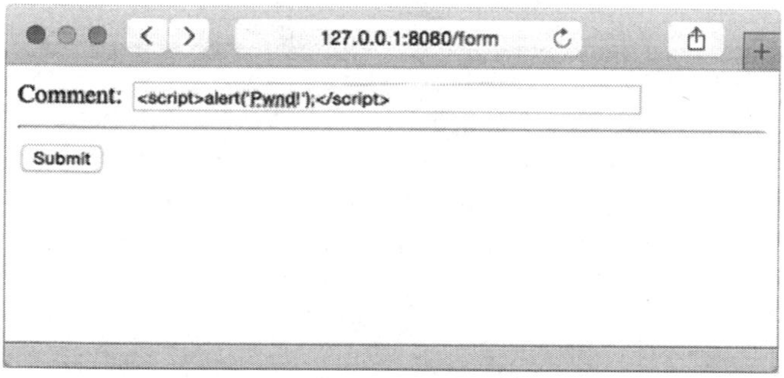


**Figure 5.9 Form for creating an XSS attack**

A web app using a different template engine that doesn't scrub the input, and displays user input directly on a web page, will get an alert message, or potentially any other malicious code that the attacker writes. As you probably realize, the Go template engine protects you from such mistakes because even if you don't scrub the input, when the input is displayed on the screen it'll be converted into escaped HTML, shown in figure 5.10.

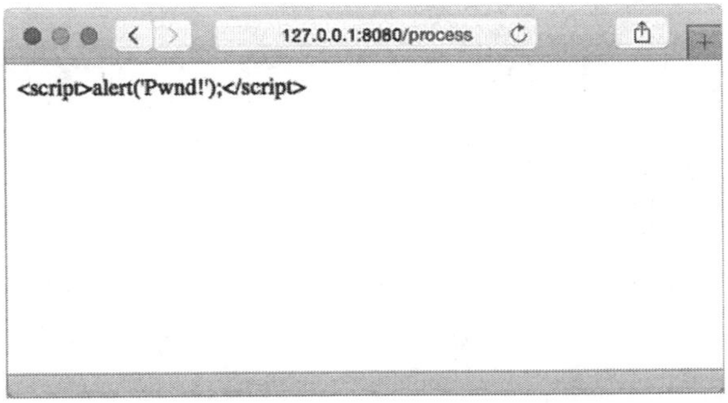

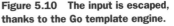

**Figure 5.10 The input is escaped, thanks to the Go template engine.**

If you inspect the source code of the page you'll see something like this:

```
<html>
  <head>
    <meta http-equiv="Content-Type" content="text/html; charset=utf-8">
    <title>Go Web Programming</title>
  </head>
  <body>
    <div>&lt;script&gt;alert(&#39;Pwnd!&#39;);&lt;/script&gt;</div>
  </body>
</html>
```

Context-awareness isn't just for HTML, it also works on XSS attacks on JavaScript, CSS, and even URLs. Does this mean we're saved from ourselves if we use the Go template engine? Well, no, nothing really saves us from ourselves, and there are ways of getting around this. In fact, Go allows us to escape from being context-aware if we really want to.

### 5.6.2 *Unescaping HTML*

Say you really want this behavior, meaning you want the user to enter HTML or JavaScript code that's executable when displayed. Go provides a mechanism to "unescape" HTML. Just cast your input string to template.HTML and use that instead, and our code is happily unescaped. Let's see how to do this. First, make a minor change to the handler:

```
func process(w http.ResponseWriter, r *http.Request) {
    t, _ := template.ParseFiles("tmpl.html")
    t.Execute(w, template.HTML(r.FormValue("comment")))
}
```

Notice that you've just typecast the comment value to the template.HTML type.

Now recompile and run the server, and then try the same attack. What happens depends on which browser you use. If you use Internet Explorer (8 and above),

Chrome, or Safari, nothing will happen—you'll get a blank page. If you use Firefox, you'll get something like figure 5.11.

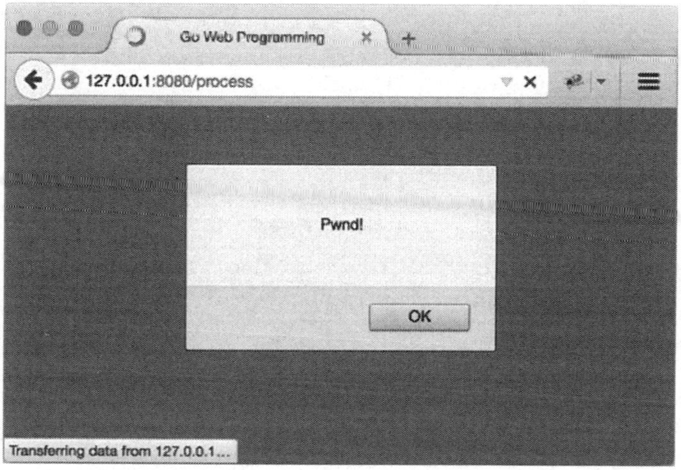


**Figure 5.11 You are pwnd!**

What just happened? By default Internet Explorer, Chrome, and Safari have built-in support for protection against certain types of XSS attacks. As a result, the simulated XSS attack doesn't work on these browsers. But you can turn off the protection by sending a special HTTP response header: *X-XSS-Protection* (originally created by Microsoft for Internet Explorer) will disable it. (Note: Firefox doesn't have default protection against these types of attacks.)

If you really want to stop the browser from protecting you from XSS attacks, you simply need to set a response header in our handler:

```
func process(w http.ResponseWriter, r *http.Request) {
    w.Header().Set("X-XSS-Protection", "0")
    t, _ := template.ParseFiles("tmpl.html")
    t.Execute(w, template.HTML(r.FormValue("comment")))
}
```

Once you do this and try the same attack again, you'll find that the attack works for Internet Explorer, Chrome, and Safari.

## 5.7 Nesting templates

We went through quite a lot of features of the Go template engine in this chapter. Before we move on, I'd like to show you how you can use layouts in your web app.

So what exactly are layouts? *Layouts* are fixed patterns in web page design that can be reused for multiple pages. Web apps often use layouts, because pages in a web app need to look the same for a consistent UI. For example, many web application designs have a header menu as well as a footer that provides additional information such as status or copyright or contact details. Other layouts include a left navigation bar or multilevel navigation menus. You can easily make the leap that layouts can be implemented with nested templates.

In an earlier section, you learned that templates can be nested using the include action. If you start writing a complicated web app, though, you'll realize that you might end up with a lot of hardcoding in your handler and a lot of template files.

Why is this so?

Remember that the syntax of the include action looks like this:

```
{{ template "name" . }}
```

where `name` is the name of the template and a string constant. This means that if you use the name of the file as the template name, it'll be impossible to have one or two common layouts, because every page will have its own layout template file—which defeats the purpose of having layouts in the first place. As an example, the file shown in the next listing won't work as a common layout template file.

**Listing 5.22 An unworkable layout file**

```
<html>
  <head>
    <meta http-equiv="Content-Type" content="text/html; charset=utf-8">
    <title>Go Web Programming</title>
  </head>
  <body>
    {{ template "content.html" }}
  </body>
</html>
```

The answer to this dilemma is that the Go template engine doesn't work this way. Although we can have each template file define a single template, with the name of the template as the name of the file, we can explicitly define a template in a template file using the define action. This listing shows our layout.html now.

**Listing 5.23 Defining a template explicitly**

```
{{ define "layout" }}

<html>
  <head>
    <meta http-equiv="Content-Type" content="text/html; charset=utf-8">
    <title>Go Web Programming</title>
  </head>
  <body>
    {{ template "content" }}
  </body>
</html>

{{ end }}
```

Notice that we start the file with `{{ define "layout" }}` and end it with `{{ end }}`. Anything within these two action tags is considered part of the layout template. This means if we have another define action tag after the `{{ end }}` we can define another template! In other words, we can define multiple templates in the same template file, as you can see in this listing.

**Listing 5.24 Defining multiple templates in a single template file**

```
{{ define "layout" }}

<html>
  <head>
    <meta http-equiv="Content-Type" content="text/html; charset=utf-8">
    <title>Go Web Programming</title>
  </head>
  <body>
    {{ template "content" }}
  </body>
</html>

{{ end }}

{{ define "content" }}

Hello World!

{{ end }}
```

The following listing shows how we use these templates in our handler.

**Listing 5.25 Using explicitly defined templates**

```
func process(w http.ResponseWriter, r *http.Request) {
    t, _ := template.ParseFiles("layout.html")
    t.ExecuteTemplate(w, "layout", "")
}
```

Parsing the template file is the same, but this time if we want to execute the template, we have to be more explicit and use the `ExecuteTemplate` method, with the name of the template we want to execute as the second parameter. The layout template nests the content template, so if we execute the layout template, we'll see `Hello World!` in the browser. Let's use cURL to get the actual HTML so that we can see it properly:

```
> curl -i http://127.0.0.1:8080/process
HTTP/1.1 200 OK
Date: Sun, 08 Feb 2015 14.09:15 GMT
Content-Length: 187
Content-Type: text/html; charset=utf-8

<html>
  <head>
```

```
    <meta http-equiv="Content-Type" content="text/html; charset=utf-8">
    <title>Go Web Programming</title>
  </head>
  <body>

Hello World!

  </body>
</html>
```

We can also define the same template in the multiple template files. To see how this works, let's remove the definition of the content template in layout.html and place it in red_hello.html, as shown in this listing. Listing 5.27 shows how to create a blue_hello.html template file.

**Listing 5.26 red_hello.html**

```
{{ define "content" }}

<h1 style="color: red;">Hello World!</h1>

{{ end }}
```

**Listing 5.27 blue_hello.html**

```
{{ define "content" }}

<h1 style="color: blue;">Hello World!</h1>

{{ end }}
```

Notice that we've just defined the content template in two places. How can we use these two templates? This listing shows our modified handler.

**Listing 5.28 A handler using the same template in different template files**

```
func process(w http.ResponseWriter, r *http.Request) {
    rand.Seed(time.Now().Unix())
    var t *template.Template
    if rand.Intn(10) > 5 {
        t, _ = template.ParseFiles("layout.html", "red_hello.html")
    } else {
        t, _ = template.ParseFiles("layout.html", "blue_hello.html")
    }
    t.ExecuteTemplate(w, "layout", "")
}
```

Note that we're actually parsing different template files (either red_hello.html or blue_hello.html) according to the random number we create. We use the same layout template as before, which includes a *content* template. Remember that the content template is defined in two different files. Which template we use depends now on which template file we parse, because both of these template files define the same template. In other words, we can switch content by parsing different template files, while maintaining the same template to be nested in the layout.

If we now recompile our server, start it, and access it through the browser, we'll randomly see either a blue or red `Hello World!` showing up in the browser (see figure 5.12).

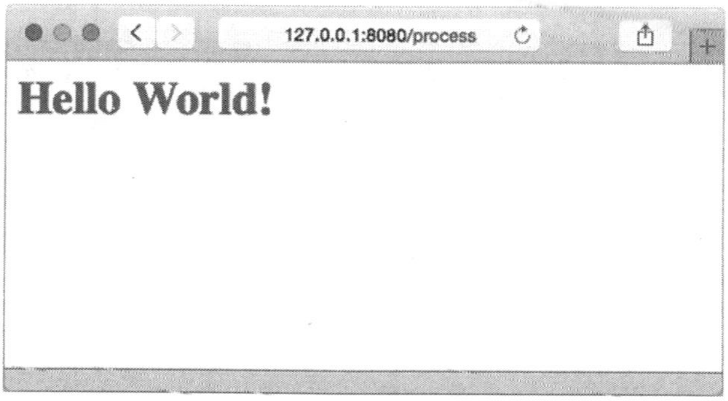


**Figure 5.12 Switching templates**

## 5.8 Using the block action to define default templates

Go 1.6 introduced a new block action that allows you to define a template and use it at the same time. This is how it looks:

```
{{ block arg }}
  Dot is set to arg
{{ end }}
```

To see how this works, I'll use the previous example and use the block action to replicate the same results. What I'll do is default to using the blue Hello World template if no templates are specified. Instead of parsing the layout.html and blue_hello.html files in the else block, as in listing 5.28, I will parse layout.html only as indicated in bold in the following listing.

**Listing 5.29 Parsing layout.html only**

```
func process(w http.ResponseWriter, r *http.Request) {
    rand.Seed(time.Now().Unix())
    var t *template.Template
    if rand.Intn(10) > 5 {
        t, _ = template.ParseFiles("layout.html", "red_hello.html")
    } else {
        t, _ = template.ParseFiles("layout.html")
    }
    t.ExecuteTemplate(w, "layout", "")
}
```

Without any further changes, this will result in a crash at random, because the template in the else block doesn't have a content template. Instead of passing it externally, I will use a block action and add it as a default content in layout.html itself, as in the code in bold in this listing.

**Listing 5.30 Using the block action to add a default content template**

```
{{ define "layout" }}

<html>
  <head>
    <meta http-equiv="Content-Type" content="text/html; charset=utf-8">
    <title>Go Web Programming</title>
  </head>
  <body>
    {{ block "content" . }}
      <h1 style="color: blue;">Hello World!</h1>
    {{ end }}
  </body>
</html>

{{ end }}
```

The block action effectively defines a template named content and also places it in the layout. If no content template is available when the overall template is executed, the content template defined by the block will be used instead.

We're done with handling requests, processing them, and generating content to respond to the requests. In the next chapter, you'll learn how you can store data in memory, in files, and in databases using Go.

## 5.9 Summary

- In a web app, template engines combine templates and data to produce the HTML that is sent back to the client.
- Go's standard template engine is in the `html/template` package.
- Go's template engine works by parsing a template and then executing it, passing a `ResponseWriter` and some data to it. This triggers the template engine to combine the parsed template with the data and send it to the `ResponseWriter`.
- Actions are instructions about how data is to be combined with the template. Go has an extensive and powerful set of actions.
- Besides actions, templates can also contain arguments, variables, and pipelines. Arguments represent the data value in a template; variables are constructs used with actions in a template. Pipelines allow chaining of arguments and functions.
- Go has a default but limited set of template functions. Customized functions can also be created by making a function map and attaching it to the template.
- Go's template engine can change the content it displays according to where the data is placed. This context-awareness is useful in defending against XSS attacks.
- Web layouts are commonly used to design a web app that has a consistent look and feel. This can be implemented in Go using nested templates.

# 6 Storing data

**This chapter covers**

- In-memory storage with structs
- File storage with CSV and gob binary files
- Relational database storage with SQL
- Go and SQL mappers

We introduced data persistence in chapter 2, briefly touching on how to persist data into a relational database, PostgreSQL. In this chapter we'll delve deeper into data persistence and talk about how you can store data in memory, files, relational databases, and NoSQL databases.

Data persistence is technically not part of web application programming, but it's often considered the third pillar of any web application—the other two pillars are templates and handlers. This is because most web applications need to store data in one form or another.

I'm generalizing but here are the places where you can store data:

- In memory (while the program is running)
- In files on the filesystem
- In a database, fronted by a server program

In this chapter, we'll go through how Go can be used to access data (create, retrieve, update, and delete—better known as CRUD) in all these places.

## 6.1 In-memory storage

In-memory storage refers not to storing data in in-memory databases but in the running application itself, to be used while the application is running. In-memory data is usually stored in data structures, and for Go, this primarily means with arrays, slices, maps, and most importantly, structs.

Storing data itself is no issue—it simply involves creating the structs, slices, and maps. If we stop to think about it, what we'll eventually manipulate is likely not to be the individual structs themselves, but *containers* for the structs. This could be arrays, slices, and maps but could also be any other types of data structures like stacks, trees, and queues.

What's more interesting is how you can retrieve the data that you need back from these containers. In the following listing, you'll use maps as containers for your structs.

**Listing 6.1 Storing data in memory**

```
package main

import (
    "fmt"
)

type Post struct {
    Id      int
    Content string
    Author  string
}

var PostById map[int]*Post
var PostsByAuthor map[string][]*Post

func store(post Post) {
    PostById[post.Id] = &post
    PostsByAuthor[post.Author] = append(PostsByAuthor[post.Author], &post)
}

func main() {

    PostById = make(map[int]*Post)
    PostsByAuthor = make(map[string][]*Post)

    post1 := Post{Id: 1, Content: "Hello World!", Author: "Sau Sheong"}
    post2 := Post{Id: 2, Content: "Bonjour Monde!", Author: "Pierre"}
    post3 := Post{Id: 3, Content: "Hola Mundo!", Author: "Pedro"}
post4 := Post{Id: 4, Content: "Greetings Earthlings!", Author:
➥ "Sau Sheong"}
```

```
    store(post1)
    store(post2)
    store(post3)
    store(post4)

    fmt.Println(PostById[1])
    fmt.Println(PostById[2])

    for _, post := range PostsByAuthor["Sau Sheong"] {
        fmt.Println(post)
    }
    for _, post := range PostsByAuthor["Pedro"] {
        fmt.Println(post)
    }
}
```

You're going to use a `Post` struct that represents a post in a forum application. Here's the data that you'll be saving in memory:

```
type Post struct {
    Id      int
    Content string
    Author  string
}
```

The main data for this `Post` struct is the content, and there are two ways of getting the post: either by a unique ID or by the name of its author. Storing posts in a map means that you're going to map a key that represents the post with the actual `Post` struct. Because you have two ways of accessing a post, you should have two maps, one each to access the post:

```
var PostById map[int]*Post
var PostsByAuthor map[string][]*Post
```

You have two variables: `PostById` maps the unique ID to a pointer to a post; `PostsByAuthor` maps the author's name to a slice of pointers to posts. Notice that you map to pointers of the posts and not to the post themselves. The reason for this is obvious: whether you're getting the post through its ID or through the author's name, you want the same post, not two different copies of it.

To store the post, you create a `store` function:

```
func store(post Post) {
    PostById[post.Id] = &post
    PostsByAuthor[post.Author] = append(PostsByAuthor[post.Author], &post)
}
```

The `store` function stores a pointer to the post into `PostById` as well as `PostsByAuthor`. Next, you create the posts themselves, a process that involves nothing more than creating structs.

```
post1 := Post{Id: 1, Content: "Hello World!", Author: "Sau Sheong"}
post2 := Post{Id: 2, Content: "Bonjour Monde!", Author: "Pierre"}
```

```
post3 := Post{Id: 3, Content: "Hola Mundo!", Author: "Pedro"}
post4 := Post{Id: 4, Content: "Greetings Earthlings!", Author: "Sau Sheong"}
store(post1)
store(post2)
store(post3)
store(post4)
```

When you execute the program, you'll see the following:

```
&{1 Hello World! Sau Sheong}
&{2 Bonjour Monde! Pierre}
&{1 Hello World! Sau Sheong}
&{4 Greetings Earthlings! Sau Sheong}
&{3 Hola Mundo! Pedro}
```

Note that you're getting back the same post regardless of whether you access it through the author or the post ID.

This process seems simple and obvious enough—trivial even. Why would we want to even talk about storing data in memory?

Very often in our web applications we start off with using relational databases (as in chapter 2) and then as we scale, we realize that we need to cache the data that we retrieve from the database in order to improve performance. As you'll see in the rest of this chapter, most of the methods used to persist data involve structs in one way or another. Instead of using an external in-memory database like Redis, we have the option of refactoring our code and storing the cache data in memory.

I'll also introduce you to storing data in structs, which is going to be the recurrent pattern for data storage for this chapter and much of the book.

## 6.2 File storage

Storing in memory is fast and immediate because there's no retrieval from disk. But there's one very important drawback: in-memory data isn't actually persistent. If you never shut down your machine or program, or if it doesn't matter if the data is lost (as in a cache), then that's probably fine. But you usually want data to be persisted when the machine or program is shut down, even if it's in cache. There are a number of ways data can be persisted, but the most common method is to store it to some sort of nonvolatile storage such as a hard disk or flash memory.

You have a number of options for storing data to nonvolatile storage. The technique we'll discuss in this section revolves around storing data to the filesystem. Specifically we'll explore two ways of storing data to files in Go. The first is through a commonly used text format, CSV (comma-separated values), and the second is specific to Go—using the gob package.

CSV is a common file format that's used for transferring data from the user to the system. It can be quite useful when you need to ask your users to provide you with a large amount of data and it's not feasible to ask them to enter the data into your forms. You can ask your users to use their favorite spreadsheet, enter all their data, and then save it as CSV and upload it to your web application. Once you have the file, you can decode the data for your purposes. Similarly, you can allow your users to get their data by creating a CSV file out of their data and sending it to them from your web application.

Gob is a binary format that can be saved in a file, providing a quick and effective means of serializing in-memory data to one or more files. Binary data files can be pretty useful too. You can use them to quickly store your structs for backup or for orderly shutdown. Just as a caching mechanism is useful, being able to store and load data temporarily in files is useful for things like sessions or shopping carts, or to serve as a temporary workspace.

Let's start with the simple exercise of opening up a file and writing to it, shown in the following listing. You'll see this repeated as we discuss saving to CSV and gob binary files.

**Listing 6.2 Reading and writing to a file**

```
package main

import (
    "fmt"
    "io/ioutil"
    "os"
)

func main() {
    data := []byte("Hello World!\n")
    err := ioutil.WriteFile("data1", data, 0644)
    if err != nil {
        panic(err)
    }
    read1, _ := ioutil.ReadFile("data1")
    fmt.Print(string(read1))

    file1, _ := os.Create("data2")
    defer file1.Close()

    bytes, _ := file1.Write(data)
    fmt.Printf("Wrote %d bytes to file\n", bytes)

    file2, _ := os.Open("data2")
    defer file2.Close()

    read2 := make([]byte, len(data))
    bytes, _ = file2.Read(read2)
    fmt.Printf("Read %d bytes from file\n", bytes)
    fmt.Println(string(read2))
}
```

Writes to file and reads from file using WriteFile and ReadFile

Writes to file and reads from file using the File struct

To reduce the amount of code on the page, in the previous listing I've replaced the errors returned by the function with a blank identifier.

In the listing, you can see two ways of writing to and reading from a file. The first is short and simple, and uses `WriteFile` and `ReadFile` from the `ioutil` package.

Writing to a file uses `WriteFile`, passing in the name of the file, the data to be written, and a number representing the permissions to set for the file. Reading from a file simply uses `ReadFile` with the filename. The data that's passed to both `WriteFile` and read from `ReadFile` is byte slices.

Writing to and reading from a file using a `File` struct is more verbose but gives you more flexibility. To write a file, you first create it using the `Create` function in the `os` package, passing it the name of the file you want to create. It's good practice to use `defer` to close the file so that you won't forget. A `defer` statement pushes a function call on a stack. The list of saved calls is then executed after the surrounding function returns. In our example, this means at the end of the main function `file2` will be closed, followed by `file1`. Once you have the `File` struct, you can write to it using the `Write` method. There are a number of other methods you can call on the `File` struct to write data to a file.

Reading a file with the `File` struct is similar. You need to use the `Open` function in the `os` package, and then use the `Read` method on the `File` struct, or any of the other methods to read the data. Reading data using the `File` struct is much more flexible because `File` has several other methods you can use to locate the correct part of the file you want to read from.

When you execute the program, you should see two files being created: data1 and data2, both containing the text "Hello World!".

### 6.2.1 Reading and writing CSV files

The CSV format is a file format in which tabular data (numbers and text) can be easily written and read in a text editor. CSV is widely supported, and most spreadsheet programs, such as Microsoft Excel and Apple Numbers, support CSV. Consequently, many programming languages, including Go, come with libraries that produce and consume the data in CSV files.

In Go, CSV is manipulated by the `encoding/csv` package. The next listing shows code for reading and writing CSV.

**Listing 6.3 Reading and writing CSV**

```
package main

import (
    "encoding/csv"
    "fmt"
    "os"
    "strconv"
)

type Post struct {
    Id      int
    Content string
    Author  string
}
```

```
func main() {
    csvFile, err := os.Create("posts.csv")
    if err != nil {
        panic(err)
    }
    defer csvFile.Close()

    allPosts := []Post{
        Post{Id: 1, Content: "Hello World!", Author: "Sau Sheong"},
        Post{Id: 2, Content: "Bonjour Monde!", Author: "Pierre"},
        Post{Id: 3, Content: "Hola Mundo!", Author: "Pedro"},
        Post{Id: 4, Content: "Greetings Earthlings!", Author: "Sau Sheong"},
    }

    writer := csv.NewWriter(csvFile)
    for _, post := range allPosts {
        line := []string{strconv.Itoa(post.Id), post.Content, post.Author}
        err := writer.Write(line)
        if err != nil {
            panic(err)
        }
    }
    writer.Flush()

    file, err := os.Open("posts.csv")
    if err != nil {
        panic(err)
    }
    defer file.Close()

    reader := csv.NewReader(file)
    reader.FieldsPerRecord = -1
    record, err := reader.ReadAll()
    if err != nil {
        panic(err)
    }

    var posts []Post
    for _, item := range record {
        id, _ := strconv.ParseInt(item[0], 0, 0)
        post := Post{Id: int(id), Content: item[1], Author: item[2]}
        posts = append(posts, post)
    }
    fmt.Println(posts[0].Id)
    fmt.Println(posts[0].Content)
    fmt.Println(posts[0].Author)
}
```

**Creating a CSV file** (annotation pointing to `csvFile, err := os.Create("posts.csv")`)

**Reading a CSV file** (annotation pointing to `file, err := os.Open("posts.csv")`)

First let's look at writing to a CSV file. You create a file called posts.csv and a variable named `csvFile`. Your objective is to write the posts in the `allPosts` variable into this file. Step one is to create a writer using the `NewWriter` function, passing in the file. Then for each post, you create a slice of strings. Finally, you call the `Write` method on the writer to write the slice of strings into the CSV file and you're done.

If the program ends here and exits, all is well and the data is written to file. Because you'll need to read the same posts.csv file next, we need to make sure that any buffered data is properly written to the file by calling the `Flush` method on the writer.

Reading the CSV file works much the same way. First, you need to open the file. Then call the `NewReader` function, passing in the file, to create a reader. Set the `FieldsPerRecord` field in the reader to be a negative number, which indicates that you aren't that bothered if you don't have all the fields in the record. If `FieldsPerRecord` is a positive number, then that's the number of fields you expect from each record and Go will throw an error if you get less from the CSV file. If `FieldsPerRecord` is 0, you'll use the number of fields in the first record as the `FieldsPerRecord` value.

You call the `ReadAll` method on the reader to read all the records in at once, but if the file is large you can also retrieve one record at a time from the reader. This results in a slice of slices, which you can then iterate through and create the `Post` structs. If you run the program now, it'll create a CSV file called posts.csv, which contains lines of comma-delimited text:

```
1,Hello World!,Sau Sheong
2,Bonjour Monde!,Pierre
3,Hola Mundo!,Pedro
4,Greetings Earthlings!,Sau Sheong
```

It'll also read from the same file and print out the data from the first line of the CSV file:

```
1
Hello World!
Sau Sheong
```

### 6.2.2 The gob package

The `encoding/gob` package manages streams of gobs, which are binary data, exchanged between an encoder and a decoder. It's designed for serialization and transporting data but it can also be used for persisting data. Encoders and decoders wrap around writers and readers, which conveniently allows you to use them to write to and read from files. The following listing demonstrates how you can use the `gob` package to create binary data files and read from them.

**Listing 6.4 Reading and writing binary data using the `gob` package**

```
package main

import (
    "bytes"
    "encoding/gob"
    "fmt"
    "io/ioutil"
)

type Post struct {
    Id      int
    Content string
```

```
    Author  string
}

func store(data interface{}, filename string) {          Store data
    buffer := new(bytes.Buffer)
    encoder := gob.NewEncoder(buffer)
    err := encoder.Encode(data)
    if err != nil {
        panic(err)
    }
    err = ioutil.WriteFile(filename, buffer.Bytes(), 0600)
    if err != nil {
        panic(err)
    }
}

func load(data interface{}, filename string) {           Load data
    raw, err := ioutil.ReadFile(filename)
    if err != nil {
        panic(err)
    }
    buffer := bytes.NewBuffer(raw)
    dec := gob.NewDecoder(buffer)
    err = dec.Decode(data)
    if err != nil {
        panic(err)
    }
}

func main() {
    post := Post{Id: 1, Content: "Hello World!", Author: "Sau Sheong"}
    store(post, "post1")
    var postRead Post
    load(&postRead, "post1")
    fmt.Println(postRead)
}
```

As before, you're using the `Post` struct and you'll be saving a post to binary, then retrieving it, using the `store` and `load` functions, respectively. Let's look at the `store` function first.

The `store` function takes an empty interface (meaning it can take anything, as well as a filename for the binary file it'll be saved to). In our example code, you'll be passing a `Post` struct. First, you need to create a `bytes.Buffer` struct, which is essentially a variable buffer of bytes that has both `Read` and `Write` methods. In other words, a `bytes.Buffer` can be both a `Reader` and a `Writer`.

Then you create a gob encoder by passing the buffer to the `NewEncoder` function. You use the encoder to encode the data (the `Post` struct) into the buffer using the `Encode` method. Finally, you write the buffer to a file.

To use the `store` function, you pass a `Post` struct and a filename to it, creating a binary data file named post1. Now let's look at the `load` function. Loading data from the binary data file post1 is the reverse of creating it. First, you need to read the raw data out from the file.

Next, you'll create a buffer from the raw data. Doing so will essentially give the raw data the `Read` and `Write` methods. You create a decoder from the buffer using the `NewDecoder` function. The decoder is then used to decode the raw data into the `Post` struct that you passed in earlier.

You define a `Post` struct called `postRead`, and then pass a reference to it into the `load` function, along with the name of the binary data file. The `load` function will load the data from the binary file into the struct.

When you run the program, a post1 file, which contains the binary data, will be created. You can open it and it'll look like gibberish. The post1 file is also read into another `Post` struct, and you'll see the struct being printed on the console:

```
{1 Hello World! Sau Sheong}
```

We're done with files. For the rest of this chapter, we'll be discussing data stored in specialized server-side programs called database servers.

## 6.3 Go and SQL

Storing and accessing data in the memory and on the filesystem is useful, but if you need robustness and scalability, you'll need to turn to *database servers*. Database servers are programs that allow other programs to access data through a client-server model. The data is normally protected from other means of access, except through the server. Typically, a client (either a library or another program) connects to the database server to access the data through a Structured Query Language (SQL). Database management systems (DBMSs) often include a database server as part of the system.

Perhaps the most well-known and popularly used database management system is the *relational database management system* (RDBMS). RDBMSs use *relational databases*, which are databases that are based on the relational model of data. Relational databases are mostly accessed through relational database servers using SQL.

Relational databases and SQL are also the most commonly used means of storing data in a scalable and easy-to-use way. I discussed this topic briefly in chapter 2, and I promised that we'll go through it properly in this chapter, so here goes.

### 6.3.1 Setting up the database

Before you start, you need to set up your database. In chapter 2 you learned how to install and set up Postgres, which is the database we're using for this section. If you haven't done so, now is a great time to do it.

Once you've created the database, you'll follow these steps:

1. Create the database user.
2. Create the database for the user.
3. Run the setup script that'll create the table that you need.

Let's start with creating the user. Run this command at the console:

```
createuser -P -d gwp
```

This command creates a Postgres database user called *gwp*. The option `-P` tells the `createuser` program to prompt you for a password for gwp, and the option `-d` tells the program to allow gwp to create databases. You'll be prompted to enter gwp's password, which I assume you'll set to gwp as well.

Next, you'll create the database for the gwp user. The database name has to be the same as the user's name. You can create databases with other names but that will require setting up permissions and so on. For simplicity's sake let's use the default database for our database user. To create a database named gwp, run this command at the console:

```
createdb gwp
```

Now that you have a database, let's create our one and only table. Create a file named setup.sql with the script shown in this listing.

**Listing 6.5 Script that creates our database**

```
create table posts (
  id      serial primary key,
  content text,
  author  varchar(255)
);
```

To execute the script, run this command on the console

```
psql -U gwp -f setup.sql -d gwp
```

and you should now have your database. Take note that you'll likely need to run this command over and over again to clean and set up the database every time before running the code.

Now that you have your database and it's set up properly, let's connect to it. The next listing shows the example we'll be going through, using a file named store.go.

**Listing 6.6 Go and CRUD with Postgres**

```
package main

import (
    "database/sql"
    "fmt"
    _ "github.com/lib/pq"
)

type Post struct {
    Id      int
    Content string
    Author  string
}
```

```
var Db *sql.DB
func init() {
    var err error
    Db, err = sql.Open("postgres", "user=gwp dbname=gwp password=gwp
    ➥ sslmode=disable")
    if err != nil {
        panic(err)
    }
}
```

**Connects to the database**

```
func Posts(limit int) (posts []Post, err error) {
    rows, err := Db.Query("select id, content, author from posts limit $1",
    ➥ limit)
    if err != nil {
        return
    }
    for rows.Next() {
        post := Post{}
        err = rows.Scan(&post.Id, &post.Content, &post.Author)
        if err != nil {
            return
        }
        posts = append(posts, post)
    }
    rows.Close()
    return
}
```

**Gets a single post**

```
func GetPost(id int) (post Post, err error) {
    post = Post{}
    err = Db.QueryRow("select id, content, author from posts where id =
    ➥ $1", id).Scan(&post.Id, &post.Content, &post.Author)
    return
}
```

**Creates a new post**

```
func (post *Post) Create() (err error) {
    statement := "insert into posts (content, author) values ($1, $2)
    ➥ returning id"
    stmt, err := Db.Prepare(statement)
    if err != nil {
        return
    }
    defer stmt.Close()
    err = stmt.QueryRow(post.Content, post.Author).Scan(&post.Id)
    return
}
```

**Updates a post**

```
func (post *Post) Update() (err error) {
    _, err = Db.Exec("update posts set content = $2, author = $3 where id =
    ➥ $1", post.Id, post.Content, post.Author)
    return
}
```

**Deletes a post**

```
func (post *Post) Delete() (err error) {
    _, err = Db.Exec("delete from posts where id = $1", post.Id)
```

```
    return
}

func main() {
    post := Post{Content: "Hello World!", Author: "Sau Sheong"}

    fmt.Println(post)                     // {0 Hello World! Sau Sheong}
    post.Create()
    fmt.Println(post)                     // {1 Hello World! Sau Sheong}

    readPost, _ := GetPost(post.Id)
    fmt.Println(readPost)                 // {1 Hello World! Sau Sheong}

    readPost.Content = "Bonjour Monde!"
    readPost.Author = "Pierre"
    readPost.Update()

    posts, _ := Posts()
    fmt.Println(posts)                    // [{1 Bonjour Monde! Pierre}]

    readPost.Delete()
}
```

### 6.3.2 *Connecting to the database*

You need to connect to the database before doing anything else. Doing so is relatively simple; in the following listing you first declare a variable `Db` as a pointer to an `sql.DB` struct, and then use the `init` function (which is called automatically for every package) to initialize it.

**Listing 6.7 Function that creates a database handle**

```
var Db *sql.DB

func init() {
    var err error
    Db, err = sql.Open("postgres", "user=gwp dbname=gwp password=gwp
      sslmode=disable")
    if err != nil {
          panic(err)
    }
}
```

The `sql.DB` struct is a handle to the database and represents a pool of zero or database connections that's maintained by the `sql` package. Setting up the connection to the database is a one-liner using the `Open` function, passing in the database driver name (in our case, it's *postgres*) and a data source name. The data source name is a string that's specific to the database driver and tells the driver how to connect to the database. The `Open` function then returns a pointer to a `sql.DB` struct.

Note that the `Open` function doesn't connect to the database or even validate the parameters yet—it simply sets up the necessary structs for connection to the database later. The connection will be set up lazily when it's needed.

Also, `sql.DB` doesn't needed to be closed (you can do so if you like); it's simply a handle and not the actual connection. Remember that this abstraction contains a pool of database connections and will maintain them. In our example, you'll be using the globally defined `Db` variable from our various CRUD methods and functions, but an alternative is to pass the `sql.DB` struct around once you've created it.

So far we've discussed the `Open` function, which returns a `sql.DB` struct given the database driver name and a data source name. How do you get the database driver? The normal way that you'd register a database driver involves using the `Register` function, with the name of the database driver, and a struct that implements the `driver.Driver` interface like this:

```
sql.Register("postgres", &drv{})
```

In this example, `postgres` is the name of the driver and `drv` is a struct that implements the `Driver` interface. You'll notice that we didn't do this earlier. Why not?

The Postgres driver we used (a third-party driver) registered itself when we imported the driver, that's why.

```
import (
    "fmt"
    "database/sql"
    _ "github.com/lib/pq"
)
```

The `github.com/lib/pq` package you imported is the Postgres driver, and when it's imported, its `init` function will kick in and register itself. Go doesn't provide any official database drivers; all database drivers are third-party libraries that should conform to the interfaces defined in the `sql.driver` package. Notice that when you import the database driver, you set the name of the package to be an underscore (_). This is because you shouldn't use the database driver directly; you should use `database/sql` only. This way, if you upgrade the version of the driver or change the implementation of the driver, you don't need to make changes to all your code.

To install this driver, run this command on the console:

```
go get "github.com/lib/pq"
```

This command will fetch the code from the repository and place it in the package repository, and then compile it along with your other code.

### 6.3.3 Creating a post

With the initial database setup done, let's start creating our first record in the database. In this example, you'll the same `Post` struct you've used in the previous few sections. Instead of storing to memory or file, you'll be storing and retrieving the same information from a Postgres database.

In our sample application, you'll use various functions to perform create, retrieve, update, and delete the data. In this section, you'll learn how to create posts using the

Create function. Before we get into the Create function, though, we'll discuss how you want to create posts.

You'll begin by creating a Post struct, with the Content and Author fields filled in. Note that you're not filling in the Id field because it'll be populated by the database (as an auto-incremented primary key).

```
post := Post{Content: "Hello World!", Author: "Sau Sheong"}
```

If you pause here and insert a fmt.Println statement to debug, you'll see that the Id field is set to 0:

```
fmt.Println(post)          ◄── {0 Hello World! Sau Sheong}
```

Now, let's create this post as a database record:

```
post.Create()
```

The Create method should return an error if something goes wrong, but for brevity's sake, let's ignore that. Let's print out the value in the variable again:

```
fmt.Println(post)          ◄── {1 Hello World! Sau Sheong}
```

This time you'll see that the Id field should be set to 1. Now that you know what you want the Create function to do, let's dive into the code.

**Listing 6.8 Creating a post**

```
func (post *Post) Create() (err error) {
    statement := "insert into posts (content, author) values ($1, $2)
    ➥ returning id "
    stmt, err := db.Prepare(statement)
    if err != nil {
        return
    }
    defer stmt.Close()
    err = stmt.QueryRow(post.Content, post.Author).Scan(&post.Id)
    if err != nil {
        return
    }
    return
}
```

The Create function is a method to the Post struct. You can see that because when you're defining the Create function, you place a reference to a Post struct between the func keyword and the name of the function, Create. The reference to a Post struct, post, is also called the receiver of the method and can be referred to without the ampersand (&) within the method.

You start the method by getting defining an SQL prepared statement. A *prepared statement* is an SQL statement template, where you can replace certain values during execution. Prepared statements are often used to execute statements repeatedly.

```
statement := "insert into posts (content, author) values ($1, $2) returning id"
```

Replace $1 and $2 with the actual values you want when creating the record. Notice that you're stating that you want the database to return the id column. Why we need to return the value of the id column will become clear soon.

To create it as a prepared statement, let's use the `Prepare` method from the `sql.DB` struct:

```
stmt, err := db.Prepare(statement)
```

This code will create a reference to an `sql.Stmt` interface (defined in the `sql.Driver` package and the struct implemented by the database driver), which is our statement.

Next, execute the prepared statement using the `QueryRow` method on the statement, passing it the data from the receiver:

```
err = stmt.QueryRow(post.Content, post.Author).Scan(&post.Id)
```

You use `QueryRow` here because you want to return only a single reference to an `sql.Row` struct. If more than one `sql.Row` is returned by the SQL statement, only the first is returned by `QueryRow`. The rest are discarded. `QueryRow` returns only the `sql.Row` struct; no errors. This is because `QueryRow` is often used with the `Scan` method on the `Row` struct, which copies the values in the row into its parameters. As you can see, the `post` receiver will have its Id field filled by the returned id field from the SQL query. This is why you need to specify the returning instruction in your SQL statement. Obviously you only need the Id field, since that's the auto-incremented value generated by the database, while you already know the Content and Author fields. As you've likely guessed by now, because the post's Id field is populated, you'll now have a fully filled `Post` struct that corresponds to a database record.

### 6.3.4 Retrieving a post

You've created the post, so naturally you need to retrieve it. As before, you want to see what you need before creating the function to do it. You don't have an existing `Post` struct, so you can't define a method on it. You'll have to define a `GetPost` function, which takes in a single Id and returns a fully filled `Post` struct:

```
readPost, _ := GetPost(1)
fmt.Println(readPost)          <-- {1 Hello World! Sau Sheong}
```

Note that this code snippet is slightly different from the overall listing; I'm making it clearer here that I'm retrieving a post by its id. This listing shows how the `GetPost` function works.

**Listing 6.9 Retrieving a post**

```
func GetPost(id int) (post Post, err error) {
    post = Post{}
    err = Db.QueryRow("select id, content, author from posts where id =
    ➥ $1", id).Scan(&post.Id, &post.Content, &post.Author)
    return
}
```

You want to return a Post struct, so you start by creating an empty one:

```
post = Post{}
```

As you saw earlier, you can chain the QueryRow method and the Scan method to copy the value of the returned results on the empty Post struct. Notice that you're using the QueryRow method on the sql.DB struct instead of sql.Stmt because obviously you don't have or need a prepared statement. It should also be obvious that you could have done it either way in the Create and GetPost functions. The only reason I'm showing you a different way is to illustrate the possibilities.

Now that you have the empty Post struct populated with the data from the database, it'll be returned to the calling function.

### 6.3.5 Updating a post

After you retrieve a post, you may want to update the information in the record. Assuming you've already retrieved readPost, let's modify it and then have the new data updated in the database as well:

```
readPost.Content = "Bonjour Monde!"
readPost.Author = "Pierre"
readPost.Update()
```

You'll create an Update method on the Post struct for this purpose, as shown in this listing.

**Listing 6.10 Updating a post**

```
func (post *Post) Update() (err error) {
    _, err = Db.Exec("update posts set content = $2, author = $3 where id =
    ➥ $1", post.Id, post.Content, post.Author)
    return
}
```

Unlike when creating a post, you won't use a prepared statement. Instead, you'll jump right in with a call to the Exec method of the sql.DB struct. You no longer have to update the receiver, so you don't need to scan the returned results. Therefore, using the Exec method on the global database variable Db, which returns sql.Result and an error, is much faster:

```
_, err = Db.Exec(post.Id, post.Content, post.Author)
```

We aren't interested in the result (which just gives the number of rows affected and the last inserted id, if applicable) because there's nothing we want to process from it, so you can ignore it by assigning it to the underscore (_). And your post will be updated (unless there's an error).

### 6.3.6 Deleting a post

So far we've been able to create, retrieve, and update posts. Deleting them when they're not needed is a natural extension. Assuming that you already have the readPost after retrieving it previously, you want to be able to delete it using a Delete method:

```
readPost.Delete()
```

That's simple enough. If you look at the Delete method in the Post struct in the following listing, there's nothing new that we haven't gone through before.

**Listing 6.11 Deleting a post**

```
func (post *Post) Delete() (err error) {
    _, err = Db.Exec("delete from posts where id = $1", post.Id)
    return
}
```

As before, when you were updating the post, you'll jump right into using the Exec method on the sql.DB struct. This executes the SQL statement, and as before, you're not interested in the returned result and so assign it to the underscore (_).

You probably noticed that the methods and functions I created are arbitrary. You can certainly change them to however you'd like. Instead of populating a Post struct with your changes, then calling the Update method on the struct, for example, you can pass the changes as parameters to the Update method. Or more commonly, if you want to retrieve posts using a particular column or filter, you can create different functions to do that.

### 6.3.7 Getting all posts

One common function is to get all posts from the database, with a given limit. In other words, you want to do the following:

```
posts, _ := Posts(10)
```

You want to get the first 10 posts from the database and put them in a slice. This listing shows how you can do this.

**Listing 6.12 Getting all posts**

```
func Posts(limit int) (posts []Post, err error) {
    rows, err := Db.Query("select id, content, author from posts limit $1",
    ➥ limit)
    if err != nil {
        return
    }
    for rows.Next() {
        post := Post{}
        err = rows.Scan(&post.Id, &post.Content, &post.Author)
        if err != nil {
            return
        }
        posts = append(posts, post)
    }
    rows.Close()
```

```
    return
}
```

You use the `Query` method on the `sql.DB` struct, which returns a `Rows` interface. The `Rows` interface is an iterator. You can call a `Next` method on it repeatedly and it'll return `sql.Row` until it runs out of rows, when it returns `io.EOF`.

For each iteration, you create a `Post` struct and scan the row into the struct, and then append it to the slice that you'll be returning to the caller.

## 6.4 Go and SQL relationships

One of the reasons relational databases are so popular for storing data is because tables can be related. This allows pieces of data to be related to each other in a consistent and easy-to-understand way. There are essentially four ways of relating a record to other records.

- *One to one* (has one)—A user has one profile, for example.
- *One to many* (has many)—A user has many forum posts, for example.
- *Many to one* (belongs to)—Many forum posts belong to one user, for example.
- *Many to many*—A user can participate in many forum threads, while a forum thread can also have many users contributing to it, for example.

We've discussed the standard CRUD for a single database table, but now let's look at how we can do the same for two related tables. For this example, we'll use a one-to-many relationship where a forum post has many comments. As you may realize, many-to-one is the inverse of one-to-many, so we'll see how that works as well.

### 6.4.1 Setting up the databases

Before we start, let's set up our database again, this time with two tables. You'll use the same commands on the console as before, but with a slightly different setup.sql script, shown in this listing.

**Listing 6.13 Setting up two related tables**

```
drop table posts cascade if exists;
drop table comments if exists;

create table posts (
  id      serial primary key,
  content text,
  author  varchar(255)
);

create table comments (
  id      serial primary key,
  content text,
  author  varchar(255),
  post_id integer references posts(id)
);
```

First, you'll see that because the tables are related, when you drop the posts table you need to cascade it; otherwise you won't be able to drop posts because the comments table depends on it. We've added the table comments, which has the same columns as posts but with an additional column, post_id, that references the column id in the posts table. This will set up post_id as a foreign key that references the primary key `id` in the posts table.

With the tables set up, let's look at the code in a single listing. The code in the following listing is found in a file named store.go.

**Listing 6.14 One-to-many and many-to-one with Go**

```
package main

import (
    "database/sql"
    "errors"
    "fmt"
    _ "github.com/lib/pq"
)

type Post struct {
    Id      int
    Content string
    Author  string
    Comments []Comment
}

type Comment struct {
    Id      int
    Content string
    Author  string
    Post    *Post
}

var Db *sql.DB

func init() {
    var err error
    Db, err = sql.Open("postgres", "user=gwp dbname=gwp password=gwp
    ➥ sslmode=disable")
    if err != nil {
        panic(err)
    }
}
```

Creates a single comment

```
func (comment *Comment) Create() (err error) {
    if comment.Post == nil {
        err = errors.New("Post not found")
        return
    }
    err = Db.QueryRow("insert into comments (content, author, post_id)
    ➥ values ($1, $2, $3) returning id", comment.Content, comment.Author,
    ➥ comment.Post.Id).Scan(&comment.Id)
```

```
    return
}

func GetPost(id int) (post Post, err error) {
    post = Post{}
    post.Comments = []Comment{}
    err = Db.QueryRow("select id, content, author from posts where id =
➥ $1", id).Scan(&post.Id, &post.Content, &post.Author)

    rows, err := Db.Query("select id, content, author from comments")
    if err != nil {
        return
    }
    for rows.Next() {
        comment := Comment{Post: &post}
        err = rows.Scan(&comment.Id, &comment.Content, &comment.Author)
        if err != nil {
            return
        }
        post.Comments = append(post.Comments, comment)
    }
    rows.Close()
    return
}

func (post *Post) Create() (err error) {
    err = Db.QueryRow("insert into posts (content, author) values ($1, $2)
➥ returning id", post.Content, post.Author).Scan(&post.Id)
    return
}

func main() {
    post := Post{Content: "Hello World!", Author: "Sau Sheong"}
    post.Create()

    comment := Comment{Content: "Good post!", Author: "Joe", Post: &post}
    comment.Create()
    readPost, _ := GetPost(post.Id)

    fmt.Println(readPost)
    fmt.Println(readPost.Comments)
    fmt.Println(readPost.Comments[0].Post)
}
```

**{1 Hello World! Sau Sheong [{1 Good post! Joe 0xc20802a1c0}]}**

**[{1 Good post! Joe c20802alc0}]**

**&{1 Hello World! Sau Sheong [{1 Good post! Joe 0xc20802a1c0}]}**

### 6.4.2 *One-to-many relationship*

As before, let's decide how to establish the relationships. First, look at the `Post` and `Comment` structs:

```
type  Post  struct {
    Id       int
    Content  string
    Author   string
    Comments []Comment
}
```

```
type Comment struct {
    Id      int
    Content string
    Author  string
    Post    *Post
}
```

Notice that Post has an additional field named Comments, which is a slice of Comment structs. Comment has a field named Post that's a pointer to a Post struct. An astute reader might ask, why are we using a field that's a pointer in Comment while we have a field that's an actual struct in Post? We don't. The Comments field in the Post struct is a slice, which is really a pointer to an array, so both are pointers. You can see why you'd want to store the relationship in the struct as a pointer; you don't really want another copy of the same Post—you want to point to the same Post.

Now that you've built the relationship, let's determine how you can use it. As mentioned earlier, this is a one-to-many as well as a many-to-one relationship. When you create a comment, you also want to create the relationship between the comment and the post it's meant for:

```
comment := Comment{Content: "Good post!", Author: "Joe", Post: &post}
comment.Create()
```

As before, you create a Comment struct, and then call the Create method on it. The relationship should be built upon creation of the comment. This means if you retrieve the post now, the relationship should be established.

```
readPost, _ := GetPost(post.Id)
```

The readPost variable should now have your newly minted comment in its Comments field. Next let's look at the Comment struct's Create method, shown in this listing.

**Listing 6.15 Creating the relationship**

```
func (comment *Comment) Create() (err error) {
    if comment.Post == nil {
        err = errors.New("Post not found")
        return
    }
    err = Db.QueryRow("insert into comments (content, author, post_id)
    ➥ values ($1, $2, $3) returning id", comment.Content, comment.Author,
    ➥ comment.Post.Id).Scan(&comment.Id)
    return
}
```

Before you create the relationship between the comment and the post, you need to make sure that the Post exists! If it doesn't, you'll return an error. The rest of the code repeats what we discussed earlier, except that now you also have to include post_id. Adding post_id will create the relationship.

With the relationship established, you want to be able to retrieve the post and be able to see the comments associated with the post. To do this, you'll modify the `GetPost` function as shown here.

**Listing 6.16 Retrieving the relationship**

```
func GetPost(id int) (post Post, err error) {
    post = Post{}
     post.Comments = []Comment{}
    err = Db.QueryRow("select id, content, author from posts where id =
    ➥ $1", id).Scan(&post.Id, &post.Content, &post.Author)

    rows, err := Db.Query("select id, content, author from comments where
    ➥ post_id = $1", id)
    if err != nil {
        return
    }
    for rows.Next() {
        comment := Comment{Post: &post}
        err = rows.Scan(&comment.Id, &comment.Content, &comment.Author)
        if err != nil {
            return
        }
        post.Comments = append(post.Comments, comment)
    }
    rows.Close()
    return
}
```

First, we need to initialize the Comments field in the `Post` struct and retrieve the post. We get all the comments related to this post and iterate through it, creating a `Comment` struct for each comment and appending it to the Comments field, and then return the post. As you can see, building up the relationships is not that difficult, though it can be a bit tedious if the web application becomes larger. In the next section, you'll see how relational mappers can be used to simplify establishing relationships.

Although we discussed the usual CRUD functions of any database application here, we've only scratched the surface of accessing an SQL database using Go. I encourage you to read the official Go documentation.

## 6.5 Go relational mappers

You've probably come to the conclusion that it's a lot of work storing data into the relational database. This is true in most programming languages; however, there's usually a number of third-party libraries that will come between the actual SQL and the calling application. In object-oriented programming (OOP) languages, these are often called object-relational mappers (ORMs). ORMs such as Hibernate (Java) and ActiveRecord (Ruby) map relational database tables and the objects in the programming language. But this isn't unique to object-oriented languages. Such mappers are found in many other programming languages, too; for example, Scala has the Activate framework and Haskell has Groundhog.

In Go, there are a number of such relational mappers (ORMs doesn't sound as accurate to me). In this section, we'll discuss a couple of them.

### 6.5.1 Sqlx

Sqlx is a third-party library that provides a set of useful extensions to the `database/sql` package. Sqlx plays well with the `database/sql` package because it uses the same interfaces and provides additional capabilities such as:

- Marshaling database records (rows) into structs, maps, and slices using struct tags
- Providing named parameter support for prepared statements

The following listing shows how Sqlx makes life easier using the `StructScan` method. Remember to get the library before starting on the code by issuing the following command on the console:

```
go get "github.com/jmoiron/sqlx"
```

**Listing 6.17 Using Sqlx**

```
package main

import (
    "fmt"
    "github.com/jmoiron/sqlx"
    _ "github.com/lib/pq"
)

type Post struct {
    Id      int
    Content string
    AuthorName string `db: author`
}

var Db *sqlx.DB

func init() {
    var err error
    Db, err = sqlx.Open("postgres", "user=gwp dbname=gwp password=gwp
    ➥ sslmode=disable")
    if err != nil {
        panic(err)
    }
}

func GetPost(id int) (post Post, err error) {
    post = Post{}
    err = Db.QueryRowx("select id, content, author from posts where id =
    ➥ $1", id).StructScan(&post)
```

```
    if err != nil {
        return
    }
    return
}

func (post *Post) Create() (err error) {
    err = Db.QueryRow("insert into posts (content, author) values ($1, $2)
    ➥ returning id", post.Content, post.AuthorName).Scan(&post.Id)
    return
}

func main() {
    post := Post{Content: "Hello World!", AuthorName: "Sau Sheong"}
    post.Create()
    fmt.Println(post)                          ◄── {1 Hello World! Sau Sheong}}
}
```

The code illustrating the difference between using Sqlx and `database/sql` is marked in bold; the other code should be familiar to you. First, instead of importing `database/sql`, you import `github.com/jmoiron/sqlx`. Normally, `StructScan` maps the struct field names to the corresponding lowercase table columns. To show how you can tell Sqlx to automatically map the correct table column to the struct field, listing 6.17 changed `Author` to `AuthorName` and used a struct tag (struct tags will be explained in further detail in chapter 7) to instruct Sqlx to get data from the correct column.

Instead of using `sql.DB`, you now use `sqlx.DB`. Both are similar, except `sqlx.DB` has additional methods like `Queryx` and `QueryRowx`.

In the `GetPost` function, instead of using `QueryRow`, you use `QueryRowx`, which returns `Rowx`. `Rowx` is the struct that has the `StructScan` method, and as you can see, it maps the table columns to the respective fields. In the `Create` method you're still using `QueryRow`, which isn't modified.

There are a few other features in Sqlx that are interesting but that I don't cover here. To learn more, visit the GitHub repository at https://github.com/jmoiron/sqlx.

Sqlx is an interesting and useful extension to `database/sql` but it doesn't add too many features. Conversely, the next library we'll explore hides the `database/sql` package and uses an ORM mechanism instead.

### 6.5.2 Gorm

The developer for Gorm delightfully calls it "the fantastic ORM for Go(lang)," and it's certainly an apt description. Gorm (Go-ORM) is an ORM for Go that follows the path of Ruby's ActiveRecord or Java's Hibernate. To be specific, Gorm follows the Data-Mapper pattern in providing mappers to map data in the database with structs. (In the relational database section earlier I used the ActiveRecord pattern.)

Gorm's capabilities are quite extensive. It allows programmers to define relationships, perform data migration, chain queries, and many other advanced features. It even has callbacks, which are functions that are triggered when a particular data event occurs, such as when data is updated or deleted. Describing the features would take another chapter, so we'll discuss only basic features. The following listing explores code using Gorm. Our simple application is again in store.go.

**Listing 6.18 Using Gorm**

```
package main

import (
    "fmt"
    "github.com/jinzhu/gorm"
    _ "github.com/lib/pq"
    "time"
)

type Post struct {
    Id        int
    Content   string
    Author    string `sql:"not null"`
    Comments  []Comment
    CreatedAt time.Time
}

type Comment struct {
    Id        int
    Content   string
    Author    string `sql:"not null"`
    PostId    int    `sql:"index"`
    CreatedAt time.Time
}

var Db gorm.DB

func init() {
    var err error
    Db, err = gorm.Open("postgres", "user=gwp dbname=gwp password=gwp
    ➥ sslmode=disable")
    if err != nil {
        panic(err)
    }
    Db.AutoMigrate(&Post{}, &Comment{})
}

func main() {
    post := Post{Content: "Hello World!", Author: "Sau Sheong"}
    fmt.Println(post)

    Db.Create(&post)
    fmt.Println(post)

    comment := Comment{Content: "Good post!", Author: "Joe"}
    Db.Model(&post).Association("Comments").Append(comment)

    var readPost Post
    Db.Where("author = $1", "Sau Sheong").First(&readPost)
      var comments []Comment
```

**{0 Hello World! Sau Sheong [] 0001-01-01 00:00:00 +0000 UTC}**

**Creates a post**

**{1 Hello World! Sau Sheong [] 2015-04-12 11:38:50.91815604 +0800 SGT}**

**Adds a comment**

**Gets comments from a post**

```
    Db.Model(&readPost).Related(&comments)
fmt.Println(comments[0])
}
```

**{1 Good post! Joe 1 2015-04-13 11:38:50.920377 +0800 SGT}**

Note that the way that you create the database handler is similar to what you've been doing all along. Also note that we no longer need to set up the database tables separately using a setup.sql file. This is because Gorm has an automatic migration capability that creates the database tables and keeps them updated whenever you change the corresponding struct. When you run the program, the database tables that are needed will be created accordingly. To run this properly you should drop the database altogether and re-create it:

```
func init() {
    var err error
    Db, err = gorm.Open("postgres", "user=gwp dbname=gwp password=gwp
      sslmode=disable")
    if err != nil {
        panic(err)
    }
    Db.AutoMigrate(&Post{}, &Comment{})
}
```

The `AutoMigrate` method is a variadic method. A variadic method or function is a method or function that can take one or more parameters. Here it's called with references to the `Post` and `Comment` structs. If you change the structs to add in a new field, a corresponding table column will be created.

Let's take a look at one of the structs, `Comment`:

```
type Comment  struct {
    Id        int
    Content   string
    Author    string `sql:"not null"`
    PostId    int
    CreatedAt time.Time
}
```

There's a field called CreatedAt, which is of type `time.Time`. If you place this field in any struct, whenever a new record is created in the database it'll be automatically populated. In this case, this is when the record is created.

You'll also notice that some of the fields have struct tags which instruct Gorm to create and map to the correct fields. In the case of the Author field, the struct tag `` `sql: "not null"` `` tells Gorm to create a column that's not `null`.

Also notice that unlike our previous example, you didn't add a Post field in the `Comments` struct. Instead, you placed a PostId field. Gorm automatically assumes that a field in this form will be a foreign key and creates the necessary relationships.

So much for the setup. Now let's take a look at creating, and retrieving, posts and comments. First, create a post:

```
post := Post{Content: "Hello World!", Author: "Sau Sheong"}
Db.Create(&post)
```

Nothing surprising here. But as you can see you're using another construct, in this case the database handler `gorm.DB`, to create the `Post` struct, following the Data-Mapper pattern. This is unlike our previous example, when you called a `Create` method on the `Post` struct, following the ActiveRecord pattern.

If you inspect the database, you'll see that a timestamp column, created_at, will be populated with the date and time it was created.

Next, you want to add a comment to the post:

```
comment := Comment{Content: "Good post!", Author: "Joe"}
Db.Model(&post).Association("Comments").Append(comment)
```

You create a comment first, and then use a combination of the `Model` method, together with the `Association` and `Append` methods, to add the comment to the post. Notice that at no time are you manually accessing the PostId.

Finally, let's look at how you can retrieve the post and the comment you created:

```
var readPost Post
Db.Where("author = $1", "Sau Sheong").First(&readPost)
var comments []Comment
Db.Model(&readPost).Related(&comments)
```

Again, you use the `Where` method on `gorm.DB` to look for the first record that has the author name `"Sau Sheong"` and push it into the `readPost` variable. This will give you the post. To get the comments, you get the post model using the `Model` method, and then get the related comments into your `comments` variable using the `Related` method.

As mentioned earlier, what we've covered briefly in this section on Gorm is only a small portion of the rich features provided by this ORM library. If you're interested, learn more at https://github.com/jinzhu/gorm.

Gorm is not the only ORM library in Go. A number of equally feature-rich libraries are available, including Beego's ORM library and GORP (which isn't exactly an ORM but close enough).

In this chapter we've covered the basic building blocks of writing a web application. In the next chapter, we switch gears and discuss how we can build web services.

## 6.6 Summary

- Caching data in memory using structs, which allows you to cache data for quicker response
- Storing and retrieving data in files, in both CSV as well as gob binary format, which allows you to process user-uploaded data or provide backup for cached data
- Performing CRUD on relational databases using `database/sql` and establishing relationships between data
- Using third-party data-accessing libraries, including Sqlx and Gorm, which give you more powerful tools to manipulate data in the database

# Part 3

# Being real

Writing code for basic server-side web applications, which you learned in the previous part, is only one of the many pieces of the web application puzzle. Most modern web applications have gone beyond a basic request-response model and evolved in many ways. Single Page Applications (SPA) provide speedy interactivity for users while getting data from web services. Mobile applications, native or hybrid both, do the same.

In this final part of the book, you will learn how to write web services using Go, that will serve SPA, mobile applications, and other web applications. You will also learn about using one of the most powerful features of Go—concurrency. You will learn how to add concurrency to your web applications to enhance its performance. You will also learn about testing web applications and all the ways Go provides support for your testing needs.

The book wraps up with showing you ways of deploying your web application, from copying the executable binaries to the intended server, to pushing your web applications to the cloud.

# 7 Go web services

> ***This chapter covers***
> - Using RESTful web services
> - Creating and parsing XML with Go
> - Creating and parsing JSON with Go
> - Writing Go web services

Web services, as you'll recall from our brief discussion in chapter 1, provide a service to other software programs. This chapter expands on this and shows how you can use Go to write or consume web services. You'll learn how to create and parse XML and JSON first, because these are the most frequently used data formats with web services. We'll also discuss SOAP and RESTful services before going through the steps for creating a simple web service in JSON.

## 7.1 Introducing web services

One of the more popular uses of Go is in writing web services that provide services and data to other web services or applications. Web services, at a basic level, are software programs that interact with other software programs. In other words, instead of having a human being as the end user, a web service has a software

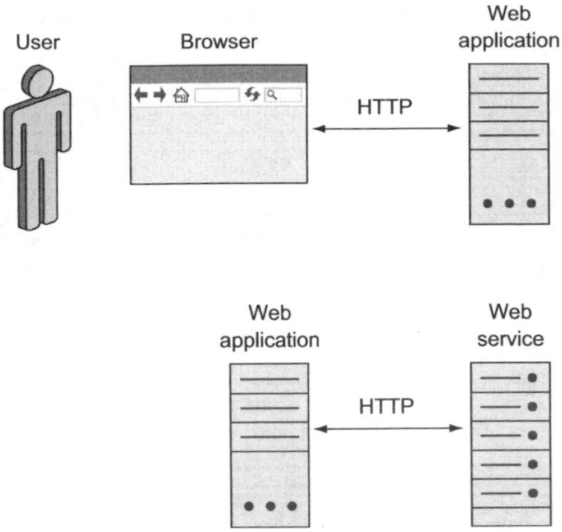

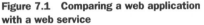

**Figure 7.1 Comparing a web application with a web service**

program as the end user. Web services, as the name suggests, communicate over HTTP (see figure 7.1).

Interestingly, though web applications are generally not solidly defined, you can find a definition of web services in a Web Services Architecture document by a W3C working group:

> *A Web service is a software system designed to support interoperable machine-to-machine interaction over a network. It has an interface described in a machine-processable format (specifically WSDL). Other systems interact with the Web service in a manner prescribed by its description using SOAP messages, typically conveyed using HTTP with an XML serialization in conjunction with other Web-related standards.*
>
> Web Service Architecture, February 11, 2004

From this description it appears as if all web services are SOAP-based. In reality, there are different types of web services, including SOAP-based, REST-based, and XML-RPC-based. The two most popular types are REST-based and SOAP-based. SOAP-based web services are mostly being used in enterprise systems; REST-based web services are more popular in publicly available web services. (We'll discuss them later in this chapter.)

SOAP-based and REST-based web services perform the same function, but each has its own strengths. SOAP-based web services have been around for a while, have been standardized by a W3C working group, and are very well documented. They're well supported by the enterprise and have a large number of extensions (collectively known as the WS-* because they mostly start with WS; for example, WS-Security and WS-Addressing). SOAP-based services are robust, are explicitly described using WSDL (Web Service Definition Language), and have built-in error handling. Together with

UDDI (Universal Description, Discovery, and Integration—a directory service), SOAP-based services can also be discovered.

SOAP is known to be cumbersome and unnecessarily complex. The SOAP XML messages can grow to be verbose and difficult to troubleshoot, and you may often need other tools to manage them. SOAP-based web services also can be heavy to process because of the additional overhead. WSDL, while providing a solid contract between the client and server, can become burdensome because every change in the web service requires the WSDL and therefore the SOAP clients to be changed. This often results in version lock-in as the developers of the web service are wary of making even the smallest changes.

REST-based web services are a lot more flexible. REST isn't an architecture in itself but a design philosophy. It doesn't require XML, and very often REST-based web services use simpler data formats like JSON, resulting in speedier web services. REST-based web services are often much simpler than SOAP-based ones.

Another difference between the two is that SOAP-based web services are function-driven; REST-based web services are data-driven. SOAP-based web services tend to be RPC (Remote Procedure Call) styled; REST-based web services, as described earlier, focus on resources, and HTTP methods are the verbs working on those resources.

ProgrammableWeb is a popular site that tracks APIs that are available publicly over the internet. As of this writing, its database contains 12,987 publicly available APIs, of which 2061 (or 16%) are SOAP-based and 6967 (54%) are REST-based.[1] Unfortunately, enterprises rarely publish the number of internal web services, so that figure is difficult to confirm.

Many developers and companies end up using both SOAP- and REST-based web services at the same time but for different purposes. In these cases, SOAP is used in internal applications for enterprise integration and REST is used for external, third-party developers. The advantage of this strategy is that both the strengths of REST (speed and simplicity) and SOAP (security and robustness) can be used where they're most effective.

## 7.2 Introducing SOAP-based web services

SOAP is a protocol for exchanging structured data that's defined in XML. SOAP was originally an acronym for Simple Object Access Protocol, terminology that is a misnomer today, as it's no longer considered simple and it doesn't deal with objects either. In the latest version, the SOAP 1.2 specification, the protocol officially became simply SOAP. SOAP is usable across different networking protocols and is independent of programming models.

SOAP is highly structured and heavily defined, and the XML used for the transportation of the data can be complex. Every operation and input or output of the service is clearly defined in the WSDL. The WSDL is the contract between the client and the server, defining what the service provides and how it's provided.

---

[1] Refer to www.programmableweb.com/category/all/apis?data_format=21176 for SOAP-based APIs and www.programmableweb.com/category/all/apis?data_format=21190 for REST-based APIs.

In this chapter we'll focus more on REST-based web services, but you should understand how SOAP-based web services work for comparison purposes.

SOAP places its message content into an envelope, like a shipping container, and it's independent of the actual means of transporting the data from one place to another. In this book, we're only looking at SOAP web services, so we're referring to SOAP messages being moved around using HTTP.

Here's a simplified example of a SOAP request message:

```
POST /GetComment HTTP/1.1
Host: www.chitchat.com
Content-Type: application/soap+xml; charset=utf-8

<?xml version="1.0"?>
<soap:Envelope
xmlns:soap="http://www.w3.org/2001/12/soap-envelope"
soap:encodingStyle="http://www.w3.org/2001/12/soap-encoding">
<soap:Body xmlns:m="http://www.chitchat.com/forum">
  <m:GetCommentRequest>
    <m:CommentId>123</m:CommentId>
  </m:GetCommentRequest >
</soap:Body>
</soap:Envelope>
```

The HTTP headers should be familiar by now. Note `Content-Type` is set to `application/soap+xml`. The request body is the SOAP message. The SOAP body contains the request message. In the example, this is a request for a comment with the ID `123`.

```
<m:GetCommentRequest>
  <m:CommentId>123</m:CommentId>
</m:GetCommentRequest >
```

This example is simplified—the actual SOAP requests are often a lot more complex. Here's a simplified example of a SOAP response message:

```
HTTP/1.1 200 OK
Content-Type: application/soap+xml; charset=utf-8

<?xml version="1.0"?>
<soap:Envelope
xmlns:soap="http://www.w3.org/2001/12/soap-envelope"
soap:encodingStyle="http://www.w3.org/2001/12/soap-encoding">
<soap:Body xmlns:m="http://www.example.org/stock">
  <m:GetCommentResponse>
    <m:Text>Hello World!</m:Text>
  </m:GetCommentResponse>
</soap:Body>
</soap:Envelope>
```

As before, the response message is within the SOAP body and is a response with the text "Hello World!"

```
<m:GetCommentResponse>
  <m:Text>Hello World!</m:Text>
</m:GetCommentResponse>
```

As you may realize by now, all the data about the message is contained in the envelope. For SOAP-based web services, this means that the information sent through HTTP is almost entirely in the SOAP envelope. Also, SOAP mostly uses the HTTP POST method, although SOAP 1.2 allows HTTP GET as well.

Here's what a simple WSDL message looks like. You might notice that WSDL messages can be detailed and the message can get long even for a simple service. That's part of the reason why SOAP-based web services aren't as popular as REST-based web services —in more complex web services, the WSDL messages can be complicated.

```
<?xml version="1.0" encoding="UTF-8"?>
<definitions  name ="ChitChat"
  targetNamespace="http://www.chitchat.com/forum.wsdl"
  xmlns:tns="http://www.chitchat.com/forum.wsdl"
  xmlns:soap="http://schemas.xmlsoap.org/wsdl/soap/"
  xmlns:xsd="http://www.w3.org/2001/XMLSchema"
  xmlns="http://schemas.xmlsoap.org/wsdl/">
  <message name="GetCommentRequest">
    <part name="CommentId" type="xsd:string"/>
  </message>
  <message name="GetCommentResponse">
    <part name="Text" type="xsd:string"/>
  </message>
  <portType name="GetCommentPortType">
    <operation name="GetComment">
      <input message="tns:GetCommentRequest"/>
      <output message="tns:GetCommentResponse"/>
    </operation>
  </portType>
  <binding name="GetCommentBinding" type="tns:GetCommentPortType">
    <soap:binding style="rpc"
      transport="http://schemas.xmlsoap.org/soap/http"/>
    <operation name="GetComment">
      <soap:operation soapAction="getComment"/>
      <input>
        <soap:body use="literal"/>
      </input>
      <output>
        <soap:body use="literal"/>
      </output>
    </operation>
  </binding>
  <service name="GetCommentService" >
    <documentation>
      Returns a comment
    </documentation>
    <port name="GetCommentPortType" binding="tns:GetCommentBinding">
      <soap:address location="http://localhost:8080/GetComment"/>
    </port>
  </service>
</definitions>
```

The WSDL message defines a service named `GetCommentService`, with a port named `GetCommentPortType` that's bound to the binding `GetCommentsBinding`. The service is defined at the location http://localhost:8080/GetComment.

```
<service name="GetCommentService" >
  <documentation>
    Returns a comment
  </documentation>
  <port name="GetCommentPortType" binding="tns:GetCommentBinding">
    <soap:address location="http://localhost:8080/GetComment"/>
  </port>
</service>
```

The rest of the message gets into the details of service. The port `GetCommentPortType` is defined with a single operation called `GetComment` that has an input message, `GetCommentRequest`, and an output message, `GetCommentResponse`.

```
<portType name="GetCommentPortType">
  <operation name="GetComment">
    <input message="tns:GetCommentRequest"/>
    <output message="tns:GetCommentResponse"/>
  </operation>
</portType>
```

This is followed by a definition of the messages themselves. The definition names the message and the parts of the message and their types.

```
<message name="GetCommentRequest">
  <part name="CommentId" type="xsd:string"/>
</message>
<message name="GetCommentResponse">
  <part name="Text" type="xsd:string"/>
</message>
```

In practice, SOAP request messages are often generated by a SOAP client that's generated from the WSDL. Similarly, SOAP response messages are often generated by a SOAP server that's also generated from the WSDL. What often happens is a language-specific client (for example, a Go SOAP client) is generated from the WSDL, and this client is used by the rest of the code to interact with the server. As a result, as long as the WSDL is well defined, the SOAP client is usually robust. The drawback is that each time we change the service, even for a small matter like changing the type of the return value, the client needs to be regenerated. This can get tedious and explains why you won't see too many SOAP web service revisions (revisions can be a nightmare if it's a large web service).

I won't discuss SOAP-based web services in further detail in the rest of this chapter, although I'll show you how Go can be used to create or parse XML.

## 7.3 Introducing REST-based web services

REST (Representational State Transfer) is a design philosophy used in designing programs that talk to each other by manipulating resources using a standard few actions (or verbs, as many REST people like to call them).

In most programming paradigms, you often get work done by defining functions that are subsequently triggered by a main program sequentially. In OOP, you do much the same thing, except that you create models (called *objects*) to represent things and you define functions (called *methods*) and attach them to those models, which you can subsequently call. REST is an evolution of the same line of thought where instead of exposing functions as services to be called, you expose the models, called *resources*, and only allow a few actions (called *verbs*) on them.

When used over HTTP, a URL is used to represent a resource. HTTP methods are used as verbs to manipulate them, as listed in table 7.1.

**Table 7.1 HTTP methods and corresponding web services**

| HTTP method | What to use it for | Example |
|---|---|---|
| POST | Creates a resource (where one doesn't exist) | POST /users |
| GET | Retrieves a resource | GET /users/1 |
| PUT | Updates a resource with the given URL | PUT /users/1 |
| DELETE | Deletes a resource | DELETE /users/1 |

The aha! moment that often comes to programmers who first read about REST is when they see the mapping between the use of HTTP methods for REST with the database CRUD operations. It's important to understand that this mapping is not a 1-to-1 mapping, nor is it the only mapping. For example, you can use both POST and PUT to create a new resource and either will be correctly RESTful.

The main difference between POST and PUT is that for PUT, you need to know exactly which resource it will replace, whereas a POST will create a new resource altogether, with a new URL. In other words, to create a new resource without knowing the URL, you'll use POST but if you want to replace an existing resource, you'll use PUT.

As mentioned in chapter 1, PUT is idempotent and the state of the server doesn't change regardless of the number of times you repeat your call. If you're using PUT to create a resource or to modify an existing resource, only one resource is being created at the provided URL. But POST isn't idempotent; every time you call it, POST will create a resource, with a new URL.

The second aha! moment for programmers new to REST comes when they realize that these four HTTP methods aren't the only ones that can be used. A lesser-known method called PATCH is often used to partially update a resource.

This is an example of a REST request:

```
GET /comment/123 HTTP/1.1
```

Note that there's no body associated in the GET, unlike in the corresponding SOAP request shown here:

```
POST /GetComment HTTP/1.1
Host: www.chitchat.com
Content-Type: application/soap+xml; charset=utf-8
```

```
<?xml version="1.0"?>
<soap:Envelope
xmlns:soap="http://www.w3.org/2001/12/soap-envelope"
soap:encodingStyle="http://www.w3.org/2001/12/soap-encoding">
<soap:Body xmlns:m="http://www.chitchat.com/forum">
  <m:GetCommentRequest>
    <m:CommentId>123</m:CommentId>
  </m:GetCommentRequest >
</soap:Body>
</soap:Envelope>
```

That's because you're using the GET HTTP method as the verb to get the resource (in this case, a blog post comment). You can return the same SOAP response earlier and it can still be considered a RESTful response because REST is concerned only about the design of the API and not the message that's sent. SOAP is all about the format of the messages. It's much more common to have REST APIs return JSON or at least a much simpler XML than SOAP messages. SOAP messages are so much more onerous to construct!

Like WSDL for SOAP, REST-based web services have WADL (Web Application Description Language) that describes REST-based web services, and even generate clients to access those services. But unlike WSDL, WADL isn't widely used, nor is it standardized. Also, WADL has competition in other tools like Swagger, RAML (Restful API Modeling Language), and JSON-home.

If you're looking at REST for the first time, you might be thinking that it's all well and good if we're only talking about a simple CRUD application. What about more complex services, or where you have to model some process or action?

How do you activate a customer account? REST doesn't allow you to have arbitrary actions on the resources, and you're more or less restricted to the list of available HTTP methods, so you can't have a request that looks like this:

```
ACTIVATE /user/456 HTTP/1.1
```

There are ways of getting around this problem; here are the two most common:

1. Reify the process or convert the action to a noun and make it a resource.
2. Make the action a property of the resource.

### 7.3.1 Convert action to a resource

Using the same example, you can convert the activate action to a resource activation. Once you do that, you can apply your HTTP methods to this resource. For example, to activate a user you can use this:

```
POST /user/456/activation HTTP/1.1

{ "date": "2015-05-15T13:05:05Z" }
```

This code will create an activation resource that represents the activation state of the user. Doing this also gives the added advantage of giving the activation resource additional properties. In our example you've added a date to the activation resource.

### 7.3.2 Make the action a property of the resource

If activation is a simple state of the customer account, you can simply make the action a property of the resource, and then use the PATCH HTTP method to do a partial update to the resource. For example, you can do this:

```
PATCH /user/456 HTTP/1.1

{ "active" : "true" }
```

This code will change the `active` property of the user resource to `true`.

## 7.4 Parsing and creating XML with Go

Now that you're armed with background knowledge of SOAP and RESTful web services, let's look at how Go can be used to create and consume them. We'll start with XML in this section and move on to JSON in the next.

XML is a popular markup language (HTML is another example of a markup language) that's used to represent data in a structured way. It's probably the most widely used format for representing structured data as well as for sending and receiving structured data. XML is a formal recommendation from the W3C, and it's defined by W3C's XML 1.0 specification.

Regardless of whether you end up writing or consuming web services, knowing how to create and parse XML is a critical part of your arsenal. One frequent use is to consume web services from other providers or XML-based feeds like RSS. Even if you'd never write an XML web service yourself, learning how to interact with XML using Go will be useful to you. For example, you might need to get data from an RSS newsfeed and use the data as part of your data source. In this case, you'd have to know how to parse XML and extract the information you need from it.

Parsing structured data in Go is quite similar, whether it's XML or JSON or any other format. To manipulate XML or JSON, you can use the corresponding XML or JSON subpackages of the encoding library. For XML, it's in the encoding/xml library.

### 7.4.1 Parsing XML

Let's start with parsing XML, which is most likely what you'll start doing first. In Go, you parse the XML into structs, which you can subsequently extract the data from. This is normally how you parse XML:

1. Create structs to contain the XML data.
2. Use `xml.Unmarshal` to unmarshal the XML data into the structs, illustrated in figure 7.2.

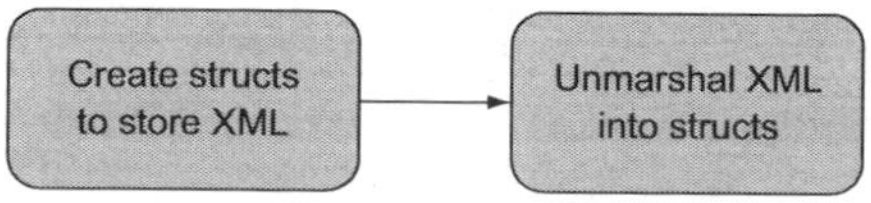

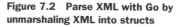

**Figure 7.2 Parse XML with Go by unmarshaling XML into structs**

Say you want to parse the post.xml file shown in this listing with Go.

**Listing 7.1 A simple XML file, post.xml**

```
<?xml version="1.0" encoding="utf-8"?>
<post id="1">
  <content>Hello World!</content>
  <author id="2">Sau Sheong</author>
</post>
```

This listing shows the code to parse the simple XML file in the code file xml.go.

**Listing 7.2 Processing XML**

```
package main

import (
  "encoding/xml"
  "fmt"
  "io/ioutil"
  "os"
)

type Post struct {     //#A
  XMLName xml.Name `xml:"post"`
  Id      string   `xml:"id,attr"`
  Content string   `xml:"content"`
  Author  Author   `xml:"author"`
  Xml     string   `xml:",innerxml"`
}

type Author struct {                          Defines structs to
  Id   string `xml:"id,attr"`                 represent the data
  Name string `xml:",chardata"`
}

func main() {
  xmlFile, err := os.Open("post.xml")
  if err != nil {
    fmt.Println("Error opening XML file:", err)
    return
  }
  defer xmlFile.Close()
  xmlData, err := ioutil.ReadAll(xmlFile)
  if err != nil {
    fmt.Println("Error reading XML data:", err)
    return
  }

  var post Post                               Unmarshals XML data
  xml.Unmarshal(xmlData, &post)               into the struct
  fmt.Println(post)
}
```

You need to define two structs, `Post` and `Author`, to represent the data. Here you've used an `Author` struct to represent an author but you didn't use a separate `Content` struct to represent the content because for `Author` you want to capture the `id` attribute. If you didn't have to capture the `id` attribute, you could define `Post` as shown next, with a string representing an `Author` (in bold):

```
type Post struct {
  XMLName xml.Name `xml:"post"`
  Id      string   `xml:"id,attr"`
  Content string   `xml:"content"`
  Author  string   `xml:"author"`
  Xml     string   `xml:",innerxml"`
}
```

So what are those curious-looking things after the definition of each field in the Post struct? They are called *struct tags* and Go determines the mapping between the struct and the XML elements using them, shown in figure 7.3.

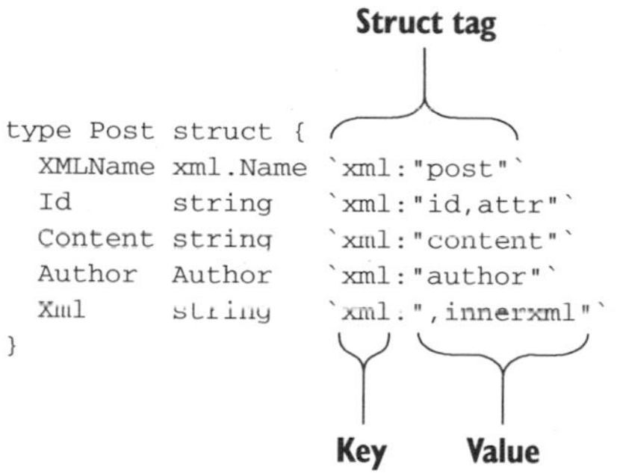


**Figure 7.3 Struct tags are used to define the mapping between XML and a struct.**

Struct tags are strings after each field that are a key-value pair. The key is a string and must not have a space, a quote ("), or a colon (:). The value must be a string between double quotes (""). For XML, the key must always be `xml`.

> **Why use backticks (`) in struct tags?**
>
> If you're wondering why backticks (`) are used to wrap around the struct tag, remember that strings in Go are created using the double quotes (") and backticks (`). Single quotes (') are used for runes (an `int32` that represents a Unicode code point) only. You're already using double quotes inside the struct tag, so if you don't want to escape those quotes, you'll have to use something else—hence the backticks.

Note that because of the way Go does the mapping, the struct and all the fields in the struct that you create must be public, which means the names need to be capitalized. In the previous code, the struct `Post` can't be just `post` and `Content` can't be `content`.

Here are some rules for the XML struct tags:

1. To store the name of the XML element itself (normally the name of the struct is the name of the element), add a field named `XMLName` with the type `xml.Name`. The name of the element will be stored in that field.
2. To store the attribute of an XML element, define a field with the same name as that attribute and use the struct tag `` `xml:"<name>,attr"` ``, where *<name>* is the name of the XML attribute.
3. To store the character data value of the XML element, define a field with the same name as the XML element tag, and use the struct tag `` `xml:",chardata"` ``.
4. To get the raw XML from the XML element, define a field (using any name) and use the struct tag `` `xml:",innerxml"` ``.
5. If there are no mode flags (like `,attr` or `,chardata` or `,innerxml`) the struct field will be matched with an XML element that has the same name as the struct's name.
6. To get to an XML element directly without specifying the tree structure to get to that element, use the struct tag `` `xml:"a>b>c"` ``, where `a` and `b` are the intermediate elements and `c` is the node that you want to get to.

Admittedly the rules can be a bit difficult to understand, especially the last couple. So let's look at some examples.

First let's look at the XML element `post` and the corresponding struct `Post`:

**Listing 7.3 Simple XML element representing a `Post`**

```
<post id="1">
  <content>Hello World!</content>
  <author id="2">Sau Sheong</author>
</post>
```

Compare it with this:

```
type Post struct {
  XMLName xml.Name `xml:"post"`
  Id      string   `xml:"id,attr"`
  Content string   `xml:"content"`
  Author  Author   `xml:"author"`
  Xml     string   `xml:",innerxml"`
}
```

Here you defined a struct `Post` with the same name XML element `post`. Although this is fine, if you wanted to know the name of the XML element, you'd be lost. Fortunately, the `xml` library provides a mechanism to get the XML element name by defining a struct field named `XMLName` with the type `xml.Name`. You'd also need to map this struct field to the element itself, in this case `` `xml:"post"` ``. Doing so stores the name of the element, `post`, into the field according to rule 1 in our list: to store the name of the XML element itself, you add a field named `XMLName` with the type `xml.Name`.

The post XML element also has an attribute named id, which is mapped to the struct field Id by the struct tag`xml:"id,attr"`. This corresponds to our second rule: to store the attribute of an XML element, you use the struct tag `xml:"<name>,attr"`.

You have the XML subelement content, with no attributes, but character data *Hello World!* You map this to the Content struct field in the Post struct using the struct tag `xml:"content"`. This corresponds to rule 5: if there are no mode flags the struct field will be matched with an XML element that has the same name as the struct's name.

If you want to have the raw XML within the XML element post, you can define a struct field, Xml, and use the struct tag `xml:",innerxml"` to map it to the raw XML within the post XML element:

```
<content>Hello World!</content>
<author id="2">Sau Sheong</author>
```

This corresponds to rule 4: to get the raw XML from the XML element, use the struct tag `xml:",innerxml"`. You also have the XML subelement author, which has an attribute id, and its subelement consists of character data *Sau Sheong*. To map this properly, you need to have another struct, Author:

```
type Author struct {
  Id    string `xml:"id,attr"`
  Name  string `xml:",chardata"`
}
```

Map the subelement to this struct using the struct tag `xml:"author"`, as described in rule 5. In the Author struct, map the attribute id to the struct field Id with `xml:"id,attr"` and the character data *Sau Sheong* to the struct field Name with `xml:",chardata"` using rule 3.

We've discussed the program but nothing beats running it and seeing the results. So let's give it a spin and run the following command on the console:

```
go run xml.go
```

You should see the following result:

```
{{ post} 1 Hello World! {2 Sau Sheong}
  <content>Hello World!</content>
  <author id="2">Sau Sheong</author>
}
```

Let's break down these results. The results are wrapped with a pair of braces ({}) because post is a struct. The first field in the post struct is another struct of type xml.Name, represented as { post }. Next, the number 1 is the Id, and "Hello World!" is the content. After that is the Author, which is again another struct, {2 Sau Sheong}. Finally, the rest of the output is simply the inner XML.

We've covered rules 1–5. Now let's look at how rule 6 works. Rule 6 states that to get to an XML element directly without specifying the tree structure, use the struct tag `xml:"a>b>c"`, where a and b are the intermediate elements and c is the node that you want to get to.

The next listing is another example XML file, with the same name post.xml, showing how you can parse it.

**Listing 7.4 XML file with nested elements**

```
<?xml version="1.0" encoding="utf-8"?>
<post id="1">
  <content>Hello World!</content>
  <author id="2">Sau Sheong</author>
  <comments>
    <comment id="1">
      <content>Have a great day!</content>
      <author id="3">Adam</author>
    </comment>
    <comment id="2">
      <content>How are you today?</content>
      <author id="4">Betty</author>
    </comment>
  </comments>
</post>
```

Most of the XML file is similar to listing 7.3, except now you have an XML subelement, `comments` (in bold), which is a container of multiple XML subelements `comment`. In this case, you want to get the list of comments in the post, but creating a struct `Comments` to contain the list of comments seems like overkill. To simplify, you'll use rule 6 to leap-frog over the `comments` XML subelement. Rule 6 states that to get to an XML element directly without specifying the tree structure, you can use the struct tag `` `xml:"a>b>c"` ``. The next listing shows the modified `Post` struct with the new struct field and the corresponding mapping struct tag.

**Listing 7.5 `Post` struct with `comments` struct field**

```
type Post struct {
  XMLName  xml.Name  `xml:"post"`
  Id       string    `xml:"id,attr"`
  Content  string    `xml:"content"`
  Author   Author    `xml:"author"`
  Xml      string    `xml:",innerxml"`
  Comments []Comment `xml:"comments>comment"`
}
```

To get a list of comments, you've specified the type of the `Comments` struct field to be a slice of `Comment` structs (shown in bold). You also map this field to the `comment` XML subelement using the struct tag `` `xml:"comments>comment"` ``. According to rule 6, this will allow you to jump right into the `comment` subelement and bypass the `comments` XML element.

Here's the code for the `Comment` struct, which is similar to the `Post` struct:

```
type Comment struct {
  Id      string `xml:"id,attr"`
```

```
  Content string `xml:"content"`
  Author  Author `xml:"author"`
}
```

Now that you've defined the structs and the mapping, you can unmarshal the XML file into your structs. The input to the `Unmarshal` function is a slice of bytes (better known as a string), so you need to convert the XML file to a string first. Remember that the XML file should be in the same directory as your Go file.

```
xmlFile, err := os.Open("post.xml")
if err != nil {
  fmt.Println("Error opening XML file:", err)
  return
}
defer xmlFile.Close()
xmlData, err := ioutil.ReadAll(xmlFile)
if err != nil {
  fmt.Println("Error reading XML data:", err)
  return
}
```

Unmarshaling XML data can be a simple one-liner (two lines, if you consider defining the variable a line of its own):

```
var post Post
xml.Unmarshal(xmlData, &post)
```

If you have experience in parsing XML in other programming languages, you know that this works well for smaller XML files but that it's not efficient for processing XML that's streaming in or even in large XML files. In this case, you don't use the `Unmarshal` function and instead use the `Decoder` struct (see figure 7.4) to manually decode the XML elements. Listing 7.6 is a look at the same example, but using `Decoder`.

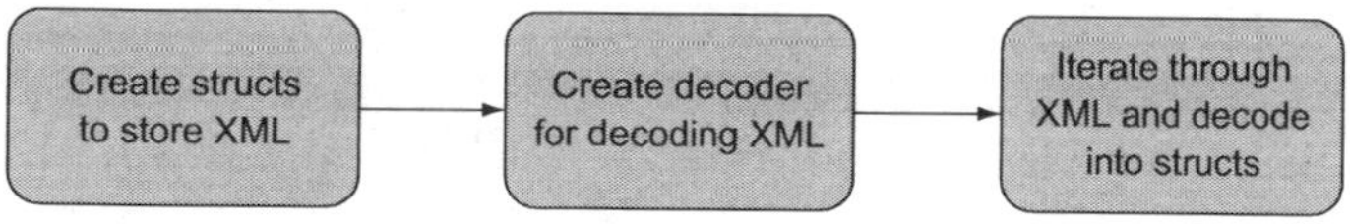


**Figure 7.4 Parsing XML with Go by decoding XML into structs**

**Listing 7.6 Parsing XML with `Decoder`**

```
package main

import (
  "encoding/xml"
  "fmt"
  "io"
  "os"
)
```

```
type Post struct {
  XMLName  xml.Name  `xml:"post"`
  Id       string    `xml:"id,attr"`
  Content  string    `xml:"content"`
  Author   Author    `xml:"author"`
  Xml      string    `xml:",innerxml"`
  Comments []Comment `xml:"comments>comment"`
}

type Author struct {
  Id   string `xml:"id,attr"`
  Name string `xml:",chardata"`
}

type Comment struct {
  Id      string `xml:"id,attr"`
  Content string `xml:"content"`
  Author  Author `xml:"author"`
}

func main() {
  xmlFile, err := os.Open("post.xml")
  if err != nil {
    fmt.Println("Error opening XML file:", err)
    return
  }
  defer xmlFile.Close()

  decoder := xml.NewDecoder(xmlFile)              // Creates decoder from XML data
  for {                                           // Iterates through XML data in decoder
    t, err := decoder.Token()                     // Gets token from decoder at each iteration
    if err == io.EOF {
      break
    }
    if err != nil {
      fmt.Println("Error decoding XML into tokens:", err)
      return
    }

    switch se := t.(type) {                       // Checks type of token
    case xml.StartElement:
      if se.Name.Local == "comment" {
        var comment Comment
        decoder.DecodeElement(&comment, &se)      // Decodes XML data into struct
      }
    }
  }
}
```

The various structs and their respective mappings remain the same. The difference is that you'll be using the `Decoder` struct to decode the XML, element by element, instead of unmarshaling the entire XML as a string.

First, you need to create a `Decoder`, which you can do by using the `NewDecoder` function and passing in an `io.Reader`. In this case use the `xmlFile` you got using `os.Open` earlier on.

Once you have the decoder, use the `Token` method to get the next token in the XML stream. A token in this context is an interface that represents an XML element. What you want to do is to continually take tokens from the decoder until you run out. So let's wrap the action of taking tokens from the decoder in an infinite `for` loop that breaks only when you run out of tokens. When that happens, `err` will not be `nil`. Instead it will contain the `io.EOF` struct, signifying that it ran out of data from the file (or data stream).

As you're taking the tokens from the decoder, you'll inspect them and check whether they're `StartElements`. A `StartElement` represents the start tag of an XML element. If the token is a `StartElement`, check if it's a comment XML element. If it is, you can decode the entire token into a `Comment` struct and get the same results as before.

Decoding the XML file manually takes more effort and isn't worth it if it's a small XML file. But if you get XML streamed to you, or if it's a very large XML file, it's the only way of extracting data from the XML.

A final note before we discuss creating XML: the rules described in this section are only a portion of the list. For details on all the rules, refer to the `xml` library documentation, or better yet, read the source `xml` library source code.

### 7.4.2 Creating XML

The previous section on parsing XML was a lengthy one. Fortunately, most of what you learned there is directly applicable to this section. Creating XML is the reverse of parsing XML. Where you unmarshal XML into Go structs, you now marshal Go structs into XML. Similarly, where you decode XML into Go structs, you now encode Go structs into XML, shown in figure 7.5.

Let's start with marshaling. The code in the file xml.go, shown in listing 7.7, will generate an XML file named post.xml.

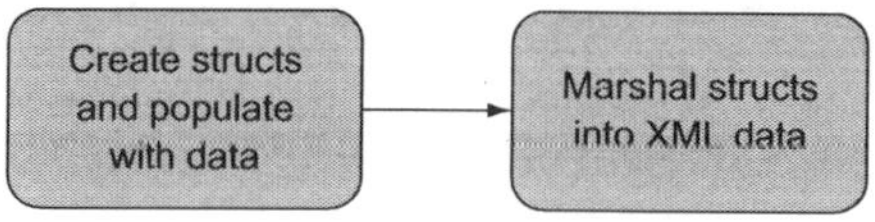


**Figure 7.5 Create XML with Go by creating structs and marshaling them into XML**

**Listing 7.7 Using the `Marshal` function to generate an XML file**

```
package main

import (
  "encoding/xml"
  "fmt"
  "io/ioutil"
)

type Post struct {
  XMLName xml.Name `xml:"post"`
  Id      string   `xml:"id,attr"`
```

```
  Content string   `xml:"content"`
  Author  Author   `xml:"author"`
}

type Author struct {
  Id   string `xml:"id,attr"`
  Name string `xml:",chardata"`
}

func main() {
  post := Post{
    Id:      "1",
    Content: " Hello World!",
    Author: Author{
      Id:   "2",
      Name: "Sau Sheong",
    },
  }
  output, err := xml.Marshal(&post)
  if err != nil {
    fmt.Println("Error marshalling to XML:", err)
    return
  }
  err = ioutil.WriteFile("post.xml", output, 0644)
  if err != nil {
    fmt.Println("Error writing XML to file:", err)
    return
  }

}
```

Creates struct with data

Marshals struct to a byte slice of XML data

As you can see, the structs and the struct tags are the same as those you used when unmarshaling the XML. Marshaling simply reverses the process and creates XML from a struct. First, you populate the struct with data. Then, using the `Marshal` function you create the XML from the `Post` struct. Here's the content of the post.xml file that's created:

```
<post id="1"><content>Hello World!</content><author id="2">Sau Sheong
    </author></post>
```

It's not the prettiest, but it's correctly formed XML. If you want to make it look prettier, use the `MarshalIndent` function:

```
output, err := xml.MarshalIndent(&post, "", "\t")
```

The first parameter you pass to `MarshalIndent` is still the same, but you have two additional parameters. The second parameter is the prefix to every line and the third parameter is the indent, and every level of indentation will be prefixed with this. Using `MarshalIndent`, you can produce prettier output:

```
<post id="1">
  <content>Hello World!</content>
  <author id="2">Sau Sheong</author>
</post>
```

Still, it doesn't look right. We don't have the XML declaration. Although Go doesn't create the XML declaration for you automatically, it does provide a constant `xml.Header` that you can use to attach to the marshaled output:

```
err = ioutil.WriteFile("post.xml", []byte(xml.Header + string(output)), 0644)
```

Prefix the output with `xml.Header` and then write it to post.xml, and you'll have the XML declaration:

```
<?xml version="1.0" encoding="UTF-8"?>
<post id="1">
    <content>Hello World!</content>
    <author id="2">Sau Sheong</author>
</post>
```

Just as you manually decoded the XML into Go structs, you can also manually encode Go structs into XML (see figure 7.6). Listing 7.8 shows a simple example.

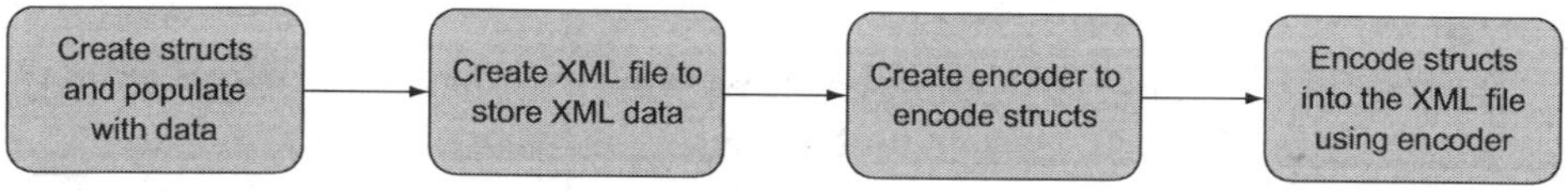


**Figure 7.6 Create XML with Go by creating structs and encoding them into XML using an encoder**

**Listing 7.8 Manually encoding Go structs to XML**

```
package main

import (
  "encoding/xml"
  "fmt"
  "os"
)

type Post struct {
  XMLName xml.Name `xml:"post"`
  Id      string   `xml:"id,attr"`
  Content string   `xml:"content"`
  Author  Author   `xml:"author"`
}

type Author struct {
  Id   string `xml:"id,attr"`
  Name string `xml:",chardata"`
}

func main() {
  post := Post{                               <- Creates struct with data
    Id:      "1",
    Content: "Hello World!",
```

```
    Author: Author{
      Id:   "2",
      Name: "Sau Sheong",
    },
  }

  xmlFile, err := os.Create("post.xml")          Creates XML file to store data
  if err != nil {
    fmt.Println("Error creating XML file:", err)
    return
  }
  encoder := xml.NewEncoder(xmlFile)             Creates encoder with XML file
  encoder.Indent("", "\t")
  err = encoder.Encode(&post)                    Encodes struct into file
  if err != nil {
    fmt.Println("Error encoding XML to file:", err)
    return
  }
}
```

As before, you first create the post struct to be encoded. To write to a file, you need to create the file using `os.Create`. The `NewEncoder` function creates a new encoder that wraps around your file. After setting up the indentation you want, use the encoder's `Encode` method, passing a reference to the post struct. This will create the XML file post.xml:

```
<post id="1">
  <content>Hello World!</content>
  <author id="2">Sau Sheong</author>
</post>
```

You're done with parsing and creating XML, but note that this chapter discussed only the basics of parsing and creating XML. For more detailed information, see the documentation or the source code. (It's not as daunting as it sounds.)

## 7.5 Parsing and creating JSON with Go

JavaScript Serialized Object Notation (JSON) is a lightweight, text-based data format based on JavaScript. The main idea behind JSON is that it's easily read by both humans and machines. JSON was originally defined by Douglas Crockford, but is currently described by RFC 7159, as well as ECMA-404. JSON is popularly used in REST-based web services, although they don't necessarily need to accept or return JSON data.

If you're dealing with RESTful web services, you'll likely encounter JSON in one form or another, either creating or consuming JSON. Consuming JSON is commonplace in many web applications, from getting data from a web service, to authenticating your web application through a third-party authentication service, to controlling other services.

Creating JSON is equally common. Go is used in many cases to create web service backends for frontend applications, including JavaScript-based frontend applications running on JavaScript libraries such as React.js and Angular.js. Go is also used to create web services for Internet of Things (IoT) and wearables such as smart watches. In many of these cases, these frontend applications are developed using JSON, and the most natural way to interact with a backend application is through JSON.

As with Go's support for XML, Go's support for JSON is from the `encoding/json` library. As before we'll look into parsing JSON first, and then we'll see how to create JSON data.

### 7.5.1 Parsing JSON

The steps for parsing JSON data are similar to those for parsing XML. You parse the JSON into structs, from which you can subsequently extract the data. This is normally how you parse JSON:

1. Create structs to contain the JSON data.
2. Use `json.Unmarshal` to unmarshal the JSON data into the structs (see figure 7.7).

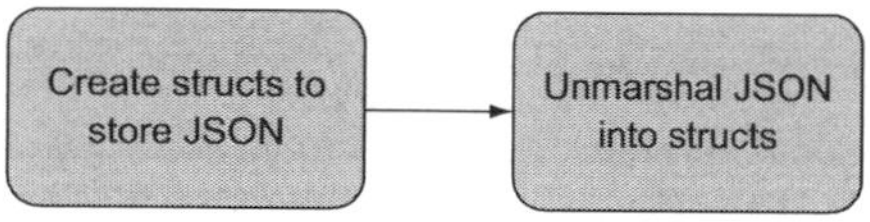

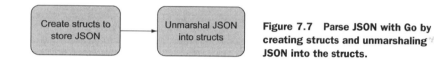

**Figure 7.7 Parse JSON with Go by creating structs and unmarshaling JSON into the structs.**

The rules for mapping the structs to JSON using struct tags are easier than with XML. There is only one common rule for mapping. If you want to store the JSON value, given the JSON key, you create a field in the struct (with any name) and map it with the struct tag `` `json:"<name>"` ``, where *<name>* is the name of the JSON key. Let's see in action.

The following listing shows the JSON file, post.json, that you'll be parsing. The data in this file should be familiar to you—it's the same data you used for the XML parsing.

**Listing 7.9 JSON file for parsing**

```
{
  "id" : 1,
  "content" : "Hello World!",
  "author" : {
    "id" : 2,
    "name" : "Sau Sheong"
  },
  "comments" : [
    {
      "id" : 3,
      "content" : "Have a great day!",
      "author" : "Adam"
    },
    {
      "id" : 4,
```

```
      "content" : "How are you today?",
      "author" : "Betty"
    }
  ]
}
```

The next listing contains the code that will parse the JSON into the respective structs, in a json.go file. Notice that the structs themselves aren't different.

**Listing 7.10 JSON file for parsing**

```
package main

import (
  "encoding/json"
  "fmt"
  "io/ioutil"
  "os"
)

type Post struct {
  Id       int       `json:"id"`
  Content  string    `json:"content"`
  Author   Author    `json:"author"`
  Comments []Comment `json:"comments"`
}

type Author struct {
  Id   int    `json:"id"`
  Name string `json:"name"`
}

type Comment struct {
  Id      int    `json:"id"`
  Content string `json:"content"`
  Author  string `json:"author"`
}

func main() {
  jsonFile, err := os.Open("post.json")
  if err != nil {
    fmt.Println("Error opening JSON file:", err)
    return
  }
  defer jsonFile.Close()
  jsonData, err := ioutil.ReadAll(jsonFile)
  if err != nil {
    fmt.Println("Error reading JSON data:", err)
    return
  }

  var post Post
  json.Unmarshal(jsonData, &post)
  fmt.Println(post)
}
```

Defines structs to represent the data

Unmarshals JSON data into the struct

You want to map the value of the key `id` to the Post struct's `Id` field, so we append the struct tag `` `json:"id"` `` after the field. This is pretty much what you need to do to map the structs to the JSON data. Notice that you nest the structs (a post can have zero or more comments) through slices. As before in XML parsing, unmarshaling is done with a single line of code—simply a function call.

Let's run our JSON parsing code and see the results. Run this at the console:

```
go run json.go
```

You should see the following results:

```
{1 Hello World! {2 Sau Sheong} [{3 Have a great day! Adam} {4 How are you
    today? Betty}]}
```

We looked at unmarshaling using the `Unmarshal` function. As in XML parsing, you can also use `Decoder` to manually decode JSON into the structs for streaming JSON data. This is shown in figure 7.8 and listing 7.11.

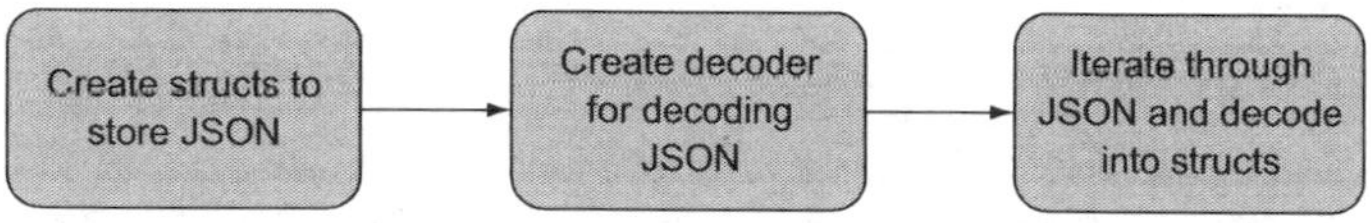


**Figure 7.8 Parse XML with Go by decoding JSON into structs**

**Listing 7.11 Parsing JSON using `Decoder`**

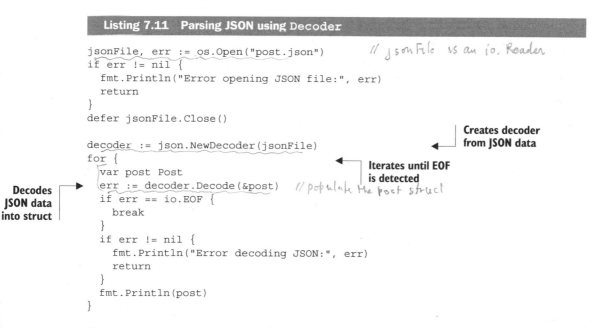

```
jsonFile, err := os.Open("post.json")
if err != nil {
  fmt.Println("Error opening JSON file:", err)
  return
}
defer jsonFile.Close()

decoder := json.NewDecoder(jsonFile)
for {
  var post Post
  err := decoder.Decode(&post)
  if err == io.EOF {
    break
  }
  if err != nil {
    fmt.Println("Error decoding JSON:", err)
    return
  }
  fmt.Println(post)
}
```

**Creates decoder from JSON data**

**Iterates until EOF is detected**

**Decodes JSON data into struct**

Here you use `NewDecoder`, passing in an `io.Reader` containing the JSON data, to create a new decoder. When a reference to the post struct is passed into the `Decode` method, the struct will be populated with the data and will be ready for use. Once the data runs out, the `Decode` method returns an `EOF`, which you can check and then exit the loop.

Let's run our JSON decoder and see the results. Run this at the console:

```
go run json.go
```

You should see the following results.

```
{1 Hello World! {2 Sau Sheong} [{1 Have a great day! Adam} {2 How are you
➥ today? Betty}]}
```

So when do we use `Decoder` versus `Unmarshal`? That depends on the input. If your data is coming from an `io.Reader` stream, like the `Body` of an `http.Request`, use `Decoder`. If you have the data in a string or somewhere in memory, use `Unmarshal`.

### 7.5.2 Creating JSON

We just went through parsing JSON, which as you can see, is very similar to parsing XML. Creating JSON is also is similar to creating XML (see figure 7.9).

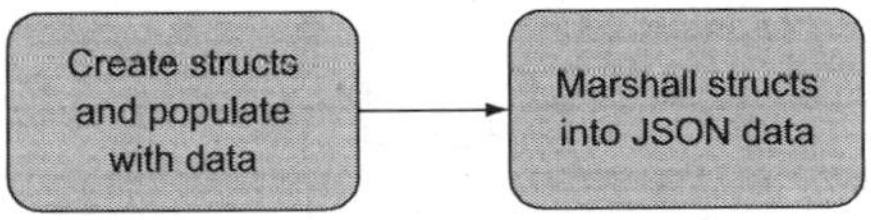


**Figure 7.9 Create JSON with Go by creating structs and marshaling them into JSON data.**

This listing contains the code for marshaling the Go structs to JSON.

**Listing 7.12 Marshaling structs to JSON**

```
package main

import (
  "encoding/json"
  "fmt"
  "io/ioutil"
)

type Post struct {
  Id       int       `json:"id"`
  Content  string    `json:"content"`
  Author   Author    `json:"author"`
  Comments []Comment `json:"comments"`
}

type Author struct {
  Id   int    `json:"id"`
  Name string `json:"name"`
}

type Comment struct {
  Id      int    `json:"id"`
```

**Creates struct with data** (annotation pointing to `type Post struct {`)

```
    Content string `json:"content"`
    Author  string `json:"author"`
}

func main() {
  post := Post{
    Id:      1,
    Content: "Hello World!",
    Author: Author{
      Id:   2,
      Name: "Sau Sheong",
    },
    Comments: []Comment{
      Comment{
        Id:      3,
        Content: "Have a great day!",
        Author:  "Adam",
      },
      Comment{
        Id:      4,
        Content: "How are you today?",
        Author:  "Betty",
      },
    },
  }

  output, err := json.MarshalIndent(&post, "", "\t\t")
  if err != nil {
    fmt.Println("Error marshalling to JSON:", err)
    return
  }
  err = ioutil.WriteFile("post.json", output, 0644)
  if err != nil {
    fmt.Println("Error writing JSON to file:", err)
    return
  }
}
```

**Marshals struct to byte slice of JSON data**

As before, the structs are the same as when you're parsing JSON. First, you create the struct. Then you call the `MarshalIndent` function (which works the same way as the one in the `xml` library) to create the JSON data in a slice of bytes. You can then save the output to file if you want to.

Finally, as in creating XML, you can create JSON manually from the Go structs using an encoder, shown in figure 7.10.

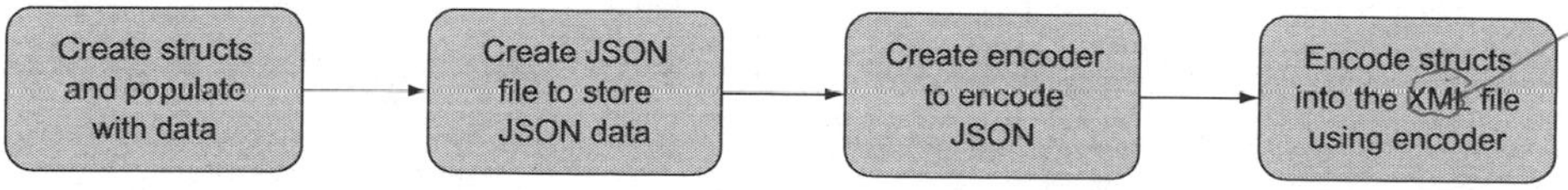


**Figure 7.10 Create JSON with Go by creating structs and encoding them into JSON using an encoder.**

The code in this listing, also in json.go, will generate JSON from the Go structs.

**Listing 7.13 Creating JSON from structs using `Encoder`**

```
package main

import (
  "encoding/json"
  "fmt"
  "io"
  "os"
)

type Post struct {                                    // Creates struct with data
  Id       int        `json:"id"`
  Content  string     `json:"content"`
  Author   Author     `json:"author"`
  Comments []Comment `json:"comments"`
}

type Author struct {
  Id   int    `json:"id"`
  Name string `json:"name"`
}

type Comment struct {
  Id      int    `json:"id"`
  Content string `json:"content"`
  Author  string `json:"author"`
}

func main() {

  post := Post{
    Id:      1,
    Content: "Hello World!",
    Author: Author{
      Id:   2,
      Name: "Sau Sheong",
    },
    Comments: []Comment{
      Comment{
        Id:      3,
        Content: "Have a great day!",
        Author:  "Adam",
      },
      Comment{
        Id:      4,
        Content: "How are you today?",
        Author:  "Betty",
      },
    },
  }
```

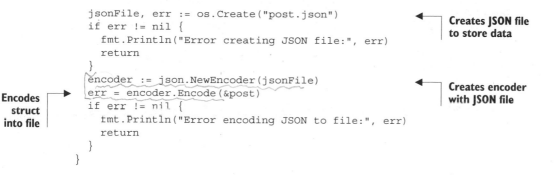

```
  jsonFile, err := os.Create("post.json")          ◄── Creates JSON file
  if err != nil {                                       to store data
    fmt.Println("Error creating JSON file:", err)
    return
  }
  encoder := json.NewEncoder(jsonFile)              ◄── Creates encoder
  err = encoder.Encode(&post)                           with JSON file
  if err != nil {
    fmt.Println("Error encoding JSON to file:", err)
    return
  }
}
```

Encodes struct into file

As before, you create a JSON file to store the JSON that's generated. You use this file to create an encoder using the NewEncoder function. Then you call the Encode method on the encoder and pass it a reference to the post struct. This will extract the data from the struct and create JSON data, which is then written to the writer you passed in earlier.

This wraps up the sections on parsing and creating XML and JSON. Going through these sections seems like plodding through similar patterns, but it provides you with the grounding you need for the next section, where you'll create a Go web service.

## 7.6 Creating Go web services

Creating a Go web service is relatively pain-free. If you've arrived here after going through the earlier chapters and the earlier sections in this chapter, the rest should just click and lightbulbs should start flickering on.

You're going to build a simple REST-based web service that allows you to create, retrieve, update, and retrieve forum posts. Another way of looking at it is you're wrapping a web service interface over the CRUD functions you built in chapter 6. You'll be using JSON as the data transport format. This simple web service will be reused to explain other concepts in the following chapters.

First, let's look at the database operations that you'll need. Essentially you're going to reuse—but simplify—the code from section 6.4. The code you need is placed in a file named data.go, shown in the following listing, with the package name main. The code isolates what you need to do with the database.

**Listing 7.14 Accessing the database with data.go**

```
package main

import (
  "database/sql"
  _ "github.com/lib/pq"
)

var Db *sql.DB

func init() {                          ◄── Connects to the Db
```

```
  var err error
  Db, err = sql.Open("postgres", "user=gwp dbname=gwp password=gwp ssl-
  mode=disable")
  if err != nil {
    panic(err)
  }
}

func retrieve(id int) (post Post, err error) {          Gets a single post
  post = Post{}
  err = Db.QueryRow("select id, content, author from posts where id = $1",
  id).Scan(&post.Id, &post.Content, &post.Author)
  return
}
                                                        Creates a new post
func (post *Post) create() (err error) {
  statement := "insert into posts (content, author) values ($1, $2) return-
  ing id"
  stmt, err := Db.Prepare(statement)
  if err != nil {
    return
  }
  defer stmt.Close()
  err = stmt.QueryRow(post.Content, post.Author).Scan(&post.Id)
  return
}

Updates a post
func (post *Post) update() (err error) {
  _, err = Db.Exec("update posts set content = $2, author = $3 where id =
  $1", post.Id, post.Content, post.Author)
  return
}
                                                        Deletes a post
func (post *Post) delete() (err error) {
  _, err = Db.Exec("delete from posts where id = $1", post.Id)
  return
}
```

As you can see, the code is similar to that of listing 6.6, with slightly different function and method names, so we won't go through it again. If you need a refresher, please flip back to section 6.4.

Now that you can do CRUD on the database, let's turn to the actual web service. The next listing shows the entire web service in a server.go file.

**Listing 7.15 Go web service in server.go**

```
package main

import (
  "encoding/json"
  "net/http"
  "path"
  "strconv"
)
```

```
type Post struct {
  Id      int    `json:"id"`
  Content string `json:"content"`
  Author  string `json:"author"`
}

func main() {
  server := http.Server{
    Addr: "127.0.0.1:8080",
  }
  http.HandleFunc("/post/", handleRequest)
  server.ListenAndServe()
}

func handleRequest(w http.ResponseWriter, r *http.Request) {
  var err error
  switch r.Method {
  case "GET":
    err = handleGet(w, r)
  case "POST":
    err = handlePost(w, r)
  case "PUT":
    err = handlePut(w, r)
  case "DELETE":
    err = handleDelete(w, r)
  }
  if err != nil {
    http.Error(w, err.Error(), http.StatusInternalServerError)
    return
  }
}

func handleGet(w http.ResponseWriter, r *http.Request) (err error) {
  id, err := strconv.Atoi(path.Base(r.URL.Path))
  if err != nil {
    return
  }
  post, err := retrieve(id)
  if err != nil {
    return
  }
  output, err := json.MarshalIndent(&post, "", "\t\t")
  if err != nil {
    return
  }
  w.Header().Set("Content-Type", "application/json")
  w.Write(output)
  return
}

func handlePost(w http.ResponseWriter, r *http.Request) (err error) {
  len := r.ContentLength
  body := make([]byte, len)
  r.Body.Read(body)
  var post Post
```

**Handler function to multiplex request to the correct function** (annotation for `handleRequest`)

**Retrieves post** (annotation for `handleGet`)

**Creates post** (annotation for `handlePost`)

```
  json.Unmarshal(body, &post)
  err = post.create()
  if err != nil {
    return
  }
  w.WriteHeader(200)
  return
}

func handlePut(w http.ResponseWriter, r *http.Request) (err error) {    // Updates post
  id, err := strconv.Atoi(path.Base(r.URL.Path))
  if err != nil {
    return
  }
  post, err := retrieve(id)
  if err != nil {
    return
  }
  len := r.ContentLength
  body := make([]byte, len)
  r.Body.Read(body)
  json.Unmarshal(body, &post)
  err = post.update()
  if err != nil {
    return
  }
  w.WriteHeader(200)
  return
}

func handleDelete(w http.ResponseWriter, r *http.Request) (err error) {    // Deletes post
  id, err := strconv.Atoi(path.Base(r.URL.Path))
  if err != nil {
    return
  }
  post, err := retrieve(id)
  if err != nil {
    return
  }
  err = post.delete()
  if err != nil {
    return
  }
  w.WriteHeader(200)
  return
}
```

The structure of the code is straightforward. You use a single handler function called `handleRequest` that will multiplex to different CRUD functions according to the method that was used. Each of the called functions takes in a `ResponseWriter` and a `Request` while returning an error, if any. The `handleRequest` handler function will also take care of any errors that are floated up from the request, and throw a 500 status code (`StatusInternalServerError`) with the error description, if there's an error.

Let's delve into the details and start by creating a post, shown in this listing.

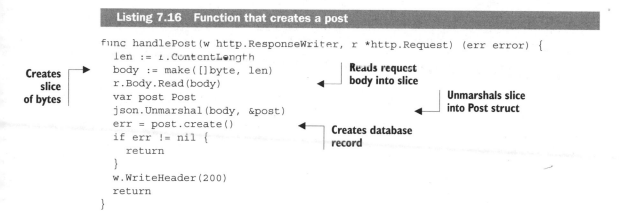

**Listing 7.16 Function that creates a post**

```
func handlePost(w http.ResponseWriter, r *http.Request) (err error) {
  len := r.ContentLength
  body := make([]byte, len)          // Creates slice of bytes
  r.Body.Read(body)                  // Reads request body into slice
  var post Post
  json.Unmarshal(body, &post)        // Unmarshals slice into Post struct
  err = post.create()                // Creates database record
  if err != nil {
    return
  }
  w.WriteHeader(200)
  return
}
```

First, you create a slice of bytes with the correct content length size, and read the contents of the body (which is a JSON string) into it. Next, you declare a `Post` struct and unmarshal the content into it. Now that you have a `Post` struct with the fields populated, you call the `create` method on it to save it to the database.

To call the web service, you'll be using cURL (see chapter 3). Run this command on the console:

```
curl -i -X POST -H "Content-Type: application/json"  -d '{"content":"My
[CA} first post","author":"Sau Sheong"}' http://127.0.0.1:8080/post/
```

You're using the `POST` method and setting the `Content-Type` header to `application/json`. A JSON string request body is sent to the URL http://127.0.0.1/post/. You should see something like this:

```
HTTP/1.1 200 OK
Date: Sun, 12 Apr 2015 13:32:14 GMT
Content-Length: 0
Content-Type: text/plain; charset=utf-8
```

This doesn't tell us anything except that the handler function didn't encounter any errors. Let's peek into the database by running this single line SQL query from the console:

```
psql -U gwp -d gwp -c "select * from posts;"
```

You should see this:

```
 id |    content    |   author
----+---------------+------------
  1 | My first post | Sau Sheong
(1 row)
```

In each of the handler functions (except for the create handler function, `postPost`), you assume the URL will contain the `id` to the targeted post. For example, when you want to retrieve a post, you assume the web service will be called by a request to a URL:

```
/post/<id>
```

where `<id>` is the `id` of the post. The next listing shows how this works in retrieving the post.

**Listing 7.17 Function that retrieves a post**

```
func handleGet(w http.ResponseWriter, r *http.Request) (err error) {
  id, err := strconv.Atoi(path.Base(r.URL.Path))
  if err != nil {
    return
  }
  post, err := retrieve(id)                        // Gets data from database into Post struct
  if err != nil {
    return
  }
  output, err := json.MarshalIndent(&post, "", "\t\t")   // Marshals the Post struct into JSON string
  if err != nil {
    return
  }
  w.Header().Set("Content-Type", "application/json")   // Writes JSON to ResponseWriter
  w.Write(output)
  return
}
```

You extract the URL's path, and then get the `id` using the `path.Base` function. The `id` is a string, but you need an integer to retrieve the post, so you convert it into an integer using `strconv.Atoi`. Once you have the `id`, you can use the `retrievePost` function, which gives you a `Post` struct that's filled with data.

Next, you convert the `Post` struct into a JSON-formatted slice of bytes using the `json.MarshalIndent` function. Then you set the `Content-Type` header to `application/json` and write the bytes to the `ResponseWriter` to be returned to the calling program.

To see how this works, run this command on the console:

```
curl -i -X GET http://127.0.0.1:8080/post/1
```

This tells you to use the GET method on the URL, with the `id` 1. The results would be something like this:

```
HTTP/1.1 200 OK
Content-Type: application/json
Date: Sun, 12 Apr 2015 13:32:18 GMT
Content-Length: 69

{
    "id": 1,
    "content": "My first post",
    "author": "Sau Sheong"
}
```

You need the results when updating the post too, shown in this listing.

**Listing 7.18 Function that updates a post**

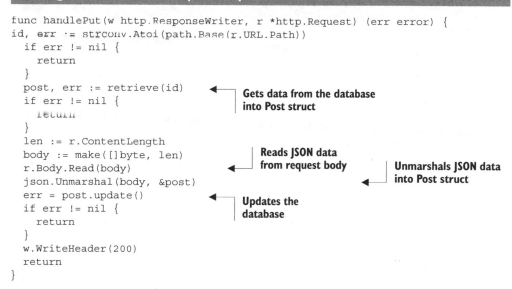

```
func handlePut(w http.ResponseWriter, r *http.Request) (err error) {
id, err := strconv.Atoi(path.Base(r.URL.Path))
  if err != nil {
    return
  }
  post, err := retrieve(id)
  if err != nil {
    return
  }
  len := r.ContentLength
  body := make([]byte, len)
  r.Body.Read(body)
  json.Unmarshal(body, &post)
  err = post.update()
  if err != nil {
    return
  }
  w.WriteHeader(200)
  return
}
```

**Gets data from the database into Post struct**

**Reads JSON data from request body**

**Unmarshals JSON data into Post struct**

**Updates the database**

Updating the post involves retrieving the post and then updating its information with the information sent through the PUT request. Once you've retrieved the post, you read the body of the request, and then unmarshal the contents into the retrieved post and call the `update` method on it.

To see this in action, run this command through the console:

```
curl -i -X PUT -H "Content-Type: application/json"  -d '{"content":"Updated
➥ post","author":"Sau Sheong"}' http://127.0.0.1:8080/post/1
```

Note that unlike when you're creating the post using POST, you need to send in the `id` of the post you want to update through the URL. You should see something like this:

```
HTTP/1.1 200 OK
Date: Sun, 12 Apr 2015 14:29:39 GMT
Content-Length: 0
Content-Type: text/plain; charset=utf-8
```

Now check the database and see what you have. Run this single line SQL query from the console again:

```
psql -U gwp -d gwp -c "select * from posts;"
```

You should see this:

```
 id |    content    |   author
----+---------------+------------
  1 | Updated post  | Sau Sheong
(1 row)
```

Deleting the post through the web service, shown in the following listing, involves simply retrieving the post and calling the `delete` method on it.

**Listing 7.19 Function that deletes a post**

```
func handleDelete(w http.ResponseWriter, r *http.Request) (err error) {
  id, err := strconv.Atoi(path.Base(r.URL.Path))
  if err != nil {
    return
  }
  post, err := retrieve(id)           // Gets data from database into Post struct
  if err != nil {
    return
  }
  err = post.delete()                 // Deletes post data in database
  if err != nil {
    return
  }
  w.WriteHeader(200)
  return
}
```

Notice that in both updating and deleting the post, you write the 200 status code to indicate all is well. If there was an error along the way, it would've been returned to the calling function (the handler function `handlePost`) and a 500 status code would've been sent back.

Let's make a final call to cURL to delete the post record:

```
curl -i -X DELETE http://127.0.0.1:8080/post/1
```

You should see something like this:

```
HTTP/1.1 200 OK
Date: Sun, 12 Apr 2015 14:38:59 GMT
Content-Length: 0
Content-Type: text/plain; charset=utf-8
```

Don't forget to run the single line SQL query again, and this time you should see nothing in the table:

```
id | content | author
----+---------+--------
(0 rows)
```

## 7.7 Summary

- A major use of Go today is to write web services, so being able to at least understand how to build web services is a valuable skill.
- There are mainly two types of web services: SOAP-based and REST-based web services:
  - SOAP is a protocol for exchanging structured data that's defined in XML. Because their WSDL messages can become quite complicated, SOAP-based web services aren't as popular as REST-based web services.

  - REST-based web services expose resources over HTTP and allow specific actions on them.
- Creating and parsing XML and JSON are similar and involve creating a struct and either generating (unmarshaling) XML or JSON from it, or creating a struct and extracting (marshaling) XML or JSON into it.

# 8 Testing your application

***This chapter covers***

- The Go testing libraries
- Unit testing
- HTTP testing
- Testing with dependency injection
- Using third-party testing libraries

Testing is one of the main critical activities in programming, but often it's neglected or left as an afterthought. Go provides basic testing capabilities that look surprisingly primitive, but as you'll learn in this chapter, Go supplies the tools to create the automated tests you need as a programmer. This chapter also covers the `check` and `Ginkgo` packages, popular Go testing libraries that extend the built-in `testing` package.

As with the web application programming libraries we've explored in the previous few chapters, Go provides only the fundamental tools. As a programmer you'll need to build on them to deliver the kind of tests that you need.

## 8.1 Go and testing

Go offers a few testing-focused libraries in the standard library. The main test library is the `testing` package, which contains most of the functions you'll see in this chapter. Another library that's interesting for web application programming is the `net/http/httptest` package. The `httptest` package, as the name suggests, is a library for testing web applications; it is based on the `testing` package.

Let's look at the main `testing` package first. It's important to start here because this package provides basic automated testing capabilities in Go. Once you understand the `testing` package, the `httptest` package will make a whole lot more sense.

The `testing` package is used with the `go test` command which is used on any Go source files that end with *_test.go*. Usually this corresponds with the name of the source code file you're testing, although that's not strictly necessary.

If you have a server.go file, you should also have a server_test.go file that contains all the tests you want to run on the server.go file. The server_test.go file must be in the same package as the server.go file.

In the test file you create functions with the following form:

```
func TestXxx(*testing.T) { … }
```

where `Xxx` is any alphanumeric string in which the first letter is capitalized. When you run the `go test` command in the console, this and other similar functions will be executed. Within these functions you can use `Error`, `Fail`, and other methods to indicate test failure. If there's no failure, the test for the function is considered to have passed. Let's take a closer look.

## 8.2 Unit testing with Go

Unit testing, as the name indicates, is a kind of automated testing that provides confidence that a unit (a modular part of a program) is correct. Although a unit often corresponds to a function or a method, it doesn't necessarily need to. A good gauge of whether a part of a program is a unit is if it can be tested independently. A unit typically takes in data and returns an output, and unit test cases correspondingly pass data into the unit and check the resultant output to see if they meet the expectations. Unit tests are usually run in suites, which are groups of unit test cases to validate a particular behavior.

In Go, unit test cases are written in _test.go files, grouped according to their functionality. Let's take a look at a basic example in main.go, where you have a function that needs to be tested, shown in the following listing. You'll reuse the code from the JSON decoding example in listings 7.8 and 7.9.

**Listing 8.1 Example JSON decoding**

```
package main

import (
  "encoding/json"
  "fmt"
  "os"
)

type Post struct {
  Id       int       `json:"id"`
  Content  string    `json:"content"`
  Author   Author    `json:"author"`
  Comments []Comment `json:"comments"`
}

type Author struct {
  Id   int    `json:"id"`
  Name string `json:"name"`
}

type Comment struct {
  Id      int    `json:"id"`
  Content string `json:"content"`
  Author  string `json:"author"`
}

func decode(filename string) (post Post, err error) {
  jsonFile, err := os.Open(filename)
  if err != nil {
    fmt.Println("Error opening JSON file:", err)
    return
  }
  defer jsonFile.Close()

  decoder := json.NewDecoder(jsonFile)
  err = decoder.Decode(&post)
  if err != nil {
    fmt.Println("Error decoding JSON:", err)
    return
  }
  return
}

func main() {
  _, err := decode("post.json")
  if err != nil {
    fmt.Println("Error:", err)
  }
}
```

**Refactored decoding code into a separate decode function**

Here you refactored out a decode function and moved the logic of opening the file and decoding it into a separate function. You then called decode from the main function, rather than placing all of the logic inside the main function. This is an important point: although most of the time you focus on writing code that implements features and delivery functionality, it's equally important that the code be testable. This often requires some form of design thinking before writing the program. Keep in mind that testing is a critical part of writing software programs. I'll come back to this point later in this chapter.

As a reminder, the following listing is the JSON file you parsed in chapter 7.

**Listing 8.2 The post.json file that you parsed**

```
{
  "id" : 1,
  "content" : "Hello World!",
  "author" : {
    "id" : 2,
    "name" : "Sau Sheong"
  },
  "comments" : [
    {
      "id" : 3,
      "content" : "Have a great day!",
      "author" : "Adam"
    },
    {
      "id" : 4,
      "content" : "How are you today?",
      "author" : "Betty"
    }
  ]
}
```

Now let's look at the main_test.go file.

**Listing 8.3 Test file for main.go**

```
package main                          ← Tests files are in same
                                        package as tested functions
import (
  "testing"
)

func TestDecode(t *testing.T) {                     Calls the function
  post, err := decode("post.json")               ← that's tested
  if err != nil {
    t.Error(err)
  }
  if post.Id != 1 {                                          ←
    t.Error("Wrong id, was expecting 1 but got", post.Id)      Checks if results are
  }                                                            expected; if not, flag
  if post.Content != "Hello World!" {                        ← error messages.
    t.Error("Wrong content, was expecting 'Hello World!' but got",
    ➥ post.Content)
  }
}
```

```
func TestEncode(t *testing.T) {
  t.Skip("Skipping encoding for now")
}
```

**Skips the test altogether**

Notice that the test file is in the same package as the program file. In this example you'll only use the `testing` package, so that's the only package you'll be importing. The function `TestDecode` takes in a parameter, `t`, that's a pointer to a `testing.T` struct. This is a test case that represents the unit testing of the `decode` function. The `testing.T` struct is one of the two main structs in the package, and it's the main struct that you'll be using to call out any failures or errors.

The `testing.T` struct has a number of useful functions:

- `Log`—Similar to `fmt.Println`; records the text in the error log.
- `Logf`—Similar to `fmt.Printf`. It formats its arguments according to the given format and records the text in the error log.
- `Fail`—Marks the test function as having failed but allows the execution to continue.
- `FailNow`—Marks the test function as having failed and stops its execution.

There are also a few convenience functions that combine these functions, as shown in figure 8.1.

| | Log | Logf |
|---|---|---|
| Fail | Error | Errorf |
| FailNow | Fatal | Fatalf |

**Figure 8.1 Convenience functions in `testing.T`, with each cell representing a single function. The functions in the white cells are combination functions. For example, the `Error` function is a combination of calling the `Fail` function, followed by the `Log` function.**

In figure 8.1, the `Error` function is a combination of calling the `Log` function, followed by the `Fail` function. The `Fatal` function is a combination of calling the `Log` function followed by the `FailNow` function.

In the test function you call the `decode` function normally, and then test the results. If the results aren't what you expect, you can call any of the `Fail`, `FailNow`, `Error`, `Errorf`, `Fatal`, or `Fatalf` functions accordingly. The `Fail` function, as you've probably guessed, tells you that the test case has failed but allows you to continue the execution of the rest of the test case. The `FailNow` function is stricter and exits the test case once it's encountered. `Fail` and `FailNow` only affect the test case they're in—in this case, the TestDecode test case.

Run the TestDecode test case now. In the console, run this command in the directory where the main_test.go file is:

```
go test
```

This will execute all _test.go files in the same directory, and you should see something like this (assuming the files are in a directory named unit_testing):

```
PASS
ok    unit_testing  0.004s
```

It's not very descriptive, so if you want more information, you can use the verbose (`-v`) flag, and if you want to know the coverage of the test case against your code, you can give it the coverage (`-cover`) flag.

```
go test -v -cover
```

which will give more information:

```
=== RUN TestDecode
--- PASS: TestDecode (0.00s)
=== RUN TestEncode
--- SKIP: TestEncode (0.00s)
  main_test.go:23: Skipping encoding for now
PASS
coverage: 46.7% of statements
ok    unit_testing  0.004s
```

### 8.2.1 Skipping test cases

Notice that you have two test cases in the same file—the second test case is TestEncode. But this test case doesn't do anything, because you don't have an encode function to test. If you're doing test-driven development (TDD), you might want to let the test case continue failing until you've written the function. If that is too irritating, Go provides a `Skip` function in `testing.T` that allows you to skip test cases if you're not ready to write them. The `Skip` function is also useful if you have test cases that run a very long time and you want to skip them if you only want to run a sanity check.

In addition to skipping tests, you can pass in a short (`-short`) flag to the `go test` command, and using some conditional logic in the test case, you can skip the running of parts of a test. Note that this is different from selective running of a specific test, which you can specify with an option in the `go test` command. The selective running of specific tests runs certain tests and skips others whereas the `-short` flag skips parts of a test (or the entire test case), depending on the way you write the test code.

Let's see how this works for the use case where you want to avoid executing a long-running test case. First, create a new test case (in the same main_test.go file). Remember to import the `time` package first:

```
func TestLongRunningTest(t *testing.T) {
  if testing.Short() {
    t.Skip("Skipping long-running test in short mode")
  }
  time.Sleep(10 * time.Second)
}
```

You set the condition that if the `-short` flag is set, you'll skip this test case. Otherwise you'll sleep for 10 seconds. Now let's run this normally and see what happens:

```
=== RUN TestDecode
--- PASS: TestDecode (0.00s)
=== RUN TestEncode
--- SKIP: TestEncode (0.00s)
  main_test.go:24: Skipping encoding for now
```

```
=== RUN TestLongRunningTest
--- PASS: TestLongRunningTest (10.00s)
PASS
coverage: 46.7% of statements
ok    unit_testing  10.004s
```

Notice that the `TestLongRunningTest` test case runs for 10 seconds, as expected. Now run this in the console

```
go test -v -cover -short
```

and run the tests again:

```
=== RUN TestDecode
--- PASS: TestDecode (0.00s)
=== RUN TestEncode
--- SKIP: TestEncode (0.00s)
  main_test.go:24: Skipping encoding for now
=== RUN TestLongRunningTest
--- SKIP: TestLongRunningTest (0.00s)
  main_test.go:29: Skipping long-running test in short mode
PASS
coverage: 46.7% of statements
ok    unit_testing  0.004s
```

As you can see, the long-running test case is now skipped.

### 8.2.2 Running tests in parallel

As mentioned earlier, unit test cases are meant to be tested independently. Sometimes this isn't possible because dependencies exist within a test suite. When it is possible, you can run unit test cases in parallel in order to speed up the tests. Let's see how to do this in Go.

Add a file named parallel_test.go, shown in this listing, in the same directory.

**Listing 8.4 Parallel testing**

```
package main

import (
  "testing"
  "time"
)

func TestParallel_1(t *testing.T) {    // Works for 1 second
  t.Parallel()                         // Calls Parallel function to run test cases in parallel
  time.Sleep(1 * time.Second)
}

func TestParallel_2(t *testing.T) {    // Works for 2 seconds
  t.Parallel()
  time.Sleep(2 * time.Second)
}
```

```
func TestParallel_3(t *testing.T) {      ← Works for 3 seconds
  t.Parallel()
  time.Sleep(3 * time.Second)
}
```

You can use the `time.Sleep` function to simulate processing, with three different test cases, working for 1, 2, and 3 seconds, respectively. To run the tests in parallel, you need to call the `Parallel` function on `testing.T` as the first statement in the test case.

Now run this in the console:

```
go test -v -short -parallel 3
```

The parallel (`-parallel`) flag indicates that you want to run a maximum of three test cases in parallel. You're still using the `-short` flag because you don't want to run the long-running test case. Let's see what happens.

```
=== RUN TestDecode
--- PASS: TestDecode (0.00s)
=== RUN TestEncode
--- SKIP: TestEncode (0.00s)
  main_test.go:24: Skipping encoding for now
=== RUN TestLongRunningTest
--- SKIP: TestLongRunningTest (0.00s)
  main_test.go:30: Skipping long-running test in short mode
=== RUN TestParallel_1
=== RUN TestParallel_2
=== RUN TestParallel_3
--- PASS: TestParallel_1 (1.00s)
--- PASS: TestParallel_2 (2.00s)
--- PASS: TestParallel_3 (3.00s)
PASS
ok     unit_testing   3.006s
```

You can see that all test cases in main_test.go and parallel_test.go are executed. Also, notice that all three parallel test cases are executed together. Even though each parallel case has a different execution time, because all three run at the same time and all finish within the timing of the longest running test, the final execution timing shows only 3.006 seconds (0.006 seconds for the first few test cases, and then 3 seconds for the longest running test case, TestParallel_3).

### 8.2.3 Benchmarking

The Go testing package provides two types of testing. You went through functional testing in the previous section, which tests the functionality of the program. The Go `testing` package also provides benchmarking, which is run to determine the performance of a unit of work.

Similar to unit testing, benchmark test cases are functions of the format:

```
func BenchmarkXxx(*testing.B) { … }
```

inside the _test.go files. Let's build some benchmark test cases in a new file named bench_test.go, shown in this listing.

**Listing 8.5 Benchmark testing**

```
package main

import (
  "testing"
)

// benchmarking the decode function
func BenchmarkDecode(b *testing.B) {
  for i := 0; i < b.N; i++ {
    decode("post.json")
  }
}
```

Loops through function to be benchmarked b.N times

As you can see, benchmarking with Go is rather straightforward. You execute the code that you want to benchmark (in this case, the decode function) b.N times in order to reliably benchmark its response time. As the code is being executed, b.N will change accordingly.

To run benchmark test cases, use the bench (-bench) flag when executing the go test command. You need to indicate which benchmark files you want to run using regular expressions as the flag parameter for the -bench flag. To run all benchmarks files, just use the dot (.):

```
go test -v -cover -short -bench .
```

Here are the results:

```
=== RUN TestDecode
--- PASS: TestDecode (0.00s)
=== RUN TestEncode
--- SKIP: TestEncode (0.00s)
main_test.go:38: Skipping encoding for now
=== RUN TestLongRunningTest
--- SKIP: TestLongRunningTest (0.00s)
main_test.go:44: Skipping long-running test in short mode
PASS
BenchmarkDecode  100000     19480 ns/op
coverage: 42.4% of statements
ok  unit_testing2.243s
```

The 100000 indicates how many loops were run (b.N). In this example, 100,000 loops were run and each loop took 19,480 nanoseconds, or 0.01948 milliseconds. The number of times a benchmark runs is dictated by Go. This number can't be specified directly by the user, although you can specify the amount of time it has to run in, therefore limiting the number of loops run. Go will run as many iterations as needed to get an accurate measurement. In Go 1.5, the test subcommand has a -test.count flag that lets you specify how many times to run each test and benchmark (the default is one time).

Notice that you're still running the functional tests. If you want to keep it simple, you can ignore the functional tests by using the run (-run) flag. The -run flag indicates which functional tests to run; if you use any name that doesn't match the functional tests, the corresponding tests will be ignored.

```
go test -run x -bench .
```

There are no functional tests named x, so no functional tests are run. This will result in the following:

```
PASS
BenchmarkDecode     100000        19714 ns/op
ok    unit_testing  2.150s
```

Knowing how fast a function runs is pretty useful, but it'll be more interesting if you can compare it with another function. In chapter 7, you learned two ways of unmarshaling JSON data into a struct: using the `Decode` function or using the `Unmarshal` function. You just benchmarked the `Decode` function; let's see how fast the `Unmarshal` function is. To do so, you need to refactor the unmarshaling code into an `unmarshal` function in main.go, shown in the next listing.

**Listing 8.6 Unmarshaling JSON data**

```
func unmarshal(filename string) (post Post, err error) {
  jsonFile, err := os.Open(filename)
  if err != nil {
    fmt.Println("Error opening JSON file:", err)
    return
  }
  defer jsonFile.Close()

  jsonData, err := ioutil.ReadAll(jsonFile)
  if err != nil {
    fmt.Println("Error reading JSON data:", err)
    return
  }
  json.Unmarshal(jsonData, &post)
  return
}
```

Now that you have an `unmarshal` function, let's benchmark it.

**Listing 8.7 Benchmarking the `Unmarshal` function**

```
func BenchmarkUnmarshal(b *testing.B) {
  for i := 0; i < b.N; i++ {
    unmarshal("post.json")
  }
}
```

Now run the benchmark again to get the results:

```
PASS
BenchmarkDecode     100000        19577 ns/op
BenchmarkUnmarshal      50000        24532 ns/op
ok    unit_testing  3.628s
```

You can see from the benchmarking results that `Decode` takes 0.019577 ms whereas `Unmarshal` takes 0.024532 ms, making `Unmarshal` about 25 % slower than `Decode`.

## 8.3 HTTP testing with Go

This is a book on web programming, so naturally there's a section on testing web applications. Although there are many ways to test web applications, I'll focus on unit testing the handlers with Go.

Unit testing web applications in Go is handled by the `testing/httptest` package. The `httptest` package provides facilities to simulate a web server, allowing you to use the client functions of the `net/http` package to send an HTTP request and capturing the HTTP response that's returned.

You'll reuse the simple web service you created in listing 7.14. As a recap, the simple web service has only one handler, named `handleRequest`, which in turn multiplexes the request to a set of functions depending on the HTTP method in the request. If an HTTP GET request comes in, `handleRequest` will multiplex the request to a `handleGet` function, shown in this listing.

**Listing 8.8 Multiplexing handler and GET handler function**

```
func handleRequest(w http.ResponseWriter, r *http.Request) {
  var err error
  switch r.Method {
  case "GET":
    err = handleGet(w, r)
  case "POST":
    err = handlePost(w, r)
  case "PUT":
    err = handlePut(w, r)
  case "DELETE":
    err = handleDelete(w, r)
  }
  if err != nil {
    http.Error(w, err.Error(), http.StatusInternalServerError)
    return
  }
}

func handleGet(w http.ResponseWriter, r *http.Request) (err error) {
  id, err := strconv.Atoi(path.Base(r.URL.Path))
  if err != nil {
    return
  }
  post, err := retrieve(id)
  if err != nil {
    return
  }
  output, err := json.MarshalIndent(&post, "", "\t\t")
```

**handleRequest, which multiplexes the request according to HTTP method** (annotation to `func handleRequest`)

**Switches to correct function** (annotation to `switch r.Method {`)

```
  if err != nil {
    return
  }
  w.Header().Set("Content-Type", "application/json")
  w.Write(output)
  return
}
```

Let's look at the unit test case (figure 8.2) to test the case where an HTTP GET request, shown in listing 8.9, comes in.

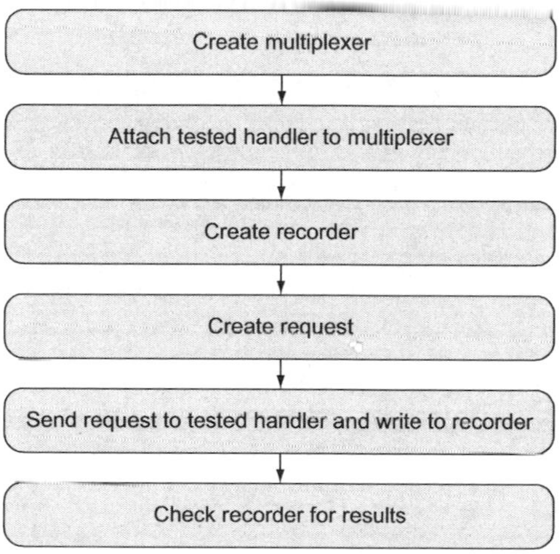


**Figure 8.2 Sequence for doing HTTP testing with Go, using the `httptest` package**

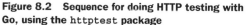

**Listing 8.9 Testing GET requests**

```
package main

import (
  "encoding/json"
  "net/http"
  "net/http/httptest"
  "testing"
)

func TestHandleGet(t *testing.T) {
  mux := http.NewServeMux()
  mux.HandleFunc("/post/", handleRequest)

  writer := httptest.NewRecorder()
  request, _ := http.NewRequest("GET", "/post/1", nil)
  mux.ServeHTTP(writer, request)

  if writer.Code != 200 {
    t.Errorf("Response code is %v", writer.Code)
  }
```

Annotations:
- `mux := http.NewServeMux()` — **Creates a multiplexer to run test on**
- `mux.HandleFunc(...)` — **Attaches handler you want to test**
- `writer := httptest.NewRecorder()` — **Captures returned HTTP response**
- `request, _ := http.NewRequest(...)` — **Creates request to handler you want to test**
- `mux.ServeHTTP(writer, request)` — **Sends request to tested handler**
- `if writer.Code != 200 {` — **Checks ResponseRecorder for results**

```
    var post Post
    json.Unmarshal(writer.Body.Bytes(), &post)
    if post.Id != 1 {
      t.Error("Cannot retrieve JSON post")
    }
}
```

Every test case runs independently and starts its own web server for testing, so you need to create a multiplexer and attach the `handleRequest` handler function to it. To capture the returned HTTP response, use the `httptest.NewRecorder` function to create a `ResponseRecorder` struct. This struct will be used to store the response for inspection.

You also need to create an HTTP request (as opposed to parsing it, as discussed in chapters 3 and 4) by calling the `http.NewRequest` function, passing it the method you want, the URL to send the request to, and an optional HTTP request body.

Once you have the response recorder and the request, send them to the multiplexer using `ServeHTTP`. When this happens, the request is sent to the `handleRequest` handler function and then to the `handleGet` function, which will process it and return an HTTP response. But instead of sending it to the browser, the multiplexer pushes it into the response recorder and you can inspect the response. The next few lines are quite self-explanatory; you can inspect the response to see if it has the results you wanted. If it doesn't, you can throw errors as per any unit test case, HTTP or otherwise.

All of these look simple, so let's try another one. This listing shows how to create a test case for a PUT request.

**Listing 8.10 Testing PUT requests**

```
func TestHandlePut(t *testing.T) {
  mux := http.NewServeMux()
  mux.HandleFunc("/post/", handleRequest)

  writer := httptest.NewRecorder()
  json := strings.NewReader(`{"content":"Updated post","author":"Sau
  Sheong"}`)
  request, _ := http.NewRequest("PUT", "/post/1", json)
  mux.ServeHTTP(writer, request)

  if writer.Code != 200 {
    t.Errorf("Response code is %v", writer.Code)
  }
}
```

As you can see, there's not much difference between this test case and the previous one, except you need to send in the JSON content. You might notice that some code in both test case functions is repeated. Such common test code (and other test fixtures) can be placed together in a setup function that prepares the test cases for execution.

Go's `testing` package provides a `TestMain` function that allows you to do whatever setup or teardown is necessary. A typical `TestMain` function looks something like this:

```
func TestMain(m *testing.M) {
  setUp()
  code := m.Run()
  tearDown()
  os.Exit(code)
}
```

where `setUp` and `tearDown` are functions you can define to do setup and teardown for all your test case functions. Note that `setUp` and `tearDown` are run only once for all test cases. The individual test case functions are called by calling the `Run` function on `m`. Calling the `Run` function returns an exit code, which you can pass to the `os.Exit` function.

This listing shows how this changes our test cases now.

**Listing 8.11 Using `TestMain` with `httptest`**

```
package main

import (
  "encoding/json"
  "net/http"
  "net/http/httptest"
  "os"
  "strings"
  "testing"
)

var mux *http.ServeMux
var writer *httptest.ResponseRecorder

func TestMain(m *testing.M) {
  setUp()
  code := m.Run()
  os.Exit(code)
}

func setUp() {
  mux = http.NewServeMux()
  mux.HandleFunc("/post/", handleRequest)
  writer = httptest.NewRecorder()
}

func TestHandleGet(t *testing.T) {
  request, _ := http.NewRequest("GET", "/post/1", nil)
  mux.ServeHTTP(writer, request)

  if writer.Code != 200 {
    t.Errorf("Response code is %v", writer.Code)
  }
  var post Post
  json.Unmarshal(writer.Body.Bytes(), &post)
```

```
    if post.Id != 1 {
        t.Errorf("Cannot retrieve JSON post")
    }
}

func TestHandlePut(t *testing.T) {
    json := strings.NewReader(`{"content":"Updated post","author":"Sau
     Sheong"}`)
    request, _ := http.NewRequest("PUT", "/post/1", json)
    mux.ServeHTTP(writer, request)

    if writer.Code != 200 {
        t.Errorf("Response code is %v", writer.Code)
    }
}
```

Notice that the setUp function sets up the global variables that are used in each of the test case functions. This makes the test case functions more concise, and any changes to how the test cases are set up are concentrated in a single place. There isn't a need for cleaning up after the tests so you simply exit after the test cases are run.

But you didn't test an important part of the web service. As you'll recall, in chapter 7 you abstracted the data layer away from the web service and placed all the data manipulation code in the data.go file. The handleGet function calls a retrieve function, whereas the handlePut function calls the retrieve function and an update method on the Post struct. When you run the unit test cases, you're actually getting and modifying data in the database. This is a dependency, and therefore the test cases aren't as independent as you'd like them to be.

How do you get around this?

## 8.4 Test doubles and dependency injection

One popular way of making the unit test cases more independent is using *test doubles*. Test doubles are simulations of objects, structures, or functions that are used during testing when it's inconvenient to use the actual object, structure, or function. It's also often used within the context of automated unit testing because it increases the independency of the code being tested.

An example is when the code being tested involves sending of emails. Naturally you don't want to send out emails during unit testing. One way of getting around that is to create test doubles that simulate sending emails. You'd create test doubles to remove the dependency of your unit test cases on an actual database.

The concept seems straightforward enough. During automated testing, you create test doubles and use them instead of using the actual functions or structs. However, this approach requires design prior to coding the program. If you don't have the idea of using test doubles in mind during design, you might not be able to do it at all. For example, in the previous section the design of the web service doesn't allow you to create test doubles for testing. This is because the dependency on the database is embedded deep into the code.

One of the ways you can design for test doubles is to use the *dependency injection* design pattern. Dependency injection is a software design pattern that allows you to decouple the dependencies between two or more layers of software. This is done through passing a *dependency* to the called object, structure, or function. This dependency is used to perform the action instead of the object, structure, or function. In Go, this dependency is often an interface type. Let's look at an example with the simple web service in chapter 7.

### 8.4.1 Dependency injection with Go

In the web service, the `handleRequest` handler function multiplexes GET requests to the `handleGet` function, which extracts the id from the URL and retrieves a `Post` struct using the `retrieve` function in `data.go`. It uses a global `sql.DB` struct to open a database connection to a PostgreSQL database and queries the `posts` table for the data.

Figure 8.3 shows the function calling flow in the web service in chapter 7. Access to the database is transparent to the rest of the functions except for the `retrieve` function, which will access the database through a global `sql.Db` instance.

As you can see, `handleRequest` and `handleGet` are dependent on `retrieve`, which in turn is dependent on `sql.DB`. The dependency on `sql.DB` is the root of the problem, so you need to remove it.

There are a few ways to decouple the dependencies (as with everything). You can start from the bottom and decouple the dependencies at the data abstraction layer, where you can get the `sql.DB` struct directly. You can also go from the top and inject the `sql.DB` into `handleRequest` itself. In this section, I'll show you how you can do it from a top-down approach.

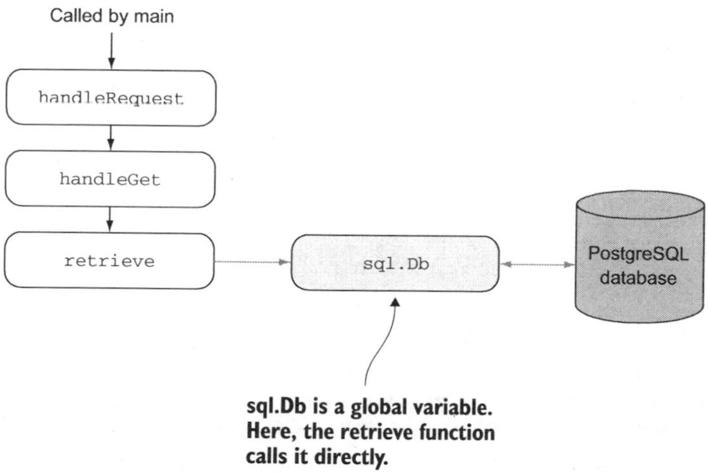


**Figure 8.3 The function calling flow of the web service in chapter 7. Access to the database is transparent to the rest of the functions except for the `retrieve` function, which will access the database through a global `sql.Db` instance.**

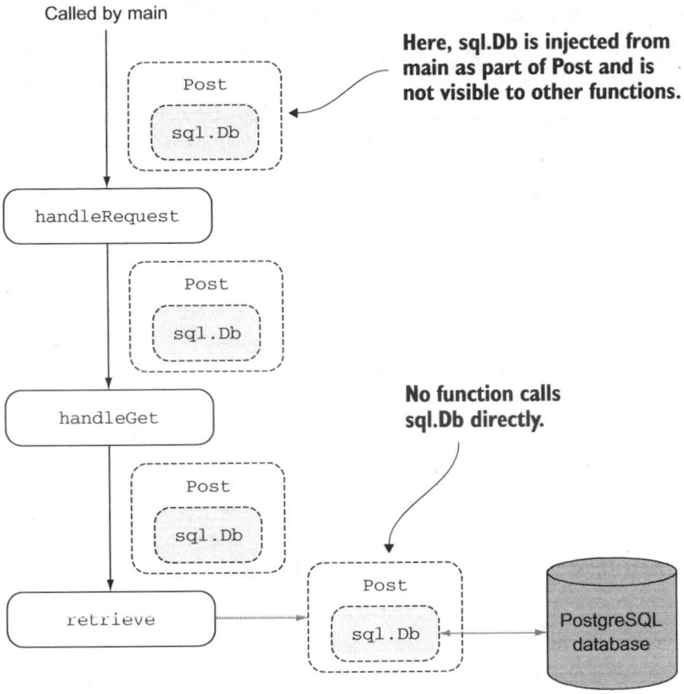


**Figure 8.4 Using the dependency injection pattern on the web service in chapter 7 by passing a pointer to a `Post` struct, which contains `sql.Db`, into the flow. The `Post` struct contains the `sql.Db` and so none of the functions in the flow are dependent on `sql.Db`.**

Figure 8.4 shows how the dependency on `sql.Db` can be removed and how it can be injected into the process flow from the main program. Note that the whole point of the exercise isn't to reject the use of `sql.Db` but to avoid the direct dependency on it, in order for you to use test doubles during testing.

Earlier I mentioned that you can inject the `sql.DB` into `handleRequest`, but you can't pass an instance or a pointer to `sql.DB` as a parameter into `handleRequest`. If you do, you're only pushing the problem upstream in the control flow. Instead you want to pass an interface (in our example, `Text`) into `handleRequest`. To retrieve a post from the database, call a method on this `Text` interface and you can assume it'll know what to do and return the necessary data you want. The next listing shows this interface.

**Listing 8.12 Interface to pass into `handlePost`**

```
type Text interface {
  fetch(id int) (err error)
  create() (err error)
  update() (err error)
  delete() (err error)
}
```

Next, let the Post struct implement the Text interface and make one of the fields in the Post struct a pointer to sql.DB. Post will implement the Text interface as long as it implements all the methods that Text has (which is already does, since you're simply reverse-engineering Text out of Post, shown in this listing).

**Listing 8.13 The new Post struct**

```
type Post struct {
  Db      *sql.DB
  Id      int    `json:"id"`
  Content string `json:"content"`
  Author  string `json:"author"`
}
```

This solves the problem of passing the sql.DB directly into handleRequest. Instead of passing sql.DB, you can pass an instance of the Post struct. The various Post methods will use the sql.DB that's a field in the struct instead. Because you're passing a Post struct into handleRequest, the function signature needs to be changed. The next listing shows the changes in the handleRequest function.

**Listing 8.14 The new handleRequest function**

```
func handleRequest(t Text) http.HandlerFunc {          // Passes in Text interface
  return func(w http.ResponseWriter, r *http.Request) {  // Returns function with correct signature
    var err error
    switch r.Method {
    case "GET":
      err = handleGet(w, r, t)                         // Passes on Text interface to actual handlers
    case "POST":
      err = handlePost(w, r, t)
    case "PUT":
      err = handlePut(w, r, t)
    case "DELETE":
      err = handleDelete(w, r, t)
    }
    if err != nil {
      http.Error(w, err.Error(), http.StatusInternalServerError)
      return
    }
  }
}
```

As you can see, handleRequest no longer follows the ServeHTTP method signature and is no longer a handler function. This is a problem—you can no longer attach it to a URL using the HandleFunc function.

To get around this, you can use the same technique first discussed in the section on handler chaining in chapter 3: get handleRequest to return a http.HandlerFunc function.

Then, in the main function instead of attaching a handler function to the URL, you can call the handleRequest function. handleRequest returns an http.HandlerFunc function, so it fits HandleFunc's method signature and you end up registering a handler function for the URL, as before. The next listing shows the modified main function.

**Listing 8.15 The modified main function**

```
func main() {

  var err error
  db, err := sql.Open("postgres", "user=gwp dbname=gwp password=gwp ssl-
  mode=disable")
  if err != nil {
    panic(err)
  }

  server := http.Server{
    Addr: ":8080",
  }
  http.HandleFunc("/post/", handleRequest(&Post{Db: db}))
  server.ListenAndServe()
}
```

Registering handleRequest, passing in Post struct

Notice that you passed the pointer to sql.DB into the handleRequest indirectly through the Post struct. This is how a dependency can be injected into handleRequest. This listing shows how it can be done for handleGet.

**Listing 8.16 The new handleGet function**

```
func handleGet(w http.ResponseWriter, r *http.Request, post Text) (err error) {
  id, err := strconv.Atoi(path.Base(r.URL.Path))
  if err != nil {
    return
  }
  err = post.fetch(id)
  if err != nil {
    return
  }
  output, err := json.MarshalIndent(post, "", "\t\t")
  if err != nil {
    return
  }
  w.Header().Set("Content-Type", "application/json")
  w.Write(output)
  return
}
```

Accepts Text interface

Retrieves data into Post struct

As you can see, there's not a whole lot of difference, except that the Post struct is sent into the function instead of being created within the function. Now rather than calling the retrieve function, which requires a global sql.DB, you can call the fetch method, shown in the following listing, on the Post struct to retrieve the data.

**Listing 8.17 The new `fetch` method**

```
func (post *Post) fetch(id int) (err error) {
  err = post.Db.QueryRow("select id, content, author from posts where id =
➥ $1", id).Scan(&post.Id, &post.Content, &post.Author)
  return
}
```

Instead of using a global `sql.DB` struct, you use the one passed to the method through the `Post` struct as a field. If you compile and run this web service now, it'll work exactly like how it worked previously. What you have done is remove a dependency (the global `sql.DB` struct) from being embedded into the code.

Quite convoluted. So how is this helpful?

The purpose is to make the unit test cases independent. If the dependency on the database is embedded into the code, the code can't be tested independently. But if you're injecting the dependency from an external source, you can test the rest of the code using a test double. Let's see how to do this.

The `handleRequest` function takes in any struct that implements the `Text` interface. This means you can create a test double that implements `Text` and pass it as a parameter into the `handleRequest` function. Create a test double called `FakePost` and that implements the few methods required to implement the `Text` interface, shown in this listing.

**Listing 8.18 The `FakePost` test double**

```
package main

type FakePost struct {
  Id      int
  Content string
  Author  string
}

func (post *FakePost) fetch(id int) (err error) {
  post.Id = id
  return
}

func (post *FakePost) create() (err error) {
  return
}

func (post *FakePost) update() (err error) {
  return
}

func (post *FakePost) delete() (err error) {
  return
}
```

Note that in the case of the `fetch` method, the `id` is set to whatever was passed in for testing purposes. The other methods can do nothing because they aren't used. You'll still need to implement them, though; otherwise it won't be considered an implementation of the Text interface. To keep the code clean, place the test double in a file named doubles.go.

Now create a test case for handleGet in server_test.go, shown in the following listing.

**Listing 8.19 Test double dependency into handlePost**

```
func TestHandleGet(t *testing.T) {
  mux := http.NewServeMux()
  mux.HandleFunc("/post/", handleRequest(&FakePost{}))

  writer := httptest.NewRecorder()
  request, _ := http.NewRequest("GET", "/post/1", nil)
  mux.ServeHTTP(writer, request)

  if writer.Code != 200 {
    t.Errorf("Response code is %v", writer.Code)
  }
  var post Post
  json.Unmarshal(writer.Body.Bytes(), &post)
  if post.Id != 1 {
    t.Errorf("Cannot retrieve JSON post")
  }
}
```

Passing a FakePost instead of a Post

Instead of passing a Post struct, this time you pass in your FakePost struct. That's all there is to it. The rest of the test case is no different from the earlier one.

To verify that it works, shut down your database and try running the test case. Your earlier test cases will fail because they need to interact with a database, but with test doubles, an actual database is no longer needed. You can now test the handleGet independently.

If handleGet works properly the test case will pass; otherwise it'll fail. Note that the test case doesn't actually test the fetch method in the Post struct, which requires the setting up (and possibly tearing down) of at least the posts table. You don't want to do so repeatedly, which would take a long time. Also, you want to isolate the different parts of the web service and test them independently to make sure they work and that you understand what went wrong. This is critical because the code continually evolves and changes. As code changes, you'll want to ensure that whatever you add later won't break what has worked before.

## 8.5 Third-party Go testing libraries

The testing package is a simple but effective library for testing Go programs, one that's used by Go for verifying the standard library itself, but areas exist where more capabilities would be welcome. A number of Go libraries are available that enhance the testing package. In this section we'll explore two popular ones, gocheck and Ginkgo. Gocheck is simpler and more integrated with the testing package while enhancing it. Ginkgo enables behavior-driven development in Go but is more complex and has a steeper learning curve.

### 8.5.1 Introducing the gocheck testing package

The gocheck project provides the check package, a test framework that builds on top of the testing package and provides a set of features that fills the feature gaps of the standard Go testing package. Some of these features are:

- Suite-based grouping of tests
- Test fixtures per test suite or test case
- Assertions, with an extensible checker interface
- More helpful error reporting
- Tight integration with the testing package

Installing the package is extremely easy. Just run this command on the console to download the package:

```
go get gopkg.in/check.v1
```

The following listing shows how you can apply the check package to the web service from chapter 7.

**Listing 8.20 server_test.go using the check package**

```
package main

import (
  "encoding/json"
  "net/http"
  "net/http/httptest"
  "testing"
  . "gopkg.in/check.v1"          // Exported identifiers can be accessed without qualifier.
)

type PostTestSuite struct {}     // Creates test suite

func init() {
  Suite(&PostTestSuite{})        // Registers test suite
}

func Test(t *testing.T) { TestingT(t) }     // Integrates with testing package

func (s *PostTestSuite) TestHandleGet(c *C) {
  mux := http.NewServeMux()
  mux.HandleFunc("/post/", handleRequest(&FakePost{}))
  writer := httptest.NewRecorder()
  request, _ := http.NewRequest("GET", "/post/1", nil)
  mux.ServeHTTP(writer, request)

  c.Check(writer.Code, Equals, 200)         // Verifies values
  var post Post
  json.Unmarshal(writer.Body.Bytes(), &post)
  c.Check(post.Id, Equals, 1)
}
```

First, you need to import the package. Note that you're importing the package as a dot (`.`) so that all the exported identifiers in the package can be accessed without a qualifier.

Next, you need to create a test suite, which is simply a struct. It can be an empty struct (as shown in the listing) or one with fields, which we'll discuss later. You must also call the `Suite` function and pass it an instance of the test suite. This will register the test suite you just created. Any method within the test suite that follows the format `TestXxx` will be considered a test case and will be executed as such.

As a final step you need to integrate with the `testing` package. You do so by creating a normal `testing` package test case; that is, a function with the format `TestXxx` that takes in a pointer to a `testing.T`. In this function you call the `TestingT` function, passing it the pointer to `testing.T`.

This will run all the test suites that have been registered using the `Suite` function and the results will be passed back to the `testing` package. With the setup done, let's look at a simple test case. We have a test case named `TestHandleGet` that is a method on the test suite and takes in a pointer to C, which has a number of interesting methods. Although we won't cover all of them in this section, interesting methods include `Check` and `Assert`, which allow you to verify the results of the values.

For example, in listing 8.20 the code checks whether the HTTP code that's returned is 200. If it's not, the test case will fail but will continue executing until the end of the test case. If you use `Assert` instead of `Check`, the test case will fail and return.

Let's see how this works. You can use the same `go test` command, but you can also use the `check` package-specific extra verbose flag (`-check.vv`) to provide more details:

```
go test -check.vv
```

This is what you get:

```
START: server_test.go:19: PostTestSuite.TestGetPost
PASS: server_test.go:19: PostTestSuite.TestGetPost  0.000s

OK: 1 passed
PASS
ok    gocheck    0.007s
```

As you can see, the extra verbosity provided more information, especially on the start of the test run. This isn't helpful in this specific test case, but you'll see later how it can be useful.

What happens if you hit an error? Let's make a slight change to the `handleGet` function and add the following statement right before you return:

```
http.NotFound(w, r)
```

This will throw an HTTP 404 status code. When you run the same `go test` command again, you'll get this:

```
START: server_test.go:19: PostTestSuite.TestGetPost
server_test.go:29:
```

```
    c.Check(post.Id, Equals, 1)
... obtained int = 0
... expected int = 1

FAIL: server_test.go:19: PostTestSuite.TestGetPost

OOPS: 0 passed, 1 FAILED
--- FAIL: Test (0.00s)
FAIL
exit status 1

FAIL  gocheck    0.007s
```

As you can see, this gives a lot more valuable information.

Another very useful feature in the check package is the ability to create test fixtures. A *test fixture* is a fixed state of the program before it's being tested. You can set up test fixtures before a test is run, and then check for the expected state.

The check package provides a set of set-up and tear-down functions for an entire test suite or for every test case. The SetupSuite function is run once when the suite starts running; the TearDownSuite function is run once after all tests have finished running. The SetupTest function is run once before every test starts running; the TearDownTest is run every time after each test has finished running.

This is how it works. You can use the same test case as before; just add a new test case for the PUT case. If you notice from the earlier code, between the two test cases a few common statements exist:

```
mux := http.NewServeMux()
mux.HandleFunc("/post/", handlePost(&FakePost{}))
writer := httptest.NewRecorder()
```

Common to all the test cases is the multiplexer and a call to the HandleFunc method on the multiplexer. HandleFunc takes in a common URL "/post/", and a call to handlePost, passing it an empty FakePost, and returns a HandlerFunc function. Finally, there's a ResponseRecorder for recording the responses to the request. This sets the stage for both test cases (and the rest of the test cases in the suite) and so can be considered test fixtures for both test cases.

The following listing shows the new server_test.go.

**Listing 8.21 Fixtures using the check package**

```
package main

import (
  "encoding/json"
  "net/http"
  "net/http/httptest"
  "testing"
    "strings"
    . "gopkg.in/check.v1"
)
```

```
type PostTestSuite struct {
  mux  *http.ServeMux
  post *FakePost
    writer *httptest.ResponseRecorder
}

func init() {
  Suite(&PostTestSuite{})
}

func Test(t *testing.T) { TestingT(t) }

func (s *PostTestSuite) SetUpTest(c *C) {
  s.post = &FakePost{}
  s.mux = http.NewServeMux()
  s.mux.HandleFunc("/post/", handleRequest(s.post))
  s.writer = httptest.NewRecorder()
}

func (s *PostTestSuite) TestGetPost(c *C) {
  request, _ := http.NewRequest("GET", "/post/1", nil)
  s.mux.ServeHTTP(s.writer, request)

  c.Check(s.writer.Code, Equals, 200)
  var post Post
  json.Unmarshal(s.writer.Body.Bytes(), &post)
  c.Check(post.Id, Equals, 1)
}

func (s *PostTestSuite) TestPutPost(c *C) {
  json := strings.NewReader(`{"content":"Updated post","author":"Sau
   Sheong"}`)
  request, _ := http.NewRequest("PUT", "/post/1", json)
  s.mux.ServeHTTP(s.writer, request)

  c.Check(s.writer.Code, Equals, 200)
  c.Check(s.post.Id, Equals, 1)
  c.Check(s.post.Content, Equals, "Updated post")
}
```

**Test fixture data stored in test suite** (annotation on PostTestSuite struct)

**Creates test fixtures** (annotation on SetUpTest)

To set up test fixtures, you must be able to store data somewhere and persist it across function calls. To use text fixtures, add fields that you want to persist into the test cases, into the test suite struct, `PostTestSuite`. As every test case in the suite is effectively a method on this struct, the text fixtures can be accessed easily. To create the text fixtures for every test case, use the `SetUpTest` function.

Notice that you're using the fields in the `PostTestSuite`, which has been defined earlier. With your test fixtures set up, you can now change your test cases accordingly. There's nothing much to change, except to remove the extra statements and switch in the structs that were set up as test fixtures. Now let's run it using the `go test` command:

```
START: server_test.go:31: PostTestSuite.TestGetPost
START: server_test.go:24: PostTestSuite.SetUpTest
PASS: server_test.go:24: PostTestSuite.SetUpTest  0.000s
```

```
PASS: server_test.go:31: PostTestSuite.TestGetPost  0.000s

START: server_test.go:41: PostTestSuite.TestPutPost
START: server_test.go:24: PostTestSuite.SetUpTest
PASS: server_test.go:24: PostTestSuite.SetUpTest  0.000s

PASS: server_test.go:41: PostTestSuite.TestPutPost  0.000s

OK: 2 passed
PASS
ok    gocheck    0.007s
```

The extra verbose option allows you to see how the test suite ran. To see the sequence of the entire test suite, let's add in the other test fixture functions:

```
func (s *PostTestSuite) TearDownTest(c *C) {
  c.Log("Finished test - ", c.TestName())
}

func (s *PostTestSuite) SetUpSuite(c *C) {
  c.Log("Starting Post Test Suite")
}

func (s *PostTestSuite) TearDownSuite(c *C) {
  c.Log("Finishing Post Test Suite")
}
```

Now rerun the test suite:

```
START: server_test.go:35: PostTestSuite.SetUpSuite
Starting Post Test Suite
PASS: server_test.go:35: PostTestSuite.SetUpSuite  0.000s

START: server_test.go:44: PostTestSuite.TestGetPost
START: server_test.go:24: PostTestSuite.SetUpTest
PASS: server_test.go:24: PostTestSuite.SetUpTest  0.000s

START: server_test.go:31: PostTestSuite.TearDownTest
Finished test - PostTestSuite.TestGetPost
PASS: server_test.go:31: PostTestSuite.TearDownTest  0.000s

PASS: server_test.go:44: PostTestSuite.TestGetPost  0.000s

START: server_test.go:54: PostTestSuite.TestPutPost
START: server_test.go:24: PostTestSuite.SetUpTest
PASS: server_test.go:24: PostTestSuite.SetUpTest  0.000s

START: server_test.go:31: PostTestSuite.TearDownTest
Finished test - PostTestSuite.TestPutPost
PASS: server_test.go:31: PostTestSuite.TearDownTest  0.000s

PASS: server_test.go:54: PostTestSuite.TestPutPost  0.000s

START: server_test.go:39: PostTestSuite.TearDownSuite
Finishing Post Test Suite
PASS: server_test.go:39: PostTestSuite.TearDownSuite  0.000s
```

```
OK: 2 passed
PASS
ok      gocheck     0.007s
```

Notice that the `SetUpSuite` and `TearDownSuite` functions are run before and after all the test cases, whereas the `SetUpTest` and `TearDownTest` functions are run within the test cases as the first and the last statements within the test case functions.

The `check` package is a simple but useful addition to your testing arsenal because it enhances the basic `testing` package. If you want to do more, try the Ginkgo test framework.

### 8.5.2 Introducing the Ginkgo testing framework

Ginkgo is *behavior-driven development* (BDD)-style testing framework in Go. It'll take a much larger space than only this section to discuss BDD, but briefly, BDD is an extension of *test-driven development* (TDD) and is a software development process (as opposed to a testing process). In BDD, software is described by its desired behavior, usually set by business requirements. *User stories* (which are requirement definitions in the language and perspective of the end user) in BDD are written from a behavioral perspective. An example of this is in describing your web service is:

```
Story: Get a post
In order to display a post to the user
As a calling program
I want to get a post

Scenario 1: using an id
Given a post id 1
When I send a GET request with the id
Then I should get a post

Scenario 2: using a non-integer id
Given a post id "hello"
When I send a GET request with the id
Then I should get a HTTP 500 response
```

Once the user story is defined, it can be converted into a test case. Test cases in BDD, as in TDD, are written before the code is written, and the aim is to develop a program that can fulfill the behavior. Admittedly, the user story used as an illustration is contrived; in a more realistic environment, BDD user stories are written at a higher-level first, and then broken down into more specific user stories after a few levels of details. The higher-level user stories are then mapped into hierarchical test suites.

Ginkgo is a feature-rich BDD-style framework. It has constructs that allow you to map user stories to test cases and is well integrated into the Go `testing` package. Ginkgo can be used to drive BDD in Go, but this section explores Ginkgo from the perspective of it being a test framework in Go.

To install Ginkgo run these two commands on the console:

```
go get github.com/onsi/ginkgo/ginkgo
go get github.com/onsi/gomega
```

The first line downloads Ginkgo and installs the command-line interface program ginkgo into `$GOPATH/bin`. The second line downloads Gomega, which is the default matcher library for Ginkgo (matchers are code that allows two different constructs like structs, maps, strings, and so on to be compared).

Before jumping into writing Ginkgo test cases, let's see how Ginkgo taps on your existing test cases. Ginkgo can convert your previous test cases into Ginkgo test cases, literally rewriting your test cases for you.

For this exercise, you'll start from the test cases from the section on dependency injection. Make a copy of the test cases if you still want them intact, because they'll be modified. After you've done that, run this in the console:

```
ginkgo convert
```

This adds in a file *xxx*_suite_test.go where *xxx* is the name of the directory, shown in this listing.

**Listing 8.22 Ginkgo test suite file**

```
package main_test

import (
  . "github.com/onsi/ginkgo"
  . "github.com/onsi/gomega"

  "testing"
)

func TestGinkgo(t *testing.T) {
  RegisterFailHandler(Fail)
  RunSpecs(t, "Ginkgo Suite")
}
```

It also changes your server_test.go file. The changed code is in bold in this listing.

**Listing 8.23 Modified test file**

```
package main

import (
  "encoding/json"
  "net/http"
  "net/http/httptest"
  "strings"
  . "github.com/onsi/ginkgo"
)

var _ = Describe("Testing with Ginkgo", func() {
  It("get post", func() {

    mux := http.NewServeMux()
    mux.HandleFunc("/post/", handleRequest(&FakePost{}))
```

```
    writer := httptest.NewRecorder()
    request, _ := http.NewRequest("GET", "/post/1", nil)
    mux.ServeHTTP(writer, request)

    if writer.Code != 200 {
      GinkgoT().Errorf("Response code is %v", writer.Code)
    }
    var post Post
    json.Unmarshal(writer.Body.Bytes(), &post)
    if post.Id != 1 {
      GinkgoT().Errorf("Cannot retrieve JSON post")
    }
  })
  It("put post", func() {

    mux := http.NewServeMux()
    post := &FakePost{}
    mux.HandleFunc("/post/", handleRequest(post))

    writer := httptest.NewRecorder()
    json := strings.NewReader(`{"content":"Updated post","author":"Sau
   Sheong"}`)
    request, _ := http.NewRequest("PUT", "/post/1", json)
    mux.ServeHTTP(writer, request)

    if writer.Code != 200 {
      GinkgoT().Error("Response code is %v", writer.Code)
    }

    if post.Content != "Updated post" {
      GinkgoT().Error("Content is not correct", post.Content)
    }
  })
})
```

Notice that you aren't using Gomega here but instead an `Error` function that's very similar to the ones you've been using in the `testing` and `check` packages. When you run the test using the `ginkgo` command:

```
ginkgo -v
```

you'll get a nicely formatted output:

```
Running Suite: Ginkgo Suite
===========================
Random Seed: 1431743149
Will run 2 of 2 specs

Testing with Ginkgo
  get post
  server_test.go:29
•
------------------------------
```

```
Testing with Ginkgo
  put post
  server_test.go:48
•
Ran 2 of 2 Specs in 0.000 seconds
SUCCESS! -- 2 Passed | 0 Failed | 0 Pending | 0 Skipped PASS

Ginkgo ran 1 suite in 577.104764ms
Test Suite Passed
```

That's pretty impressive! But if you're starting from no test cases at all, it seems silly to try to create the `testing` package test cases and then convert them. Let's see how to write Ginkgo test cases from scratch.

Ginkgo provides some utilities to get you started. First, clear off your previous test files, including the Ginkgo test suite file. Then run these two commands on the console, in the directory of your program:

```
ginkgo bootstrap
ginkgo generate
```

The first line will create the Ginkgo test suite file; the second line generates the skeleton for the test case file that you want to generate, shown in the following listing.

**Listing 8.24 Ginkgo test file**

```
package main_test

import (
  . "<path/to/your/go_files>/ginkgo"

  . "github.com/onsi/ginkgo"
  . "github.com/onsi/gomega"
)

var _ = Describe("Ginkgo", func() {

})
```

Note that you aren't using the `main` package anymore because Ginkgo isolates test cases from that package. Also, you're importing a number of libraries into the top-level namespace using the dot (`.`) import. This is optional, and Ginkgo documentation provides details on how to opt out of doing this. If you're doing this, you should remember to export any functions in the `main` package that need to be tested through Ginkgo. The next example tests the `HandleRequest` function, so it must be exported; that is, the function name's first character must be in upper case.

Also notice that Ginkgo uses the `var _ = trick` to call the `Describe` function. This is a common trick to avoid requiring an `init` function (which you used earlier on) and calling the `Describe` function in it.

The next listing shows how to write the code. You'll be mapping your earlier user story to Ginkgo code.

**Listing 8.25 Ginkgo test case with Gomega matchers**

```
package main_test

import (
  "encoding/json"
  "net/http"
  "net/http/httptest"
  . "github.com/onsi/ginkgo"
  . "github.com/onsi/gomega"
  . "gwp/Chapter_8_Testing_Web_Applications/test_ginkgo"
)

var _ = Describe("Get a post", func() {          // User story
  var mux *http.ServeMux
  var post *FakePost
  var writer *httptest.ResponseRecorder

  BeforeEach(func() {
    post = &FakePost{}
    mux = http.NewServeMux()
    mux.HandleFunc("/post/", HandleRequest(post))
    writer = httptest.NewRecorder()
  })

  Context("Get a post using an id", func() {     // Scenario 1 / Using Gomega matcher
    It("should get a post", func() {
      request, _ := http.NewRequest("GET", "/post/1", nil)
      mux.ServeHTTP(writer, request)

      Expect(writer.Code).To(Equal(200))         // Asserting correctness with Gomega

      var post Post
      json.Unmarshal(writer.Body.Bytes(), &post)

      Expect(post.Id).To(Equal(1))
    })
  })

  Context("Get an error if post id is not an integer", func() {   // Scenario 2
    It("should get a HTTP 500 response", func() {
      request, _ := http.NewRequest("GET", "/post/hello", nil)
      mux.ServeHTTP(writer, request)

      Expect(writer.Code).To(Equal(500))
    })
  })

})
```

Note that you're using the Gomega matchers in this example. (Gomega is an assertion library built by the same people who wrote Ginkgo, and matchers are test assertions.) The test fixtures are set before calling the `Context` functions (and running the scenarios) just as in the section on the `check` package:

```
var mux *http.ServeMux
var post *FakePost
var writer *httptest.ResponseRecorder

BeforeEach(func() {
  post = &FakePost{}
  mux = http.NewServeMux()
  mux.HandleFunc("/post/", HandleRequest(post))
  writer = httptest.NewRecorder()
})
```

**Exported from main to be tested here**

Note that `HandleRequest` is now capitalized and exported from the `main` package. The test scenarios are similar to the ones you had before, but now with Gomega assertion and matchers. Making assertions with Gomega looks like this:

```
Expect(post.Id).To(Equal(1))
```

where `post.Id` is what you want to test, the `Equal` function is a matcher, and `1` is the expected result. With your test scenarios written, let's see how the results look like when you run the `ginkgo` command:

```
Running Suite: Post CRUD Suite
==============================
Random Seed: 1431753578
Will run 2 of 2 specs

Get a post using an id
  should get a post
  test_ginkgo_test.go:35
•
------------------------------
Get a post using a non-integer id
  should get a HTTP 500 response
  test_ginkgo_test.go:44
•
Ran 2 of 2 Specs in 0.000 seconds
SUCCESS! -- 2 Passed | 0 Failed | 0 Pending | 0 Skipped PASS

Ginkgo ran 1 suite in 648.619232ms
Test Suite Passed
```

The next chapter discusses how you can use one of Go's key strengths—concurrency—in a web application.

## 8.6 Summary

- Go provides a built-in test tool using `go test`, and the `testing` package for unit testing.
- The `testing` package provides basic testing and benchmarking capabilities.
- Unit testing web applications in Go is handled by the `testing/httptest` package.
- You can use test doubles to make test cases more independent.
- One of the ways you can design for test doubles is to use the dependency injection design pattern.
- There are many third-party test libraries in Go, including the `Gocheck` package, which extends the basic Go testing capabilities, and Ginkgo, which implements behavior-driven style testing.

# 9 Leveraging Go concurrency

**This chapter covers**

- Understanding concurrency and parallelism principles
- Introducing goroutines and channels
- Using concurrency in web applications

One of the things that Go is well known for is its ability to make writing concurrent programs easier and less susceptible to errors. This chapter introduces concurrency and discusses Go's concurrency model and design. We'll talk about the two main features of Go that provide concurrency: goroutines and channels. You'll see an example of using Go concurrency in a web application to improve the app's performance.

## 9.1 Concurrency isn't parallelism

*Concurrency* is when two or more tasks start, run, and end within the same period of time and these tasks can potentially interact with each other. The tasks are considered to be concurrent to each other, as opposed to being sequential. Concurrency is a large and complex topic, and this chapter gives only a simple introduction.

A concept that's similar but distinctly different is parallelism. It's easy to get confused because in both cases multiple tasks can be running at the same time. In concurrency, the tasks don't necessarily need to start or end together—their execution overlaps. These tasks are scheduled and often (though not necessarily) communicate to share data as well as coordinate the execution times.

In *parallelism*, tasks start and are executed at the same time. Usually a larger problem is split into smaller chunks and processed simultaneously to improve performance. Parallelism usually requires independent resources (for example, CPUs); concurrency uses and shares the same resources. Intuitively, parallelism is easier to understand because we're talking about starting and doing multiple tasks at the same time. Parallelism is what the name indicates—parallel lines of processing that don't overlap.

> *Concurrency is about dealing with lots of things at once. Parallelism is about doing lots of things at once.*
>
> —Rob Pike, co-creator of Go

Another way to think of concurrency is by visualizing two checkout lanes at the supermarket, lining up for just one checkout counter (figure 9.1). A person from each lane takes a turn to pay for their purchases.

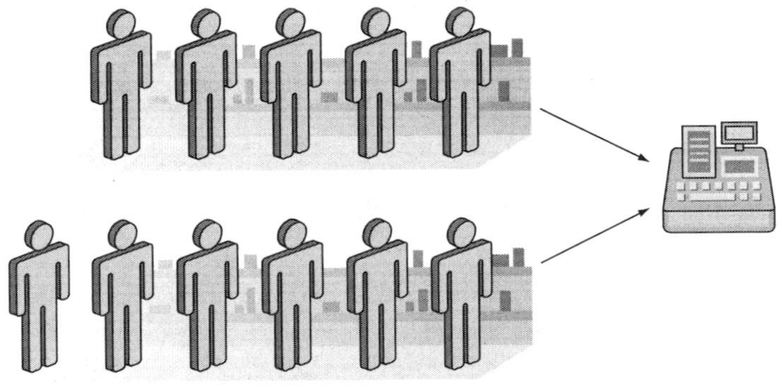

**Figure 9.1 Concurrency—two lines, one checkout counter**

With parallelism, we have the same two lanes, but now the customers are queuing up for two checkout counters, separately (figure 9.2).

Although these concepts aren't the same, it doesn't mean that they're mutually exclusive. Go can be used to create concurrent and parallel programs. Parallel programs that have to run tasks at the same time will need the environment variable `GOMAXPROCS` to be set to more than 1. Prior to Go 1.5, `GOMAXPROCS` was set to 1 by default. Since Go 1.5, GOMAXPROCS is set to the number of CPUs available in the system. Concurrent programs can run within a single CPU and tasks scheduled to run independently. You'll

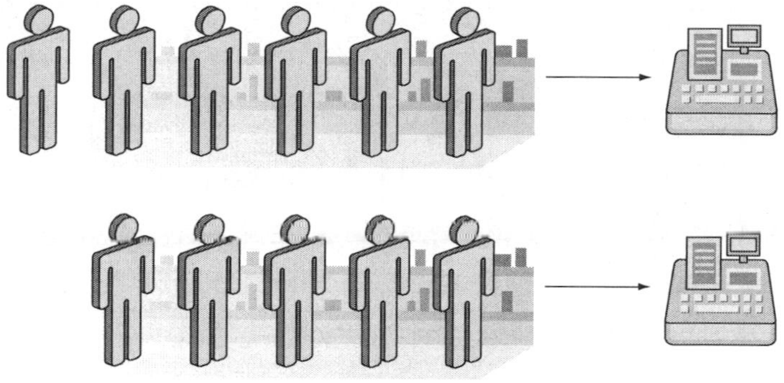

Figure 9.2 Parallelism—two lines, two checkout counters

see an example of this later in this chapter. What's important to note now is that although Go can be used to create parallel programs, it was created with concurrency in mind and not parallelism.

Go's support for concurrency is supported by two main constructs—*goroutines* and *channels*. In the following sections, I'll describe how goroutines and channels, along with some of the standard libraries, allow you to create concurrent programs.

## 9.2 Goroutines

Goroutines are functions that run independently with other goroutines. This might seem similar to threads—and in fact, goroutines are multiplexed on threads—but they aren't threads. A lot more goroutines than threads can be running, because goroutines are lightweight. A goroutine starts with a small stack (8 K as of Go 1.4) and it can grow (or shrink) as needed. Whenever a goroutine is blocked, it blocks the OS thread it's multiplexed on, but the runtime moves other goroutines on the same blocked thread to another unblocked thread.

### 9.2.1 Using goroutines

Using goroutines is pretty simple. Add the keyword `go` in front of any function (either named or anonymous) and the function becomes a goroutine. Let's see, in the following listing, how this works in a file named goroutine.go.

**Listing 9.1 Demonstrating goroutines**

```
package main

func printNumbers1() {
  for i := 0; i < 10; i++ {
    fmt.Printf("%d ", i)
  }
}
```

```
func printLetters1() {
  for i := 'A'; i < 'A'+10; i++ {
    fmt.Printf("%c ", i)
  }
}

func print1() {
  printNumbers1()
  printLetters1()
}

func goPrint1() {
  go printNumbers1()
  go printLetters1()
}

func main() {
}
```

The previous listing has two functions, `printNumbers1` and `printLetters1`. These do nothing but loop and print numbers or letters. The function `printNumbers1` prints from 0 to 9; `printLetters1` prints from A to J. A function named `print1` calls `printNumbers1` and `printLetters1` consecutively, and another function named `goPrint1` calls `printNumbers1` and `printLetters1` as goroutines.

For this example, the `main` function doesn't do anything because you'll be running the code using test cases. This way, you can take advantage of the timing that's captured and printed; otherwise you'd need to write the necessary code to find out how fast they run, and there's no actual testing of the code.

To run the test cases, shown in this listing, use a separate test file named goroutine_test.go.

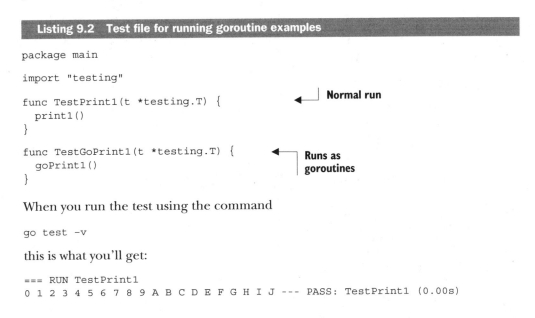

**Listing 9.2 Test file for running goroutine examples**

```
package main

import "testing"

func TestPrint1(t *testing.T) {       // Normal run
  print1()
}

func TestGoPrint1(t *testing.T) {     // Runs as goroutines
  goPrint1()
}
```

When you run the test using the command

```
go test -v
```

this is what you'll get:

```
=== RUN TestPrint1
0 1 2 3 4 5 6 7 8 9 A B C D E F G H I J --- PASS: TestPrint1 (0.00s)
```

```
=== RUN TestGoPrint1
--- PASS: TestGoPrint1 (0.00s)
PASS
```

What happened to the second test case and why didn't you get any output? The answer is because the second test case ended before the goroutines could output anything. To see it run properly, you need to add a delay to the end of the second test case:

```
func TestGoPrint1(t *testing.T) {
    goPrint1()
    time.Sleep(1 * time.Millisecond)
}
```

This time the second test case produces its output before the test case ends:

```
=== RUN TestPrint1
0 1 2 3 4 5 6 7 8 9 A B C D E F G H I J --- PASS: TestPrint1 (0.00s)
=== RUN TestGoPrint1
0 1 2 3 4 5 6 7 8 9 A B C D E F G H I J --- PASS: TestGoPrint1 (0.00s)
PASS
```

Both run the same way with the same output, which doesn't tell you much. The reason you get the same results is that `printNumbers1` and `printLetters1` ran so quickly, it made no difference whether or not the functions were running independently. To simulate processing work, you'll add a time delay using the `Sleep` function in the `time` package, and re-create the two functions as `printNumbers2` and `printLetters2` in goroutine.go, as shown next.

**Listing 9.3 Goroutines doing some work**

```
func printNumbers2() {
  for i := 0; i < 10; i++ {
    time.Sleep(1 * time.Microsecond
    fmt.Printf("%d ", i)
  }
}

func printLetters2() {
  for i := 'A'; i < 'A'+10; i++ {
    time.Sleep(1 * time.Microsecond)
    fmt.Printf("%c ", i)
  }
}

func goPrint2() {
  go printNumbers2()
  go printLetters2()
}
```

**Adding delay of 1 ms to simulate work**

Notice that you simulated processing work being done by adding a time delay of 1 microsecond every iteration of the loop. Correspondingly in the goroutine_test.go file, you add another test. As before, you add in 1 millisecond of delay in order to see the output properly:

```
func TestGoPrint2(t *testing.T) {
    goPrint2()
    time.Sleep(1 * time.Millisecond)
}
```

Run the test again and you'll get these results:

```
=== RUN TestPrint1
0 1 2 3 4 5 6 7 8 9 A B C D E F G H I J --- PASS: TestPrint1 (0.00s)
=== RUN TestGoPrint1
0 1 2 3 4 5 6 7 8 9 A B C D E F G H I J --- PASS: TestGoPrint1 (0.00s)
=== RUN TestGoPrint2
A 0 B 1 C D 2 E 3 F 4 G H 5 I 6 J 7 8 9 --- PASS: TestGoPrint2 (0.00s)
PASS
```

Look at the last line of output. Notice that this time around, instead of running the `printNumbers2` function first and then running `printLetters2`, the printouts to the screen are interlaced!

If you run this code again, the last line produces a different result. In fact, `printNumbers2` and `printLetters2` run independently and fight to print to the screen. Running repeatedly will produce different results each time. If you're using a Go version prior to Go 1.5, you might get the same results each time. Why?

This is because the default behavior in versions prior to Go 1.5 is to use just one CPU (even though you might have more than one CPU in my computer), unless stated otherwise. Since Go 1.5, the default behavior is the reverse—the Go runtime uses as many CPUs as the computer has. To use just one CPU, use this command:

```
go test -v -cpu 1
```

If you do so, you'll start to get the same results each time.

### 9.2.2 Goroutines and performance

Now that you know how goroutines behave, let's consider goroutine performance. You'll use the same functions but won't print to the screen (because doing so would clutter the output) by commenting out the `fmt.Println` code. The following listing shows the benchmark cases for the `print1` and `goPrint1` functions in the goroutine_test.go file.

**Listing 9.4 Benchmarking functions with and without goroutines**

```
func BenchmarkPrint1(b *testing.B) {        // Normal run
  for i := 0; i < b.N; i++ {
    print1()
  }
}
```

```
func BenchmarkGoPrint1(b *testing.B) {
  for i := 0; i < b.N; i++ {
    goPrint1()
  }
}
```

Run as goroutines

When you run the benchmark (and skip the functional test cases):

```
go test -run x -bench . -cpu 1
```

this is what you see:

```
BenchmarkPrint1    100000000         13.9 ns/op
BenchmarkGoPrint1    1000000         1090 ns/op
```

(For this example, I'm running the code on a single CPU first. I'll explain why later in this chapter.) As you can see, the `print1` function runs quickly and completes in 13.9 nanoseconds. What is surprising, though, is that if you run the same functions as goroutines, it's almost 10 times slower, with 1,090 nanoseconds! Why? Remember, *there's no such thing as a free lunch.* Starting up goroutines has a cost no matter how lightweight it is. The functions `printNumbers1` and `printLetters1` are so trivial and it ran so quickly that the costs of using goroutines outweigh those of running them sequentially.

What if you do some work in every iteration of the loop as in `printNumbers2` and `printLetters2`? Let's look at the benchmark cases in goroutine_test.go, in this listing.

**Listing 9.5 Benchmarking functions that are doing work with and without goroutines**

```
func BenchmarkPrint2(b *testing.B) {
  for i := 0; i < b.N; i++ {
    print2()
  }
}
```

Normal run

```
func BenchmarkGoPrint2(b *testing.B) {
  for i := 0; i < b.N; i++ {
    goPrint2()
  }
}
```

Runs as goroutines

When you run the benchmark tests again, this is what you get:

```
BenchmarkPrint2      10000      121384 ns/op
BenchmarkGoPrint2    1000000      17206 ns/op
```

You can see the marked difference now. Running `printNumbers2` and `printLetters2` sequentially is about seven times slower than running them as goroutines. Let's try both benchmarks again, but this time loop 100 times instead of 10 times:

```
func printNumbers2() {
  for i := 0; i < 100; i++ {
    time.Sleep(1 * time.Microsecond)
    // fmt.Printf("%d ", i)
```

Looping 100 times instead of 10 times

```
    }
}

func printLetters2() {
    for i := 'A'; i < 'A'+100; i++ {
        time.Sleep(1 * time.Microsecond)
        // fmt.Printf("%c ", i)
    }
}
```

Looping 100 times instead of 10 times

Here's the output:

```
BenchmarkPrint1   20000000           86.7 ns/op
BenchmarkGoPrint1   1000000           1177 ns/op
BenchmarkPrint2        2000        1184572 ns/op
BenchmarkGoPrint2   1000000          17564 ns/op
```

The benchmark for the print1 function is 13 times slower, but for goPrint1 the difference is trivial. Running with a load is even more drastic—the difference between running sequentially is now 67 times! The benchmark for print2 is almost 10 times slower than before (which makes sense since we're running it 10 times more) whereas for goPrint2, the difference between running it 10 times and 100 times is almost imperceptible.

Note that we're still using just one CPU. What happens if you switch to using two CPUs (but still loop 100 times)?

```
go test -run x -bench . -cpu 2
```

Here's what you get:

```
BenchmarkPrint1-2   20000000           87.3 ns/op
BenchmarkGoPrint2-2   5000000           391 ns/op
BenchmarkPrint2-2        1000       1217151 ns/op
BenchmarkGoPrint2-2    200000          8607 ns/op
```

The benchmark for print1 is no different than running it with one or four CPUs because the functions are called sequentially, and even if you give it four CPUs, it can only ever use just one of them. The benchmark for goPrint1 is fantastic; the improvement is almost three times, because the workload is shared now with two CPUs. As expected, the benchmark for print2 is almost the same as before because it can't use more than one CPU. The benchmark for goPrint2 is twice as fast as earlier, which is as expected since the workload is now shared between two CPUs.

Time to get adventurous. What happens if you give it four CPUs instead of two?

```
BenchmarkPrint1-4   20000000             90.6 ns/op
BenchmarkGoPrint1-4   3000000            479 ns/op
BenchmarkPrint2-4        1000        1272672 ns/op
BenchmarkGoPrint2-4    300000           6193 ns/op
```

As you'd expect, the benchmarks for the print1 and print2 functions are about the same. Surprisingly, though, the benchmark for goPrint1 is worse than with two CPUs (though it's still better than with just one CPU) whereas the benchmark for `goPrint2` is better than with two CPUs (though the improvement is just a disappointing 40 %). The benchmarks are worse because of the same issue I mentioned earlier: scheduling and running on multiple CPUs have a cost, and if the processing doesn't warrant the high cost, it can make the performance worse.

The moral of the story? Increasing the number of CPUs doesn't necessarily mean better performance. It's important to understand your code and do lots of benchmarking.

### 9.2.3 Waiting for goroutines

You saw how goroutines are run independently, and in a previous example, you also saw how the goroutines started in the program would end unceremoniously when the program ended. You got away with it by adding a time delay using the `Sleep` function, but that's a very hacky way of handling it. Although the danger of a program ending before the goroutines can complete is less probable in any serious code (because you'll know right away and change it), you may often encounter a need to ensure all goroutines complete before moving on to the next thing.

Go provides a simple mechanism called the *WaitGroup*, which is found in the `sync` package. The mechanism is straightforward:

- Declare a WaitGroup.
- Set up the WaitGroup's counter using the `Add` method.
- Decrement the counter using the `Done` method whenever a goroutine completes its task.
- Call the `Wait` method, which will block until the counter is 0.

The following listing shows an example. You'll be using the same `printNumbers2` and `printLetters2` functions that previously needed a one-microsecond delay.

**Listing 9.6 Using WaitGroups**

```
package main

import "fmt"
import "time"
import "sync"

func printNumbers2(wg *sync.WaitGroup) {
  for i := 0; i < 10; i++ {
    time.Sleep(1 * time.Microsecond)
    fmt.Printf("%d ", i)
  }
  wg.Done()                                    // Decrement counter
}

func printLetters2(wg *sync.WaitGroup) {
  for i := 'A'; i < 'A'+10; i++ {
```

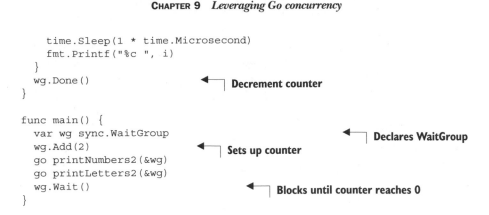

```
    time.Sleep(1 * time.Microsecond)
    fmt.Printf("%c ", i)
  }
  wg.Done()                          // Decrement counter
}

func main() {
  var wg sync.WaitGroup              // Declares WaitGroup
  wg.Add(2)                          // Sets up counter
  go printNumbers2(&wg)
  go printLetters2(&wg)
  wg.Wait()                          // Blocks until counter reaches 0
}
```

When you run the program it'll print out `0 A 1 B 2 C 3 D 4 E 5 F 6 G 7 H 8 I 9 J` nicely. How does it work? First, we define a `WaitGroup` variable called `wg`. Next, we call the `Add` method on `wg`, passing it a value of 2, which increments the counter by 2. As you call the `printNumbers2` and `printLetters2` goroutines, respectively, you decrement the counter. The WaitGroup will block at the location where you call the `Wait` method until the counter becomes 0. Once the `Done` method is called twice, the WaitGroup will unblock and the program ends.

What happens if you forget to decrement the counter in one of the goroutines? The WaitGroup blocks until the runtime detects all goroutines are asleep, after which it'll panic.

```
0 A 1 B 2 C 3 D 4 E 5 F 6 G 7 H 8 I 9 J fatal error: all goroutines are
     asleep - deadlock!
```

The WaitGroup feature is pretty nifty and it's an important tool to have in your toolbox when writing concurrent programs.

## 9.3 Channels

In the previous section, you saw how the `go` keyword can be used to convert normal functions into goroutines and execute them independently. In the last subsection, you also saw how to use WaitGroups to synchronize between independently running goroutines. In this section, you'll learn how goroutines can communicate with each other using channels.

You can think of a channel as a box. Goroutines can talk to each other only through this box. If a goroutine wants to pass something to another goroutine, it must place something in this box for the corresponding goroutine to retrieve, shown in figure 9.3.

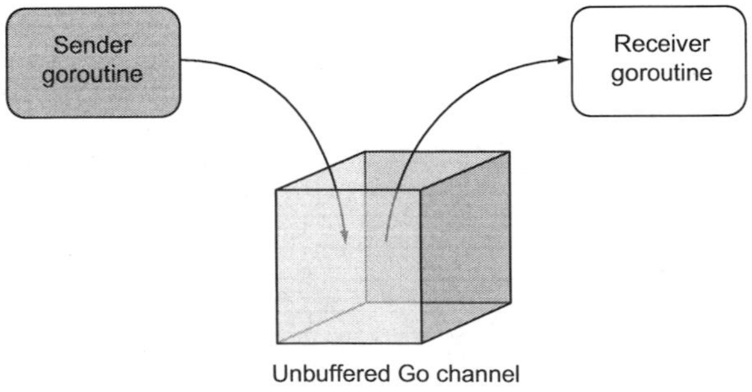


**Figure 9.3 Unbuffered Go channel as a box**

*Channels* are typed values that allow goroutines to communicate with each other. Channels are allocated using `make`, and the resulting value is a reference to an underlying data structure. This, for example, allocates a channel of integers:

```
ch := make(chan int)
```

Channels are, by default, unbuffered. If an optional integer parameter is provided, a *buffered channel* of the given size is allocated instead. This creates a buffered channel of integers with the size 10:

```
ch := make(chan int, 10)
```

Unbuffered channels are synchronous. You can think of unbuffered channels as a box that can contain only one thing at a time. Once a goroutine puts something into this box, no other goroutines can put anything in, unless another goroutine takes out whatever is inside it first. This means if another goroutine wants to put in something else when the box contains something already, it will block and go to sleep until the box is empty.

Similarly, if a goroutine tries to take out something from this box and it's empty, it'll block and go to sleep until the box has something in it.

The syntax for putting things into a channel is quickly recognizable, visually. This puts an integer 1 into the channel `ch`:

```
ch <- 1
```

Taking out the value from a channel is equally recognizable. This removes the value from the channel and assigns it to the variable `i`:

```
i := <- ch
```

Channels can be directional. By default, channels work both ways (*bidirectional*) and values can be sent to or received from it. But channels can be restricted to *send-only* or *receive-only*. This allocates a send-only channel of strings:

```
ch := make(chan <- string)
```

This allocates a receive-only channel of strings:

```
ch := make(<-chan string)
```

Although channels can be allocated to be directional, they can also be allocated as bidirectional but returned as directional. You'll see an example of this near the end of this chapter.

### 9.3.1 Synchronization with channels

As you can imagine, channels are useful when you want to synchronize between two goroutines—especially when you have one goroutine dependent on another. Let's jump into some code now and use the WaitGroup example to show how synchronization can be done using channels instead, shown in this listing.

**Listing 9.7 Synchronizing goroutines using channels**

```
package main

import "fmt"
import "time"

func printNumbers2(w chan bool) {
  for i := 0; i < 10; i++ {
    time.Sleep(1 * time.Microsecond)
    fmt.Printf("%d ", i)
  }
  w <- true                                   // Places Boolean value into channel to unblock
}

func printLetters2(w chan bool) {
  for i := 'A'; i < 'A'+10; i++ {
    time.Sleep(1 * time.Microsecond)
    fmt.Printf("%c ", i)
  }
  w <- true
}

func main() {
  w1, w2 := make(chan bool), make(chan bool)
  go printNumbers2(w1)
  go printLetters2(w2)
  <-w1                                        // Channel blocks until something's in it
  <-w2
}
```

Let's look at the `main` function first. You created two channels of type `bool`: `w1` and `w2`. Then, you ran both `printNumbers2` and `printLetters2` as goroutines, passing them the channel. As soon the goroutines are launched, you try to remove something from the channel `w1`. Because there's nothing in this channel, the program will block here. Before the function `printNumbers2` completes, though, you place a `true` value into the channel `w1`. This results in the program unblocking and continuing to the second channel, `w2`. A similar thing happens and `w2` gets a `true` value in `printLetters2`, resulting in `w2` being unblocked, and the program exits.

Notice that you took out the value from `w1` and `w2` but they aren't used, because you're only interested in unblocking the program once the goroutines complete.

This is a simple example. You can see that the goroutines aren't communicating with each other—you only used the channels to synchronize them. Let's look at another example, this time with a message passing between goroutines.

### 9.3.2 Message passing with channels

The following listing has two functions running as independent goroutines: a thrower and a catcher. The thrower throws a number in sequence by sending the number to a channel that's being passed into the goroutine. The catcher catches by receiving from the same channel and printing it out.

**Listing 9.8 Passing messages with channels**

```
package main

import (
  "fmt"
  "time"
)

func thrower(c chan int) {
  for i := 0; i < 5; i++ {
    c <- i                              // Places something into channel
    fmt.Println("Threw  >>", i)
  }
}

func catcher(c chan int) {
  for i := 0; i < 5; i++ {
    num := <-c                          // Takes something out of channel
    fmt.Println("Caught <<", num)
  }
}

func main() {
  c := make(chan int)
  go thrower(c)
  go catcher(c)
  time.Sleep(100 * time.Millisecond)
}
```

When you run this program, here's what you get:

```
Caught << 0
Threw  >> 0
Threw  >> 1
Caught << 1
Caught << 2
Threw  >> 2
Threw  >> 3
Caught << 3
Caught << 4
Threw  >> 4
```

It might seem strange that sometimes the `Caught` statement is run before the `Threw`, but that's not important—it's just the runtime scheduling between the print statements after sending or receiving from the channel. What's more important to notice is that the numbers are in sequence, meaning once the number is "thrown" from the thrower, the same number must be "caught" by the catcher before proceeding to the next number.

### 9.3.3 Buffered channels

Unbuffered or synchronous channels seem simple enough. What about buffered channels? Buffered channels are asynchronous, first-in, first-out (FIFO) message queues. Think of buffered channels as a large box that can contain a number of similar things. A goroutine can continually add things into this box without blocking until there's no more space in the box. Similarly, another goroutine can continually remove things from this box (in the same sequence it was put in) and will only block when it runs out of things to remove, shown in figure 9.4.

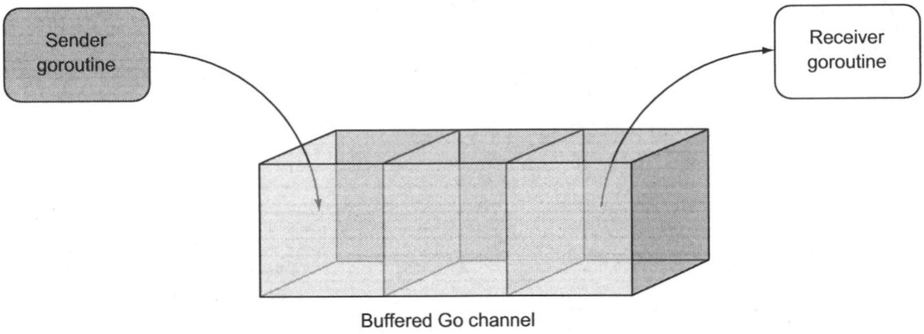


**Figure 9.4 Buffered channel as a box**

Let's see how this works with our thrower and catcher example. You convert the unbuffered channel you allocated:

```
c := make(chan int)
```

into a buffered channel of size 3:

```
c := make(chan int, 3)
```

When you run the program again, this is what you see:

```
Threw  >> 0
Threw  >> 1
Threw  >> 2
Caught << 0
Caught << 1
Caught << 2
Threw  >> 3
Threw  >> 4
Caught << 3
Caught << 4
```

You can see that the buffer fills up with three numbers before it blocks, as the catcher receives the three numbers in sequence. Buffered channels are useful when limiting throughput. If you have a limited number of processes to work on your problem and you want to throttle the number of requests coming in to your processes, buffered channels allow you to do exactly that.

### 9.3.4 Selecting channels

Go has a special keyword, `select`, that allows you to select one of many channels to receive from or send to. Think of the `select` statement like a `switch` statement but for channels, shown in this listing.

**Listing 9.9 Selecting channels**

```
package main

import (
  "fmt"
)

func callerA(c chan string) {
  c <- "Hello World!"
}

func callerB(c chan string) {
  c <- "Hola Mundo!"
}

func main() {
  a, b := make(chan string), make(chan string)
  go callerA(a)
  go callerB(b)
  for i := 0; i < 5; i++ {
    select {
    case msg := <-a:
      fmt.Printf("%s from A\n", msg)
    case msg := <-b:
      fmt.Printf("%s from B\n", msg)
    }
  }
}
```

There are two functions, `callerA` and `callerB`, each of which takes in a channel of strings and sends a message into it. These two functions are called as goroutines. You loop five times (the number of loops is arbitrary), and in each iteration the Go runtime determines whether you receive from channel `a` or channel `b`, depending on the channel that has a value at the time of selection. If both are available, the Go runtime will randomly pick one.

But when you run this program, you get a deadlock:

```
Hello World! from A
Hola Mundo! from B
fatal error: all goroutines are asleep - deadlock!
```

This is because once one goroutine has received from a channel, any other goroutine receiving from it will be blocked and go to sleep. In the example, you receive from channel `a` first, and it blocks. In the next iteration of the loop, you receive from channel `b` and it blocks. At this point you have received from both goroutines, so all goroutines are blocked and asleep, and therefore deadlocked, and the runtime will panic.

So how can you prevent a deadlock? `select` can have a default case that will be called when all channels in the select are blocked (the code is shown in bold):

```
select {
case msg := <-a:
fmt.Printf("%s from A\n", msg)
case msg := <-b:
  fmt.Printf("%s from B\n", msg)
default:
  fmt.Println("Default")
}
```

If neither channel is available when the `select` is executed, Go will run the default block. In the preceding code, both channels will be blocked once the messages are received, so the default will be executed until the loop ends. If you run this now, though, it'll show only the defaults, because the `select` is called too quickly and the loop ends before any channels can be received properly. You'll have to add a one-microsecond delay just before each time `select` is called (the code appears in bold):

```
for i := 0; i < 5; i++ {
  time.Sleep(1 * time.Microsecond)
  select {
  case msg := <-a:
    fmt.Printf("%s from A\n", msg)
  case msg := <-b:
    fmt.Printf("%s from B\n", msg)
  default:
    fmt.Println("Default")
  }
}
```

If you run this program now, the deadlock is now gone:

```
Hello World! from A
Hola Mundo! from B
Default
Default
Default
```

As you can see, after both channels are received, they're blocked and the default block is run.

It might seem odd that I'm asking you to add in a time delay. This is because I want to show you how `select` is used—in most cases you'll want to loop indefinitely. In that case, there's a different problem. After both channels block, the program will call `default` indefinitely. You could escape by breaking out of the `for` loop by counting the number of times the default is called. But there's a better way of doing this.

Channels can be closed using the `close` built-in function. Closing a channel indicates to the receiver that no more values will be sent to the channel. You can't close a receive-only channel, and sending to or closing an already closed channel causes a panic. A closed channel is never blocked and always returns the zero value for the channel's type.

In the following listing let's see how closing a channel and checking if a channel is closed helps to break the infinite loop.

**Listing 9.10 Closing channels**

```
package main

import (
  "fmt"
)

func callerA(c chan string) {
  c <- "Hello World!"
  close(c)
}

func callerB(c chan string) {
  c <- "Hola Mundo!"
  close(c)
}

func main() {
  a, b := make(chan string), make(chan string)
  go callerA(a)
  go callerB(b)
  var msg string
  ok1, ok2 := true, true
  for ok1 || ok2 {
    select {
    case msg, ok1 = <-a:
      if ok1 {
        fmt.Printf("%s from A\n", msg)
      }
    case msg, ok2 = <-b:
      if ok2 {
        fmt.Printf("%s from B\n", msg)
      }
    }
  }
}
```

**Closes channel after function is called**

**ok1 and ok2 become false when channels close**

Now you'll notice that you no longer loop just five times, and you've also done away with the one-microsecond delay. To close the channel, use the `close` built-in function, right after sending a string to the channel. Unlike closing files or sockets, remember that this doesn't disable the channel altogether—it simply tells any goroutines receiving from this channel that nothing else will come through.

In the `select` statement, you use the multivalue form of receiving a value from a channel:

```
case value, ok11 = <-a
```

The variable `value` will be assigned the value from the channel `a`, whereas `ok1` is a Boolean that indicates whether the channel is still open. If the channel is closed, `ok1` will be `false`.

One final note on closing channels: it's perfectly all right not to close them. As mentioned earlier, closing channels just means telling the receiver that nothing else is coming through. In the following code, you now know whether the channel is closed. If it is, you no longer print anything. This is what you'll get as the result:

```
Hello World! from A
Hola Mundo! from B
```

## 9.4 Concurrency for web applications

So far we've been discussing Go concurrency in a standalone program. Whatever works as a standalone program will obviously work in a web application as well. In this section you'll switch over to a web application and learn how concurrency can be used to improve Go web applications. You'll encounter some of the basic techniques shown in the previous sections, as well as other concurrency patterns in a more practical web application.

You'll create a photo mosaic-generating web application. A *photo mosaic* is a picture (usually a photograph) that has been divided into (usually equal-sized) rectangular sections, each of which is replaced with another picture (called a *tile picture*). If you view it from far away or if you squint at it, then the original picture can be seen. If you look closer, you'll see that the picture is made up of many hundreds or even thousands of smaller tile pictures.

The basic idea is simple: the web application allows a user to upload a *target picture*, which will be used to create a photo mosaic. To make things simple, let's assume that tile pictures are already available and are correctly sized.

### 9.4.1 Creating the photo mosaic

Let's start with the photo mosaic algorithm. The steps can be followed without the use of any third-party libraries.

1. Build a tile database, a hash of tile pictures, by scanning a directory of pictures and then using the filename as the key and the average color of the picture as the value. The average color is a 3-tuple calculated from getting the red, green, and blue (RGB) of every pixel and adding up all the reds, greens, and blues, and then dividing by the total number of pixels.
2. Cut the target picture into smaller pictures of the correct tile size.
3. For every tile-sized piece of the target picture, assume the average color to be the color of the top-left pixel of that piece.
4. Find the corresponding tile in the tile database that's the nearest match to the average color of the piece of the target picture, and place that tile in the corresponding position in the photo mosaic. To find the nearest match, calculate the

Euclidean distance between the two color 3-tuples by converting each color 3-tuple into a point in a 3-dimensional space.

5 Remove the tile from the tile database so that each tile in the photo mosaic is unique.

The next listing shows the mosaic-creating code in a single source file named mosaic.go. Let's look at each function in this file.

**Listing 9.11 The averageColor function**

```
func averageColor(img image.Image) [3]float64 {        ◄── Finds the average
  bounds := img.Bounds()                                    color of the picture
  r, g, b := 0.0, 0.0, 0.0
  for y := bounds.Min.Y; y < bounds.Max.Y; y++ {
    for x := bounds.Min.X; x < bounds.Max.X; x++ {
      r1, g1, b1, _ := img.At(x, y).RGBA()
      r, g, b = r+float64(r1), g+float64(g1), b+float64(b1)
    }
  }
  totalPixels := float64(bounds.Max.X * bounds.Max.Y)
  return [3]float64{r / totalPixels, g / totalPixels, b / totalPixels}
}
```

First is the averageColor function, which takes the red, green, and blue of each pixel in the image, adds them all up, and then divides each sum by the total number of pixels in the image. Then you create a 3-tuple (actually a 3-element array) consisting of these numbers.

Next, as in the following listing, you have the resize function. The resize function resizes an image to a new width.

**Listing 9.12 The resize function**

```
func resize(in image.Image, newWidth int) image.NRGBA {     ◄── Resizes an image
  bounds := in.Bounds()                                          to its new width
  ratio := bounds.Dx()/ newWidth
  out := image.NewNRGBA(image.Rect(bounds.Min.X/ratio, bounds.Min.X/ratio,
  ➥ bounds.Max.X/ratio, bounds.Max.Y/ratio))
  for y, j := bounds.Min.Y, bounds.Min.Y; y < bounds.Max.Y; y, j = y+ratio,
   j+1 {
    for x, i := bounds.Min.X, bounds.Min.X; x < bounds.Max.X; x, i =
    ➥ x+ratio, i+1 {
      r, g, b, a := in.At(x, y).RGBA()
      out.SetNRGBA(i, j, color.NRGBA{uint8(r>>8), uint8(g>>8), uint8(b>>8),
      ➥ uint8(a>>8)})
    }
  }
  return *out
}
```

The `tilesDB` function creates a database of the tile picture by scanning the directory where the tile pictures are located, shown in this listing.

**Listing 9.13 The `tilesDB` function**

```
func tilesDB() map[string][3]float64 {
  fmt.Println("Start populating tiles db ...")
  db := make(map[string][3]float64)
  files, _ := ioutil.ReadDir("tiles")
  for _, f := range files {
    name := "tiles/" + f.Name()
    file, err := os.Open(name)
    if err == nil {
      img, _, err := image.Decode(file)
      if err == nil {
        db[name] = averageColor(img)
      } else {
        fmt.Println("error in populating TILEDB:", err, name)
      }
    } else {
      fmt.Println("cannot open file", name, err)
    }
    file.Close()
  }
  fmt.Println("Finished populating tiles db.")
  return db
}
```

Populates a tiles database in memory

The tile database is a map with a string as the key a 3-tuple (in this case, a 3-element array) as the value. You open each image file in the directory and then get the average color of the image to create an entry in the map. The tile database is used to find the correct tile picture in the tile picture director and it is passed into the `nearest` function, along with the target color 3-tuple.

```
func nearest(target [3]float64, db *map[string][3]float64) string {
  var filename string
  smallest := 1000000.0
  for k, v := range *db {
    dist := distance(target, v)
    if dist < smallest {
      filename, smallest = k, dist
    }
  }
  delete(*db, filename)
  return filename
}
```

Finds the nearest matching image

Each entry in the tile database is compared with the target color and the entry with the smallest distance is returned as the nearest tile, and also removed from the tile database. The `distance` function, shown in the next listing, calculates the Euclidean distance between two 3-tuples.

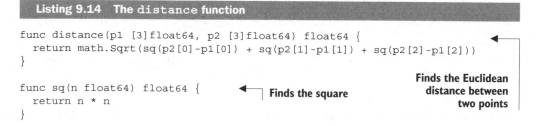

**Listing 9.14 The `distance` function**

```
func distance(p1 [3]float64, p2 [3]float64) float64 {
  return math.Sqrt(sq(p2[0]-p1[0]) + sq(p2[1]-p1[1]) + sq(p2[2]-p1[2]))
}

func sq(n float64) float64 {
  return n * n
}
```

- Finds the Euclidean distance between two points
- Finds the square

Scanning and loading the tile database every time a photo mosaic is created can be pretty cumbersome. You want to do that only once, and clone the tile database every time a photo mosaic is created. The source tile database, TILEDB, shown in the following listing, is then created as a global variable and populated upon start of the web application.

**Listing 9.15 The `cloneTilesDB` function**

```
var TILESDB map[string][3]float64

func cloneTilesDB() map[string][3]float64 {
  db := make(map[string][3]float64)
  for k, v := range TILESDB {
    db[k] = v
  }
  return db
}
```

- Clones the tile database each time the photo mosaic is generated.

### 9.4.2 The photo mosaic web application

With the mosaic-generating functions in place, you can begin writing your web application. Place the web application in a source code file named main.go, shown next.

**Listing 9.16 The photo mosaic web application**

```
package main

import (
  "bytes"
  "encoding/base64"
  "fmt"
  "html/template"
  "image"
  "image/draw"
  "image/jpeg"
  "net/http"
  "os"
  "strconv"
  "sync"
  "time"
)
```

```
func main() {
  mux := http.NewServeMux()
  files := http.FileServer(http.Dir("public"))
  mux.Handle("/static/", http.StripPrefix("/static/", files))
  mux.HandleFunc("/", upload)
  mux.HandleFunc("/mosaic", mosaic)
  server := &http.Server{
    Addr:    "127.0.0.1:8080",
    Handler: mux,
  }

  TILESDB = tilesDB()
  fmt.Println("Mosaic server started.")
  server.ListenAndServe()
}


func upload(w http.ResponseWriter, r *http.Request) {
  t, _ := template.ParseFiles("upload.html")
  t.Execute(w, nil)
}


func mosaic(w http.ResponseWriter, r *http.Request) {
  t0 := time.Now()

  r.ParseMultipartForm(10485760)
  file, _, _ := r.FormFile("image")              // Gets uploaded file and tile size
  defer file.Close()
  tileSize, _ := strconv.Atoi(r.FormValue("tile_size"))

  original, _, _ := image.Decode(file)           // Decodes uploaded target image
  bounds := original.Bounds()

  newimage := image.NewNRGBA(image.Rect(bounds.Min.X, bounds.Min.X,
   bounds.Max.X, bounds.Max.Y))

  db := cloneTilesDB()                           // Clones tile database

  sp := image.Point{0, 0}                        // Sets up source point for each tile
  for y := bounds.Min.Y; y < bounds.Max.Y; y = y + tileSize {   // Iterates through target image
    for x := bounds.Min.X; x < bounds.Max.X; x = x + tileSize {

      r, g, b, _ := original.At(x, y).RGBA()
      color := [3]float64{float64(r), float64(g), float64(b)}

      nearest := nearest(color, &db)
      file, err := os.Open(nearest)
      if err == nil {
        img, _, err := image.Decode(file)
        if err == nil {

          t := resize(img, tileSize)
          tile := t.SubImage(t.Bounds())
          tileBounds := image.Rect(x, y, x+tileSize, y+tileSize)
```

```
          draw.Draw(newimage, tileBounds, tile, sp, draw.Src)
        } else {
          fmt.Println("error:", err, nearest)
        }
      } else {
        fmt.Println("error:", nearest)
      }
      file.Close()
    }
  }

  buf1 := new(bytes.Buffer)
  jpeg.Encode(buf1, original, nil)
  originalStr := base64.StdEncoding.EncodeToString(buf1.Bytes())

  buf2 := new(bytes.Buffer)
  jpeg.Encode(buf2, newimage, nil)
  mosaic := base64.StdEncoding.EncodeToString(buf2.Bytes())
  t1 := time.Now()
  images := map[string]string{
    "original": originalStr,
    "mosaic":   mosaic,
    "duration": fmt.Sprintf("%v ", t1.Sub(t0)),
  }
  t, _ := template.ParseFiles("results.html")
  t.Execute(w, images)
}
```

**Encodes in JPEG, deliver to browser in base64 string**

The main logic for creating the photo mosaic resides in the `mosaic` function, which is a handler function. First, you get the uploaded file and the tile size from the form. Next, you decode the uploaded target image and create a new photo mosaic image. You clone the source tile database and set up the source point for each tile (the source point is needed by the `image/draw` package later). You're now ready to iterate through each tile-sized piece of the target image.

For every piece, you pick the top-left pixel and assume that's the average color. Then you find the nearest tile in the tile database that matches this color. The tile database gives you a filename, so you open the tile picture and resize it to the tile size. The resultant tile is drawn into the photo mosaic you created earlier.

Once the photo mosaic is created, you encode it into JPEG format and then encode it once again into a base64 string.

The original target picture and the photo mosaic are then sent to the results.html template to be displayed on the next page. As you can see, the image is displayed using a data URL with the base64 content that's embedded in the web page itself (the code is shown in bold in the following listing). Data URLs are used as an alternative to a normal URL that points to another resource. In a data URL, the data itself is embedded into the URL.

**Listing 9.17 The results template**

```
<!DOCTYPE html>
<html>
  <head>
    <meta http-equiv="Content-Type" content="text/html; charset=utf-8">
    <title>Mosaic</title>
    ...
  </head>
  <body>
    <div class='container'>
        <div class="col-md-6">
          <img src="data:image/jpg;base64,{{ .original }}" width="100%">
          <div class="lead">Original</div>
        </div>
        <div class="col-md-6">
          <img src="data:image/jpg;base64,{{ .mosaic }}" width="100%">
          <div class="lead">Mosaic – {{ .duration }} </div>
        </div>
        <div class="col-md-12 center">
          <a class="btn btn-lg btn-info" href="/">Go Back</a>
        </div>
    </div>
    <br>
  </body>
</html>
```

Figure 9.5 shows the mosaic that's created if you build it and then run it with only one CPU, assuming your code is in a directory named mosaic:

```
GOMAXPROCS=1 ./mosaic
```

**Figure 9.5 Basic photo mosaic web application**

Now that you have the basic mosaic-generating web application, let's create the concurrent version of it.

### 9.4.3 Concurrent photo mosaic web application

One of the more frequent uses of concurrency is to improve performance. The web application from the previous section created a mosaic from a 151 KB JPEG image in about 2.25 seconds. The performance isn't fantastic and can be improved using concurrency. You'll use the algorithm in this example to build concurrency into the photo mosaic web application:

1. Split the original image into four quarters.
2. Process them at the same time.
3. Combine the results into a single mosaic.

For a diagrammatic point of view, see figure 9.6.

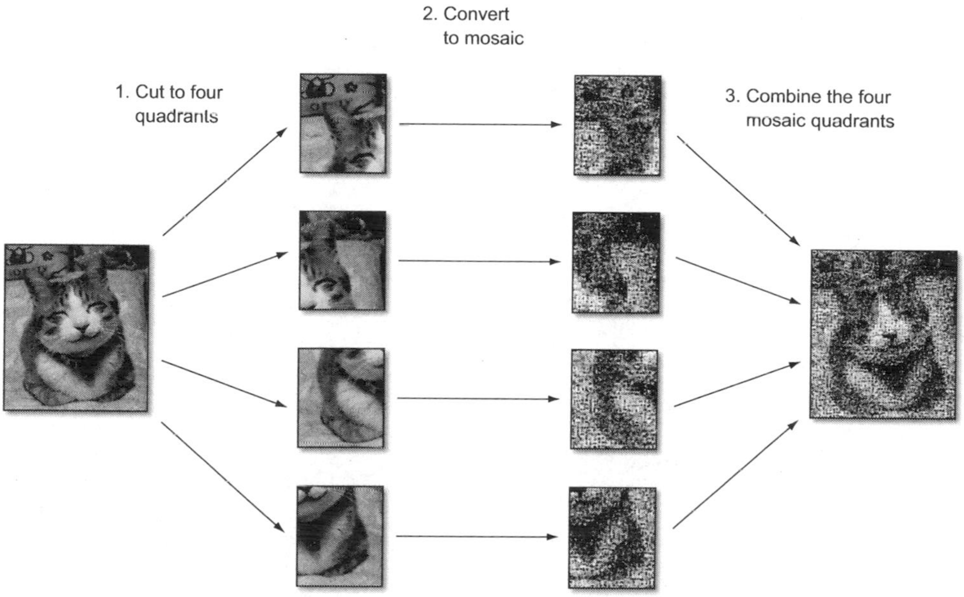


**Figure 9.6 Concurrency algorithm for generating mosaics faster**

A word of caution: this is not the only way that performance can be improved or concurrency can be achieved, but only one relatively straightforward way.

The main change is in the `mosaic` handler function. The earlier program had a single handler function that created the photo mosaic. In the concurrent version of the web application, you need to break up that function into two separate ones, called cut and combine, respectively. Both functions are called from the mosaic handler function, shown here.

**Listing 9.18 The mosaic handler function**

```
func mosaic(w http.ResponseWriter, r *http.Request) {
  t0 := time.Now()
  r.ParseMultipartForm(10485760) // max body in memory is 10MB
  file, _, _ := r.FormFile("image")
  defer file.Close()
  tileSize, _ := strconv.Atoi(r.FormValue("tile_size"))
  original, _, _ := image.Decode(file)
  bounds := original.Bounds()
  db := cloneTilesDB()

  c1 := cut(original, &db, tileSize, bounds.Min.X, bounds.Min.Y,
  ➥ bounds.Max.X/2, bounds.Max.Y/2)
  c2 := cut(original, &db, tileSize, bounds.Max.X/2, bounds.Min.Y,
  ➥ bounds.Max.X, bounds.Max.Y/2)
  c3 := cut(original, &db, tileSize, bounds.Min.X, bounds.Max.Y/2,
  ➥ bounds.Max.X/2, bounds.Max.Y)
  c4 := cut(original, &db, tileSize, bounds.Max.X/2, bounds.Max.Y/2,
  ➥ bounds.Max.X, bounds.Max.Y)
  c := combine(bounds, c1, c2, c3, c4)

  buf1 := new(bytes.Buffer)
  jpeg.Encode(buf1, original, nil)
  originalStr := base64.StdEncoding.EncodeToString(buf1.Bytes())

  t1 := time.Now()
  images := map[string]string{
    "original": originalStr,
    "mosaic":   <-c,
    "duration": fmt.Sprintf("%v ", t1.Sub(t0)),
  }

  t, _ := template.ParseFiles("results.html")
  t.Execute(w, images)
}
```

Fanning out, cutting up image for independent processing

Fanning in, combining images

Cutting up the image is handled by the cut function, in what is known as the *fan-out* pattern (figure 9.7).

The original image is cut up into four quadrants to be processed separately. As you may notice, these are regular functions and not goroutines, so how can they run concurrently? The answer is because the cut function creates a goroutine from an anonymous function and returns a channel.

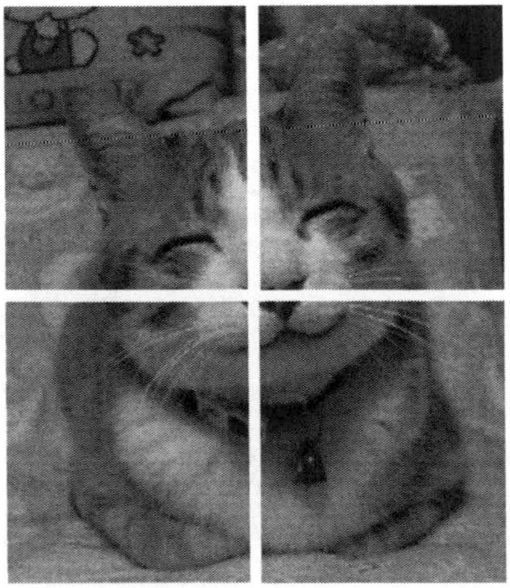

**Figure 9.7 Splitting the target picture into four quadrants**

Here's where you need to be careful. Remember that you're converting an application to a concurrent one, with multiple goroutines running at the same time. If you have some resources that are shared, the changes can possibly cause a race condition.

> **Race condition**
>
> A *race condition* exists when the program depends on a specific sequence or timing for it to happen and specific sequence or timing can't be guaranteed. As a result, the behavior of the program becomes erratic and unpredictable.
>
> Race conditions commonly appear in concurrent programs that modify a shared resource. If two or more processes or threads try to modify the shared resource at the same time, the one that gets to the resource first will behave as expected but the other processes won't. Because we can't predict which process gets the resource first, the system won't behave consistently.
>
> Race conditions are notoriously difficult to debug, although they aren't difficult to fix once the problem is identified.

In this case, you do have a shared resource: the original image that was uploaded to the mosaic application. The `nearest` function finds the best-fitting tile image and removes it from the tile database in order not to have duplicate tiles. This means if the `cut` goroutines happen to find the same tile as the best fitting, at the same time, there will be a race condition.

To eliminate the race condition, you can use a common technique called *mutual exclusion, mutex* for short. Mutex refers to the requirement that only one process (in our case, a goroutine) can access a critical section at the same time. In the case of the concurrent mosaic application, you need to implement mutex on the nearest function.

To do this, you can use Go's `Mutex` struct in the `sync` package. First, define a `DB` struct, where the struct encapsulates both the actual tile store as well as a `mutex` flag, shown next.

**Listing 9.19 The `DB` struct**

```
type DB struct {
  mutex *sync.Mutex
  store map[string][3]float64
}
```

Next, change the `nearest` function into a method on the `DB` struct, shown here.

**Listing 9.20 The `nearest` method**

```
func (db *DB) nearest(target [3]float64) string {
  var filename string
  db.mutex.Lock()
  smallest := 1000000.0
```

**Sets mutex flag by locking it** (annotation to `db.mutex.Lock()`)

```
    for k, v := range db.store {
      dist := distance(target, v)
      if dist < smallest {
        filename, smallest = k, dist
      }
    }
    delete(db.store, filename)
    db.mutex.Unlock()                          // Unsets mutex flag by unlocking it
    return filename
}
```

In the new nearest method, you can lock the section that searches for the best-fitting tile. You shouldn't just lock the delete function because doing so will still cause a race condition—another goroutine can find the same tile just before it's removed from the database.

Next is the cut function.

**Listing 9.21 The cut function**

```
func cut(original image.Image, db *DB, tileSize, x1, y1, x2, y2 int) <-chan
  image.Image {                                // Passes in reference to DB struct instead of map
  c := make(chan image.Image)                  // Returns channel
  sp := image.Point{0, 0}
  go func() {                                  // Creates anonymous goroutine
    newimage := image.NewNRGBA(image.Rect(x1, y1, x2, y2))
    for y := y1; y < y2; y = y + tileSize {
      for x := x1; x < x2; x = x + tileSize {
        r, g, b, _ := original.At(x, y).RGBA()
        color := [3]float64{float64(r), float64(g), float64(b)}
        nearest := db.nearest(color)           // Calls nearest method on DB to get best-fitting tile
        file, err := os.Open(nearest)
        if err == nil {
          img, _, err := image.Decode(file)
          if err == nil {
            t := resize(img, tileSize)
            tile := t.SubImage(t.Bounds())
            tileBounds := image.Rect(x, y, x+tileSize, y+tileSize)
            draw.Draw(newimage, tileBounds, tile, sp, draw.Src)
          } else {
            fmt.Println("error:", err)
          }
        } else {
          fmt.Println("error:", nearest)
        }
        file.Close()
      }
    }
    c <- newimage.SubImage(newimage.Rect)
  }()
  return c
}
```

The logic is the same as in the original photo mosaic web application. You created a channel in the `cut` function and started an anonymous goroutine that sends the results to this channel and then returns the channel. This way, the channel is immediately returned to the `mosaic` handler function, and the completed photo mosaic segment is sent to the channel when the processing is done. You may notice that although you've created the return channel as bidirectional, you can typecast it to be returned as a receive-only channel.

You've cut the original image into four separate pieces and converted each piece into a part of a photo mosaic. It's time to put them together again, using what's commonly known as the *fan-in* pattern, in the `combine` function, shown here.

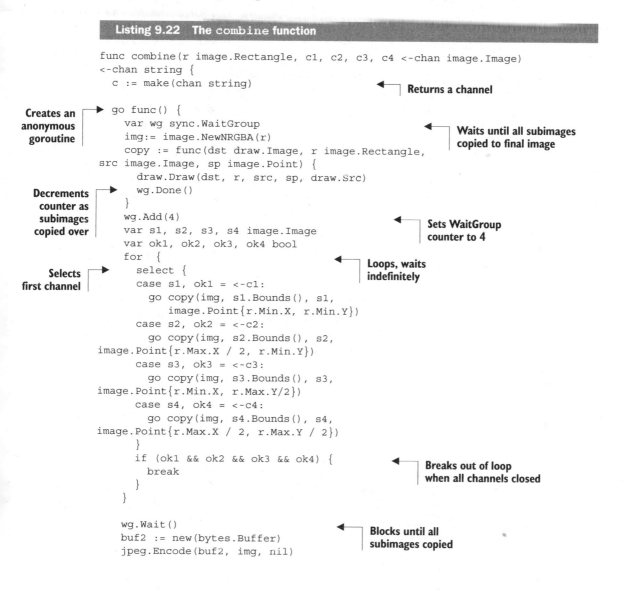

**Listing 9.22 The `combine` function**

```
func combine(r image.Rectangle, c1, c2, c3, c4 <-chan image.Image)
<-chan string {
  c := make(chan string)

  go func() {
    var wg sync.WaitGroup
    img:= image.NewNRGBA(r)
    copy := func(dst draw.Image, r image.Rectangle,
src image.Image, sp image.Point) {
      draw.Draw(dst, r, src, sp, draw.Src)
      wg.Done()
    }
    wg.Add(4)
    var s1, s2, s3, s4 image.Image
    var ok1, ok2, ok3, ok4 bool
    for  {
      select {
      case s1, ok1 = <-c1:
        go copy(img, s1.Bounds(), s1,
          image.Point{r.Min.X, r.Min.Y})
      case s2, ok2 = <-c2:
        go copy(img, s2.Bounds(), s2,
image.Point{r.Max.X / 2, r.Min.Y})
      case s3, ok3 = <-c3:
        go copy(img, s3.Bounds(), s3,
image.Point{r.Min.X, r.Max.Y/2})
      case s4, ok4 = <-c4:
        go copy(img, s4.Bounds(), s4,
image.Point{r.Max.X / 2, r.Max.Y / 2})
      }
      if (ok1 && ok2 && ok3 && ok4) {
        break
      }
    }

    wg.Wait()
    buf2 := new(bytes.Buffer)
    jpeg.Encode(buf2, img, nil)
```

Returns a channel

Creates an anonymous goroutine

Waits until all subimages copied to final image

Decrements counter as subimages copied over

Sets WaitGroup counter to 4

Loops, waits indefinitely

Selects first channel

Breaks out of loop when all channels closed

Blocks until all subimages copied

```
        c <- base64.StdEncoding.EncodeToString(buf2.Bytes())
    }()
    return c
}
```

As in the cut function, the main logic in combining the images resides in an anonymous goroutine, and you create and return a receive-only channel. As a result, you can encode the original image while combining the four photo mosaic segments.

In the anonymous goroutine, you create another anonymous function and assign it to a variable copy. This function copies a photo mosaic segment into the final photo mosaic and will be run as a goroutine later. Because the copy function is called as a goroutine, you won't be able to control it when it completes. To synchronize the completion of the copying, you use a WaitGroup. You create a WaitGroup, wg, and then set the counter to 4 using the Add method. Each time the copy function completes, it will decrement the counter using the Done method. You call the Wait method just before encoding the image to allow all the copy goroutines to complete and you have a complete photo mosaic image.

Remember that the input to the combine function includes the four channels coming from the cut function containing the photo mosaic segments, and you don't know when the channels have segments. You could try to receive each one of those channels in sequence, but that wouldn't be very concurrent. What I like to do is to start processing whichever segment that comes first, and the select statement fits the bill nicely.

You loop indefinitely, and in each iteration, you select the channel that's ready with a value. (If more than one is available, Go randomly assigns you one.) You use the image from this channel and start a goroutine with the copy function. You're using the multivalue format for receiving values from the channel, meaning the second variable (ok1, ok2, ok3, or ok4) tells you if you've successfully received from the channel. The for loop breaks once you've successfully received on all channels.

Moving on, and referring to the WaitGroup wg you used earlier, remember that even though you received all the photo mosaic segments successfully, you have in turn started four separate goroutines, which might not have completed at that time. The Wait method on the WaitGroup wg blocks the encoding of the assembled photo mosaic until the photo mosaic is completed.

Now that you have the concurrent mosaic application, let's run it. For now, run go build and then execute it with just one CPU, assuming that your code is in a directory named mosaic_concurrent:

```
GOMAXPROCS=1 ./mosaic_concurrent
```

You can see the results in figure 9.8, which uses the same target picture and tile pictures when you run it with a single CPU.

If you're sharp-eyed, you might see the slight differences in the photo mosaic that's generated (it works better on the e-book version where you can see the color

**Figure 9.8 Photo mosaic web application with concurrency**

differences). The final photo mosaic is assembled from four separate pieces and the algorithm doesn't smooth out the rough edges. But you can see the difference in performance—where the basic photo mosaic web application took 2.25 seconds, the one using concurrency takes only a quarter of that time, about 646 ms.

You might be wondering now if what I've just shown you is a case of parallel programming instead of concurrent programming. What's done here *seems* to be just breaking up a function into four goroutines that are run independently.

Keep in mind that you didn't just break up a long-running function into separate `cut` functions running goroutines—you also assembled their output with the `combine` function that wraps a goroutine. Whenever any one of the `cut` functions completes its processing, it will send the results to the `combine` function to be copied into a single image.

Remember that I asked you to run both the original and the concurrent web applications with only one CPU. As mentioned earlier in this chapter, concurrency is *not* parallelism—I've shown you how to take a simple algorithm and break it down into a concurrent one, with no parallelism involved. None of the goroutines are running in parallel (there's only one CPU), even though they're running independently.

For our grand finale, now run it with multiple CPUs and, in the process, automatically get parallelism for free. To do this, run the application normally:

```
./mosaic_concurrent
```

**Figure 9.9 Photo mosaic web application with concurrency and eight CPUs**

Figure 9.9 shows what you should get as a result.

As you can see from the numbers, the performance has improved three times, from 646 ms to 216 ms! And if we compare that with our original non-concurrent photo mosaic web application with 2.25 seconds, that's a 10 times performance improvement!

There's no difference between the original and the concurrent web applications in terms of the photo mosaic algorithm. In fact, between the two applications, the mosaic.go source file was hardly modified. The main difference is concurrency, and that's a testament to how powerful it is.

We're done with programming our web applications. The next chapter discusses how you can take your web applications and web services and deploy them.

## 9.5 Summary

- The Go web server itself is concurrent and each request to the server runs on a separate goroutine.
- Concurrency is not parallelism—they are complementary concepts but not the same. Concurrency is when two or more tasks start, run, and end within the same period of time and these tasks can potentially interact with each other while parallelism is simply multiple tasks running at the same time.
- Go supports concurrency directly with two main features: goroutines and channels. Go doesn't support parallelism directly.
- Goroutines are used to write concurrent programs, whereas channels are used to provide the communications between goroutines.
- Unbuffered channels are synchronous and are blocked when they contain data but not received while buffered channels can be asynchronous until buffer is full.

- A `select` statement can be used to choose one out of a number of channels—the first channel that is ready to be received will be selected.
- WaitGroups can also be used to synchronize between channels.
- Concurrent web applications can be highly performant, depending on the algorithm used, even on a single CPU, compared with non-concurrent web applications.
- Concurrent web applications can potentially get the benefits of parallelism automatically.

# 10 Deploying Go

**This chapter covers**

- Deploying Go web apps to standalone servers
- Deploying Go web apps to the cloud
- Deploying Go web apps in Docker containers

Now that you've learned how to develop a web application with Go, the next logical step is to deploy it. Deploying web applications is quite different from deploying other types of applications. Desktop and mobile applications are deployed on the end users' devices (smart phones tables, laptops, and so forth) but web applications are deployed on servers that are accessed through a client (usually a browser) on the end users' device.

Deploying Go web apps can be simple because the executable program is compiled into a single binary file. Also, because Go programs can be compiled into a statically linked binary file that doesn't need any other libraries, they can be a single executable file. But web apps are usually not just a single executable binary; most often they consist of template files as well as static files like JavaScript, images, and style sheets. In this chapter we'll explore a few ways of deploying Go web apps to the internet, mostly through cloud providers. You'll learn how to deploy to

- A server that's either fully owned by you, physical, or virtual (on an Infrastructure-as-a-Service provider, Digital Ocean)
- A cloud Platform-as-a-Service (PaaS) provider, Heroku
- Another cloud PaaS provider, Google App Engine
- A dockerized container, deployed to a local Docker server, and also to a virtual machine on Digital Ocean

> **Cloud computing**
>
> Cloud computing, or "the cloud," is a model of network and computer access that provides a pool of shared resources (servers, storage, network, and others). This allows the users of these resources to avoid up-front costs and the providers of the resources to use the resources more effectively for a larger number of users. Cloud computing has gained traction over the past years and is now a regular model used by most large infrastructure and service providers, including Amazon, Google, and Facebook.

It's important to remember that there are many different ways of deploying a web app and in each of the methods you'll be learning in this chapter, there are many variations. The methods described in this chapter are based on a single person deploying the web app. The processes are usually a lot more involved in a production environment, which includes additiona tasks like running test suites, continual integration, staging servers, and so on.

This chapter also introduces many concepts and tools, each of them worthy of an entire book. Therefore, it's impossible to cover all of these technologies and services. This chapter aims to cover only a small portion, and if you want to learn more, take this as a starting point.

In our examples, you'll be using the simple web service in section 7.6. Wherever possible, you'll use PostgreSQL (except in Google App Engine, where you'll use Google Cloud SQL, which is MySQL based). The base assumption is that the setup of the database is done beforehand, on a separate database server, so setting up the database isn't covered here. If you need some brief guidance, review section 2.6.

## 10.1 Deploying to servers

Let's start with the simplest deployment: creating an executable binary and then running it off a server that's on the internet. Whether this server is a physical server connected to the internet or a virtual machine (VM) that's been created on a provider like Amazon Web Services (AWS) or Digital Ocean, it's the same. In this section, you'll learn how to deploy to a server that's running Ubuntu Server 14.04.

AWS
DigitalOcean

Heroku

### IaaS, PaaS, and SaaS

Cloud computing providers offer their services through different models. NIST (National Institute of Standards and Technology, US Department of Commerce) defines three service models that are widely used today: Infrastructure-as-a-Service (IaaS), Platform-as-a-Service (PaaS), and Software-as-a-Service (SaaS).

IaaS, the most basic of the three models, describes providers that offer their users the basic computing capabilities, including compute, storage, and networking. Examples of IaaS services include the AWS Elastic Cloud Computing (EC2) service, Google's Compute Engine, and Digital Ocean's Droplets.

PaaS is a model that describes providers that offer their users capabilities to deploy applications to the infrastructure, using their tools. Examples include Heroku, AWS's Elastic Beanstalk, and Google's App Engine.

SaaS is a model that describes providers that offer application services to the users. Most services used by consumers today can be considered SaaS services, but in the context of this book, SaaS services include Heroku's Postgres database service (which provides a cloud-based Postgres service), AWS's Relational Database Service (RDS), and Google's Cloud SQL.

In this book, and in this chapter, you'll learn how you can use IaaS and PaaS providers to deploy Go web applications.

Our simple web service from chapter 7 consists of two files: data.go (listing 10.1), which contains all the connections to the database, as well as the functions that read from and write to the database, and server.go (listing 10.2), which contains the `main` function and all the processing logic for the web service.

**Listing 10.1 Accessing the database with data.go**

```
package main

import (
  "database/sql"
  _ "github.com/lib/pq"
)

var Db *sql.DB

func init() {
  var err error
  Db, err = sql.Open("postgres", "user=gwp dbname=gwp password=gwp
  ➥ sslmode=disable")
  if err != nil {
    panic(err)
  }
}

func retrieve(id int) (post Post, err error) {
  post = Post{}
```

```
    err = Db.QueryRow("select id, content, author from posts where id =
    ➥ $1", id).Scan(&post.Id, &post.Content, &post.Author)
    return
}

func (post *Post) create() (err error) {
    statement := "insert into posts (content, author) values ($1, $2)
    ➥ returning id"
    stmt, err := Db.Prepare(statement)
    if err != nil {
      return
    }
    defer stmt.Close()
    err = stmt.QueryRow(post.Content, post.Author).Scan(&post.Id)
    return
}

func (post *Post) update() (err error) {
    _, err = Db.Exec("update posts set content = $2, author = $3 where id =
    ➥ $1", post.Id, post.Content, post.Author)
    return
}

func (post *Post) delete() (err error) {
    _, err = Db.Exec("delete from posts where id = $1", post.Id)
    return
}
```

**Listing 10.2 Go web service in server.go**

```
package main

import (
  "encoding/json"
  "net/http"
  "path"
  "strconv"
)

type Post struct {
  Id      int    `json:"id"`
  Content string `json:"content"`
  Author  string `json:"author"`
}

func main() {
  server := http.Server{
    Addr: "127.0.0.1:8080",
  }
  http.HandleFunc("/post/", handleRequest)
  server.ListenAndServe()
}

func handleRequest(w http.ResponseWriter, r *http.Request) {
  var err error
```

```
  switch r.Method {
  case "GET":
    err = handleGet(w, r)
  case "POST":
    err = handlePost(w, r)
  case "PUT":
    err = handlePut(w, r)
  case "DELETE":
    err = handleDelete(w, r)
  }
  if err != nil {
    http.Error(w, err.Error(), http.StatusInternalServerError)
    return
  }
}

func handleGet(w http.ResponseWriter, r *http.Request) (err error) {
  id, err := strconv.Atoi(path.Base(r.URL.Path))
  if err != nil {
    return
  }
  post, err := retrieve(id)
  if err != nil {
    return
  }
  output, err := json.MarshalIndent(&post, "", "\t\t")
  if err != nil {
    return
  }
  w.Header().Set("Content-Type", "application/json")
  w.Write(output)
  return
}

func handlePost(w http.ResponseWriter, r *http.Request) (err error) {
  len := r.ContentLength
  body := make([]byte, len)
  r.Body.Read(body)
  var post Post
  json.Unmarshal(body, &post)
  err = post.create()
  if err != nil {
    return
  }
  w.WriteHeader(200)
  return
}

func handlePut(w http.ResponseWriter, r *http.Request) (err error) {
  id, err := strconv.Atoi(path.Base(r.URL.Path))
  if err != nil {
    return
  }
  post, err := retrieve(id)
  if err != nil {
    return
```

```
    }
    len := r.ContentLength
    body := make([]byte, len)
    r.Body.Read(body)
    json.Unmarshal(body, &post)
    err = post.update()
    if err != nil {
      return
    }
    w.WriteHeader(200)
    return
}

func handleDelete(w http.ResponseWriter, r *http.Request) (err error) {
    id, err := strconv.Atoi(path.Base(r.URL.Path))
    if err != nil {
      return
    }
    post, err := retrieve(id)
    if err != nil {
      return
    }
    err = post.delete()
    if err != nil {
      return
    }
    w.WriteHeader(200)
    return
}
```

First, you compile the code:

```
go build
```

Assuming that you have the code in a directory called ws-s, this command will produce the executable binary ws-s in the same directory. To deploy the web service ws-s, copy the ws-s file into the server. Anywhere will do as long as it's accessible.

To run the web service, log into the server and run it from the console:

```
./ws-s
```

But wait! You're running it in the foreground, which means you can't do anything else or it will shut down the service. You can't even run it in the background using the `&` or `bg` command because once you log out, the web service gets killed.

One way of getting around this issue is to use the `nohup` command, which tells the OS to ignore the HUP (hangup) signal that is sent to your web service once you log out:

```
nohup ./ws-s &
```

This command will run the web service in the background, and there's no fear of it being killed. The web service is still connected to the console; it just ignores any signals to hang up or quit. If it crashes, you won't be alerted, and you'll need to log in to restart it. If the server is restarted, you'll have to restart the web service.

An alternative to running nohup is to use an init daemon like Upstart or systemd. In Unix-based OSes, init is the first process that's run when the system is booted up and continues running until the system is shut down. It's the direct or indirect ancestor of all other processes and is automatically started by the kernel.

In this section, you'll be using Upstart, an event-based replacement for init, created for Ubuntu. Although systemd is gaining adoption, Upstart is generally simpler to use, and for our purposes, both perform the same things.

To use Upstart, create an Upstart job configuration file, shown next, and place it in the etc/init directory. For the simple web service, you'll create ws.conf and place it in the etc/init directory.

Upstart job config file

**Listing 10.3 Listing 10.3 Upstart job configuration file for the simple web service**

```
respawn
respawn limit 10 5

setuid sausheong
setgid sausheong

exec /go/src/github.com/sausheong/ws-s/ws-s
```

The Upstart job configuration file in the listing is straightforward. Each Upstart job consists of one or more command blocks called *stanzas*. The first stanza, respawn, indicates that if the job fails, it should be respawned, or restarted. The second stanza, respawn limit 10 5, sets parameters for respawn, indicating that it will try to respawn only 10 times, waiting 5 seconds in between. After 10 tries, Upstart will stop trying to respawn the job and consider the job to have failed. The third and fourth stanzas set the user and group that will be used to run the process. The last stanza is the executable that's run by Upstart when the job starts.

To start the Upstart job, you start it from the console:

```
sudo start ws
ws start/running, process 2011
```

This command will trigger Upstart to read the /etc/init/ws.conf job configuration file and start the job. Upstart job configuration files can have a number of other stanzas, and Upstart jobs can be configured in a variety of ways, all of which are beyond the scope of this book. This section provides only a flavor of how a simple Upstart job can be used to run a Go web application.

To test this point, let's try a simple experiment. You'll try to kill the Upstart job after it's started:

```
ps -ef | grep ws
sausheo+ 2011 1 0 17:23 ? 00:00:00 /go/src/github.com/sausheong/ws-s/ws-s

sudo kill -0 2011

ps -ef | grep ws
sausheo+ 2030 1 0 17:23 ? 00:00:00 /go/src/github.com/sausheong/ws-s/ws-s
```

Notice that before we killed the process, the ID for the job was `2011`, whereas after you tried killing the process, the process PID became `2030`. This is because Upstart detects that the process went down, so Upstart will try to restart it.

Finally, most web applications are deployed to the standard HTTP port (port 80). When it is time to do the final deployment, you should be changing the port number from 8080 to 80, or use some mechanism to proxy or redirect traffic to port 80 to port 8080.

## 10.2 Deploying to Heroku

I've just shown you how easy it is to deploy a simple Go web service to a server and also how the web service can be managed by the init daemon. In this section, you'll see that it's just as easy to deploy to Heroku, a PaaS provider.

Heroku allows you to deploy, run, and manage applications written in a few programming languages, including Go. An *application*, as defined by Heroku, is a collection of source code written in one of Heroku's supported languages, as well as its dependencies.

Heroku's premise is simple and requires only a couple of things:

- A configuration file or mechanism that defines the dependencies. For example, in Ruby this would be a Gemfile file, in Node.js a package.json file, and in Java a pom.xml file.
- A Procfile that defines what to be run. More than one executable can be run at the same time.

Heroku uses the command line extensively and provides a command-line "toolbelt" to deploy, run, and manage applications. In addition, Heroku uses Git to push source code to the server to be deployed. When the Heroku platform receives the code through Git, it builds the application and retrieves the dependencies that are specified, and then assembles them into a *slug*. These slugs are then run on Heroku *dynos*, Heroku's terminology for isolated, lightweight virtualized Unix containers.

Although some of the management and configuration activities can later be done through a web interface, Heroku's main interface is still through its command-line toolbelt. So the first thing you need to do to use Heroku, after registering for an account, is to download the toolbelt at https://toolbelt.heroku.com.

There are many reasons why you'd want to use a PaaS (Heroku is an atypical PaaS) to deploy your web application. As a web application programmer, you'll find the most direct reason is that your infrastructure and systems layers are now abstracted and managed for you. Although in a large-scale production environment such as in corporate IT infrastructure this is not usually an issue, PaaS has become a boon for smaller companies and startups where there's less need for up-front capital cost commitments.

Once you have downloaded the toolbelt, log into Heroku using the credentials you received when registering for an account:

```
heroku login
Enter your Heroku credentials.
```

```
Email: <your email>
Password (typing will be hidden):
Authentication successful.
```

Figure 10.1 shows how you can deploy the same simple web service to Heroku.

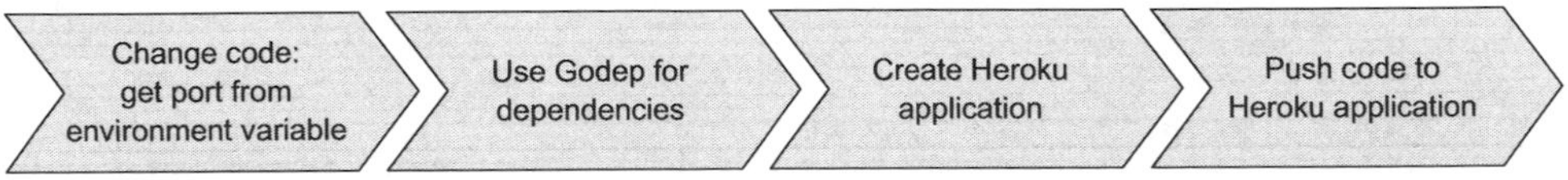


**Figure 10.1 Steps to deploy a web application on Heroku. First, change the code to use the port from the environment settings and use Godep to include dependencies. Then create the Heroku application and push the code to Heroku.**

To deploy the web service, you need to make a simple code change. Remember you bound your web server to the address :8080 previously. When deploying on Heroku, you have no control over the port to use; you must get the port by reading the environment variable `PORT`. Therefore, instead of this `main` function in the server.go file:

```
func main() {
  server := http.Server{
    Addr: ":8080",
  }
  http.HandleFunc("/post/", handlePost)
  server.ListenAndServe()
}
```

you use this `main` function:

```
func main() {
  server := http.Server{
    Addr: ":" + os.Getenv("PORT"),//
  }
  http.HandleFunc("/post/", handlePost)
  server.ListenAndServe()
}
```

**Gets port number from environment variable**

That's all the code changes you need to make; everything else is the same. Next, you need to tell Heroku about your web service's dependencies. Heroku uses godep (https://github.com/tools/godep) to manage Go dependencies. To install godep, use the standard `go get` command:

```
go get github.com/tools/godep
```

Once godep is installed, you need to use it to bring in your dependencies. In the root directory of your web service, run this command:

```
godep save
```

This command will create a directory named Godeps, retrieve all the dependencies in your code, and copy their source code into the directory Godeps/_workspace. It will also create a file named Godeps.json that lists all your dependencies. This listing shows an example of the Godeps.json file.

**Listing 10.4 Godeps.json file**

```
{
  "ImportPath": "github.com/sausheong/ws-h",
  "GoVersion": "go1.4.2",
  "Deps": [
    {
      "ImportPath": "github.com/lib/pq",
      "Comment": "go1.0-cutoff-31-ga33d605",
      "Rev": "a33d6053e025943d5dc89dfa1f35fe5500618df7"
    }
  ]
}
```

Because the web service depends only on the Postgres database driver, it lists only that as a dependency.

The last thing that you need to do is define a Procfile, shown in the next listing, which is nothing more than a file that describes which executable or main function to run.

**Listing 10.5 Godeps.json file**

```
web: ws-h
```

That's it! What the listing says is that the web process is associated with the ws-h executable binary, so that's what's going to be executed when the Heroku build completes.

Now that you have all this in place, the next step is to push everything up to Heroku. Heroku allows you to use different mechanisms to push code, including GitHub integration, Dropbox Sync, Heroku's own APIs, and standard Git. In this example, you'll use standard Git to push your simple web service to Heroku.

Before you push the code, you must create an application:

```
heroku create ws-h
```

This command will create a Heroku application called ws-h, which will finally be shown as https://ws-h.herokuapp.com. Naturally since we've used this already, you won't be able to do so again. You can choose another name, or you can drop the name altogether and let Heroku generate a random application name for you.

```
heroku create
```

Using `heroku create` will initialize a local Git repository for the web service and add the remote Heroku repository. Once you've created the application, you can use Git to push the code to the application:

```
git push heroku master
```

This will push your code to Heroku, triggering a build and deploy. And that's all you need to do! Heroku also provides a number of nifty application management tools for scaling and managing releases, as well as configuration tools to add new services.

## 10.3 Deploying to Google App Engine

Another popular PaaS for Go web applications is the Google App Engine (GAE). Google has a number of services in its Google Cloud Platform suite of products, including the App Engine and the Compute Engine. The App Engine is a PaaS service; a Compute Engine, like AWS's EC2 and Digital Ocean's Droplets, is an IaaS service. Using EC2 or Droplets isn't much different from having your own VM or running your own server, and we've covered that. This section explores Google's powerful PaaS service, GAE.

There are a number of reasons why you'd use GAE as compared with any other PaaS, including Heroku. The main reasons are performance and scalability. GAE allows you to build applications that can automatically scale and load balance according to its load. Google also provides a large number of tools and capabilities built into the GAE. For example, it can allow your application to authenticate into Google Accounts and it provides services to send emails, create logs, and serve and manipulate images. Integration into other Google APIs is also more straightforward using GAE.

With any advantages there are also a number of disadvantages. For one, you have read-only access to the filesystem, you can't have a request lasting more than 60 seconds (GAE will kill it if you do), and you can't have direct network access or make other kinds of system calls. This means you can't (at least not easily) access many services outside of Google's sandboxed application environment.

Figure 10.2 shows a high-level overview of the steps for deploying a web application on the GAE.

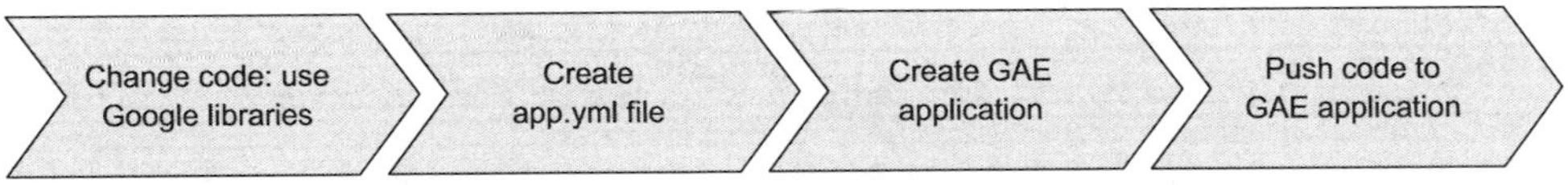


**Figure 10.2 Steps to deploy on the Google App Engine. First change the code to use Google libraries and create the app.yml configuration file. Then create the application and push it to the GAE.**

As with all other Google services, you'll need a Google account to start with. Unlike Heroku, much of the management and servicing of the web application is done through the web interface (figure 10.3), called the Google Developer Console (https://console.developers.google.com).

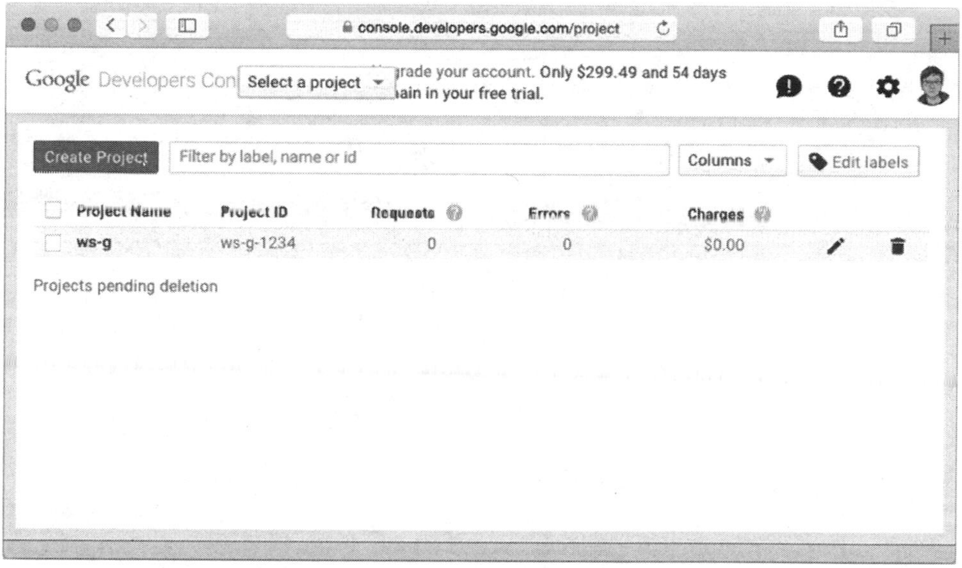


**Figure 10.3 Use the Google Developer Console to create your GAE web application.**

Although a command-line interface is available that's equivalent to the developer console, Google's command-line tools aren't integrated, unlike in Heroku. To use the GAE, you'll need to download the appropriate GAE SDK for Go at https://cloud.google.com/appengine/downloads.

> **Google App Engine and other Google services**
>
> GAE and other Google services like the Google Cloud SQL are *not* free. Google provides a 60-day free trial and $300 worth of services during the trial period so you can go through the exercises in this chapter without cost. After the trial period, you will have to pay for the services themselves.

Once you have the tools in place, you need to configure the datastore for the GAE. As mentioned earlier, Google restricts direct network access so connecting to a PostgreSQL server directly isn't possible. As an alternative, Google provides the Google Cloud SQL service, which is based on MySQL and is directly accessible through the `cloudsql` package. This is what you'll be using for this section.

To use Google Cloud SQL, you'll need to create a database instance using the Developer Console (figure 10.4). From the console, you can click the project that you created (mine is called ws-g-1234), and then from the left navigation panel, click Storage, then Cloud SQL. Clicking the New Instance button will give you a number of options for creating the database instance. Most of the default options are fine, but

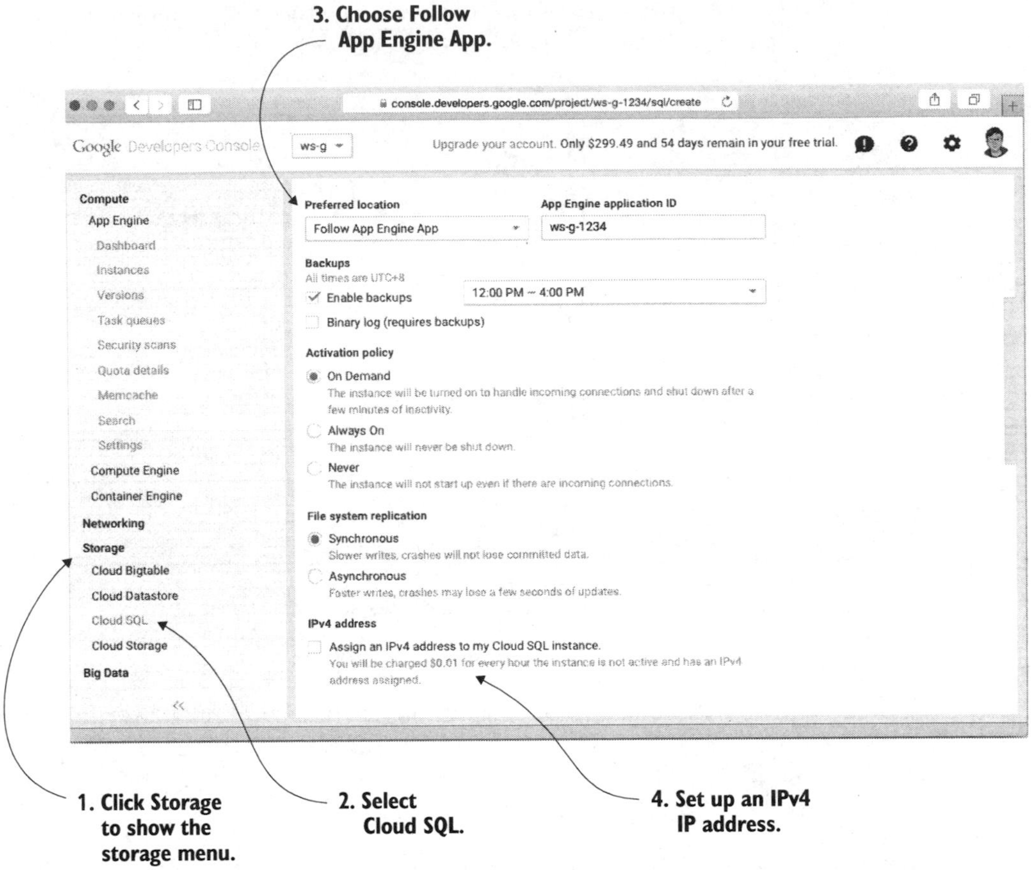


**Figure 10.4 Creating a Google Cloud SQL database instance using the Developer Console**

you need to set the preferred location option to Follow App Engine App and use the default project application ID. If you don't, your GAE application won't be able to access the database instance.

You'll also need to add an IPv4 address, unless your desktop or laptop (or server), as well as the internet provider you're using, has IPv6 network connectivity. This is because Google provides an IPv6 to your database instance by default and for free (although an IPv4 address will cost you some money and you won't have one by default).

Besides these settings, it's okay to use the defaults. Just specify a name for your instance and you're all set.

As you may have guessed, with all these modifications, code change is inevitable. Here's a high-level list of things you'll need to do to make your code deployable to GAE:

- Change the package name from `main` to another package name.
- Remove the `main` function.

- Move the handler registration statement(s) into an init function.
- Use a MySQL database driver instead of PostgreSQL.
- Change the SQL queries to MySQL format.

Because GAE will take over your entire application, you won't have control over how it's started or which port it runs on. In fact, you're not going to be writing a standalone application at all—what you'll be writing is simply a package to be deployed on GAE. As a result, you'll need to change the package name to something other than `main` (`main` is only for standalone Go programs).

Next, remove the `main` function and move your code into an init function. In other words, the `main` function we had earlier

```
func main() {
  server := http.Server{
    Addr: ":8080",
  }
  http.HandleFunc("/post/", handlePost)
  server.ListenAndServe()
}
```

should be modified and its processing logic placed in an init function:

```
func init() {
  http.HandleFunc("/post/", handlePost)
}
```

Notice that the code that specifies the starting address and port, as well as the code that starts up the web server, is no longer needed.

Switch to a MySQL database driver instead of a PostgreSQL driver. In data.go you need to import a MySQL database driver and use the correct data connection string:

```
import (
  "database/sql"
  _ "github.com/ziutek/mymysql/godrv"
)
func init() {
  var err error
  Db, err = sql.Open("mymysql", "cloudsql:<app ID>:<instance name>*<database
  name>/<user name>/<password>")
  if err != nil {
    panic(err)
  }
}
```

In addition, you'll need to switch to the correct MySQL SQL queries. Although the syntax is similar, there's enough difference between MySQL and PostgreSQL such that it won't work without any changes. For example, instead of using `$1`, `$2`, and so on to represent the replaced variables, you have to use `?`. So, instead of (code in bold)

```
func retrieve(id int) (post Post, err error) {
  post = Post{}
```

```
  err = Db.QueryRow("select id, content, author from posts where id =
  ➥ $1", id).Scan(&post.Id, &post.Content, &post.Author)
  return
}
```

change the SQL query to (code in bold)

```
func retrieve(id int) (post Post, err error) {
  post = Post{}
  err = Db.QueryRow("select id, content, author from posts where id = ?",
  ➥ id).Scan(&post.Id, &post.Content, &post.Author)
  return
}
```

Changing $n to ? in MySQL query format

With all the code changes done, the next action is to create an app.yaml file, shown in the following listing, to describe the application.

**Listing 10.6 app.yaml file for deploying to GAE**

```
application: ws-g-1234
version: 1
runtime: go
api_version: go1

handlers:
- url: /.*
  script: _go_app
```

The file is quite self-descriptive, and the only thing you have to change in this file, normally, should be the name of the application. And that's it! Now let's test our brand-new GAE web application.

You may realize by now that with all these changes, there's no chance at all that you'll be able to run this application on your development machine. Nothing to fear. Google provides developers with a GAE SDK that allows developers to run the application locally.

Assuming that you've installed the SDK by following the instructions on the download site, you can run your GAE web application by issuing this command on your console, in the application root directory:

```
goapp serve
```

The SDK provides the environment that's needed to run your web application locally so you can test the application. It also provides an admin site running locally to inspect what you've just written. Just go to http://localhost:8000 to look at the admin site. Unfortunately, as of this writing Cloud SQL isn't supported in the development environment, so you can't test the web service locally. A good alternative is to switch to a local MySQL server for testing, and then to the Cloud SQL database for production.

When you're happy with your work, you can deploy it to Google's servers. Deployment is easy by issuing this command:

```
goapp deploy
```

The SDK will push your code to Google's servers, compile it, and deploy it. And if everything is fine, your application will be live on the internet! Assuming your application is named ws-g-1234 (like mine), your application will be at http://ws-g-1234.appspot.com.

Let's test our newly deployed simple web service. Use curl and send a POST request to the server to create a record:

```
curl -i -X POST -H "Content-Type: application/json"  -d '{"content":"My first
     post","author":"Sau Sheong"}' http://ws-g-1234.appspot.com/post/
HTTP/1.1 200 OK
Content-Type: text/html; charset=utf-8
Date: Sat, 01 Aug 2015 06:46:59 GMT
Server: Google Frontend
Content-Length: 0
Alternate-Protocol: 80:quic,p=0
```

Now, use curl again to get the same record:

```
curl -i -X GET http://ws-g-1234.appspot.com/post/1
HTTP/1.1 200 OK
Content-Type: application/json
Date: Sat, 01 Aug 2015 06:44:29 GMT
Server: Google Frontend
Content-Length: 69
Alternate-Protocol: 80:quic,p=0

{
    "id": 1,
    "content": "My first post",
    "author": "Sau Sheong"
}
```

The GAE is powerful and has a lot of capabilities to help developers create and deploy scalable web applications to the internet. But it's Google's playground, and if you want to play in it, you have to follow its rules.

## 10.4 Deploying to Docker

The previous section included a brief introduction to Docker and discussed how you can dockerize your Go web application and push it out as a Docker container on the many Docker hosting services available. This section will focus entirely on deploying a simple Go web service to a local Docker host and then to a Docker host on the cloud.

### 10.4.1 What is Docker?

Docker is quite a phenomenon. Since its release as an open source project by PaaS company dotCloud in 2013, its adoption by large and small companies has been amazing. Technology companies like Google, AWS, and Microsoft have embraced it. AWS has the EC2 Container Service, Google provides the Google Container Engine, and many other cloud providers like Digital Ocean, Rackspace, and even IBM have thrown

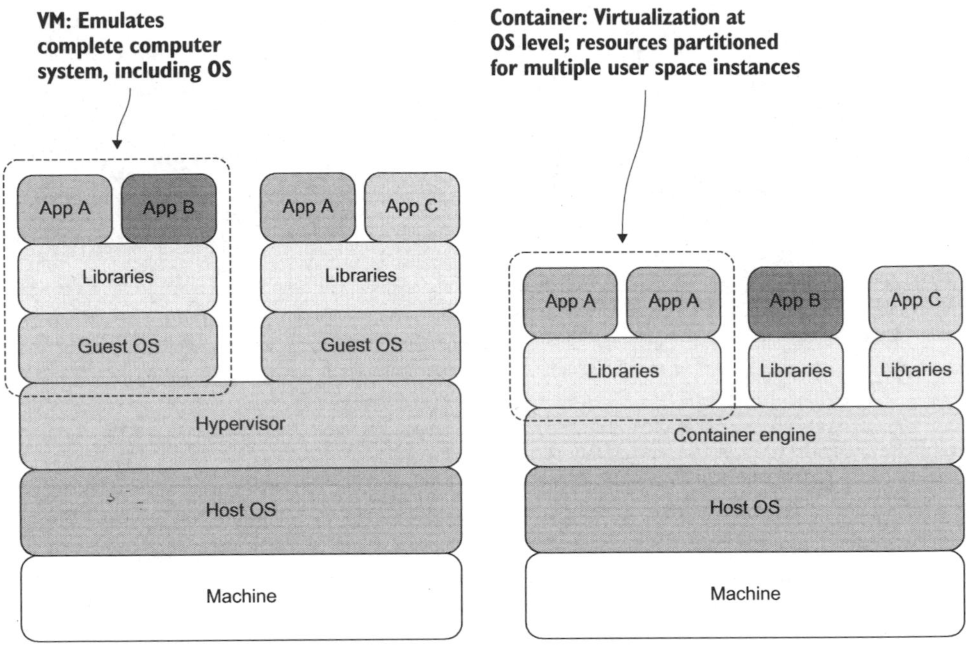


**Figure 10.5 Containers are a different take on infrastructure virtualization, providing virtualization at the OS level and allowing resources to be partitioned through multiple isolated user space instance**

in support for Docker. Traditional companies like BBC and banks such as ING and Goldman Sachs have started using Docker internally.

Docker is an open platform for building, shipping, and running applications on containers. Containers aren't a new technology—they've been around since the early days of Unix, and Linux containers, which Docker was originally based on, were introduced in 2008. Heroku dynos are also containers.

Containers are a different spin on the virtualization of infrastructure (figure 10.5). VMs provide emulation of the complete computer system, including the entire OS, but containers provide virtualization at the OS level, allowing computer resources to be partitioned through multiple isolated user space instances. As a result, the resource requirements of a container are much less than a VM and the container is much faster to start up and deploy.

Docker is essentially software for managing containers, making it easier for developers to use them. It's not the only available software to do that—there are many others, including chroot, Linux containers (LXC), Solaris Zones, CoreOS, and lmctfy—but it's probably the most well-known to-date.

### 10.4.2 Installing Docker

Docker only works on Linux-based OSes today, though there are workarounds to make the Docker tool available on OS X and Windows. To install Docker, go to https://docs.docker.com/engine/installation, select where you want to install Docker, and follow the instructions. For Ubuntu Server 14.04, the instruction is as simple as this:

```
wget -qO- https://get.docker.com/ | sh
```

To verify that Docker is installed properly, run this command on the console:

```
sudo docker run hello-world
```

This command will pull the hello-world image from a remote repository and run it as a container locally.

### 10.1.3 Docker concepts and components

The *Docker engine*, or Docker (figure 10.6), consists of a number of components. The first, which you used earlier in testing the Docker installation, is the *Docker client*. This is the command-line interface that allows you to interact with the Docker daemon.

The *Docker daemon* is the process that sits on the host OS that answers requests for service and orchestrates the management of containers. *Docker containers*, containers for short, are lightweight virtualization of all the programs that are needed to run a particular application, including the OS. Containers are lightweight because though the application and other bundled programs believe they have the OS (and in fact the whole hardware) to themselves, they actually don't. Instead, the share the same host OS.

Docker containers are built on *Docker images*, which are read-only templates that help to launch containers. You run containers from images. Docker images can be built in different ways. One way of doing it involves using a set of instructions contained in a single file called the Dockerfile.

Docker images can be stored locally in the same computer as the Docker daemon (also called the Docker host),

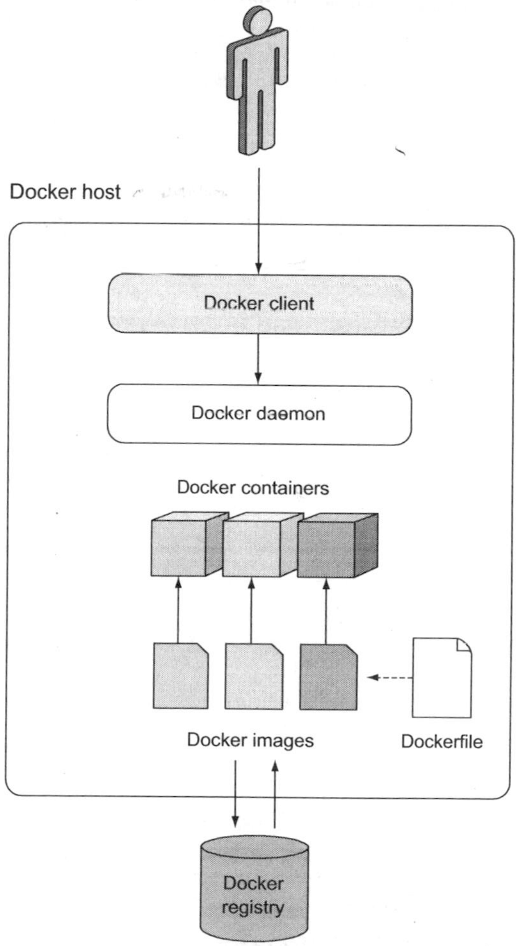


**Figure 10.6 The Docker engine consists of the Docker client, the Docker daemon, and various Docker containers, which are instantiated as Docker images. Docker images can be created through Dockerfiles and can be stored in the Docker registry.**

or they can be hosted in a *Docker registry*, a repository of Docker images. You can run your own private Docker registry or use *Docker Hub* (https://hub.docker.com) as your registry. Docker Hub hosts both public and private Docker images, though the latter usually requires a subscription.

If you install Docker on a Linux OS like Ubuntu, the Docker daemon and the Docker client are installed in the same machine. With other types of OSes, Docker can install the client on one type of OS (for example, OS X or Windows), and the daemon will be installed somewhere else, usually in a VM sitting in that OS. An example of this is when you install Docker on OS X, the Docker client is installed in OS X and the Docker daemon will be installed in a VM inside VirtualBox (an x86-based hypervisor).

Docker containers are run from Docker images and run on the Docker host.

Now that you have an overall understanding of Docker, let's see how you can deploy a simple Go web service into a Docker container. We'll be using the same simple web service we've used in the previous three sections.

### 10.4.4 Dockerizing a Go web application

Despite the plethora of technologies, dockerizing a Go web application is surprisingly easy. There's no need for messing with the code because the web service will have full access to the whole container, so the only work is entirely in the configuration and use of Docker. Figure 10.7 shows a high-level overview of the steps for dockerizing your web application and deploying it both locally and to a cloud provider.

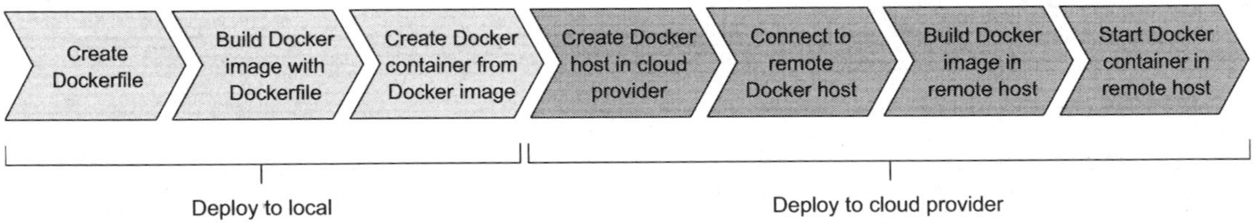


**Figure 10.7 Steps to dockerize and deploy a Go web application locally and to a cloud provider. To dockerize an application locally, use a Dockerfile to create the image and then start a container from the image. To move the image to the cloud, create a Docker host in the cloud provider, and then connect to it, build the image in the remote host, and start a container from it.**

For this section, we'll use the name ws-d as the name of the web service. First, shown in the next listing, create a Dockerfile file in the root application directory.

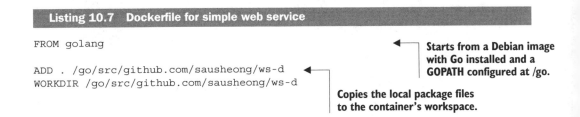

**Listing 10.7 Dockerfile for simple web service**

```
FROM golang

ADD . /go/src/github.com/sausheong/ws-d
WORKDIR /go/src/github.com/sausheong/ws-d
```

Starts from a Debian image with Go installed and a GOPATH configured at /go. (annotates `FROM golang`)

Copies the local package files to the container's workspace. (annotates `ADD`)

**Builds the ws-d command inside the container.**

```
RUN go get github.com/lib/pq
RUN go install github.com/sausheong/ws-d

ENTRYPOINT /go/bin/ws-d

EXPOSE 8080
```

**Runs the ws-d command by default when the container starts.**

**Documents that the service listens on port 8080.**

The first line tells Docker to start from the golang image, which is a Debian image with the latest Go installed, and a workspace configured at /go. The next two lines copy the local code (in the current directory) to the container and set the working directory accordingly. After that, you use the `RUN` command to tell Docker to get the PostgreSQL driver and build the web service code, placing the executable binaries in /go/bin. Once you have that, use the `ENTRYPOINT` command to tell Docker to run `/go/bin/ws-d` by default whenever the container is started. Finally, use `EXPOSE` to expose the port 8080 to other containers. Note that this doesn't open up port 8080 to the public; it simply opens up the port to other containers in the same machine.

Now build the image from the Dockerfile:

```
docker build –t ws-d .
```

This command will execute the Dockerfile and build a local image based on the instructions in it. Once this is done, you can issue the `docker images` command and you should see this:

```
REPOSITORY      TAG         IMAGE ID          CREATED             VIRTUAL SIZE
ws-d            latest      65e8437fce6b      10 minutes ago      534.7 MB
```

Now that you have the image, you can now run the image to create and start the container:

```
docker run --publish 80:8080 --name simple_web_service --rm  ws-d
```

This code will create a container, using the name simple_web_service from the image ws-d. The flag `--publish 80:8080` opens up the HTTP port 80 and maps it to the exposed port 8080 earlier, whereas the flag `--rm` tells Docker that once the container exits, it should be removed. If this flag isn't set, when the container exits it will still remain and can be simply started up again. To see whether your container has been created, issue

```
docker ps
```

You should see your container in the list of active containers:

```
CONTAINER ID   IMAGE ...  PORTS                    NAMES
eeb674e289a4   ws-d  ...  0.0.0.0:80->8080/tcp     simple_web_service
```

Some of the columns have been omitted to fit the page, but you can see that your container is now running on the local Docker host. You can run a quick test to see if your service works. Use curl and send a POST request to the server to create a record:

```
curl -i -X POST -H "Content-Type: application/json"  -d '{"content":"My first
     post","author":"Sau Sheong"}' http://127.0.0.1/post/
HTTP/1.1 200 OK
Content-Type: text/html; charset=utf-8
Date: Sat, 01 Aug 2015 06:46:59 GMT
Server: Google Frontend
Content-Length: 0
Alternate-Protocol: 80:quic,p=0
```

Now, use curl again to get the same record:

```
curl -i -X GET http://127.0.0.1/post/1
HTTP/1.1 200 OK
Content-Type: application/json
Date: Sat, 01 Aug 2015 06:44:29 GMT
Server: Google Frontend
Content-Length: 69
Alternate-Protocol: 80:quic,p=0

{
    "id": 1,
    "content": "My first post",
    "author": "Sau Sheong"
}
```

### 10.4.5 Pushing your Docker container to the internet

Dockerizing the simple web service sounds great, but it's still running locally. What you want is to have it running on the internet. There are a number of ways of doing this, but using the Docker machine is probably the most simple (at the moment, because Docker is still evolving).

*Docker machine* is a command-line interface that allows you to create Docker hosts, either locally or on cloud providers, both public and private. As of this writing, the list of public cloud providers include AWS, Digital Ocean, Google Compute Engine, IBM Softlayer, Microsoft Azure, Rackspace, Exoscale, and VMWare vCloud Air. It can also create hosts on private clouds, including clouds running on OpenStack, VMWare, and Microsoft Hyper-V (which covers most of the private cloud infrastructure to date).

Docker Machine isn't installed along with the main Docker installation; you need to install it separately. You can install it by either cloning the repository from https://github.com/docker/machine or downloading the binary for your platform from https://docs.docker.com/machine/install-machine. For Linux you can use the following command to get the binary:

```
curl -L https://github.com/docker/machine/releases/download/v0.3.0/docker-
➥ machine_linux-amd64 /usr/local/bin/docker-machine
```

Then make it executable:

```
chmod +x /usr/local/bin/docker-machine
```

Once you've downloaded Docker Machine and made it executable, you can use it to create a Docker host in any of the cloud providers. One of the easiest is probably Digital Ocean, a virtual private server (VPS) provider known for its ease-of-use and low cost. (A VPS is a VM sold as a service by a provider.) In May 2015, Digital Ocean became the second-largest hosting company in the world, in terms of web-facing servers, after AWS.

To create a Docker host on Digital Ocean, you'll first need to sign up for a Digital Ocean account. Once you have an account, go to the Applications & API page at https://cloud.digitalocean.com/settings/applications.

On this page there is a Generate New Token button (figure 10.8), which you can click to generate a token. Enter any name you want, and remember to keep the Write check box selected. Then click the Generate Token button to create a personal access token, which is something like a username and password rolled into one, used for API authentication. The token is only shown when you create it—it won't be shown again—so you should store it someplace safe.

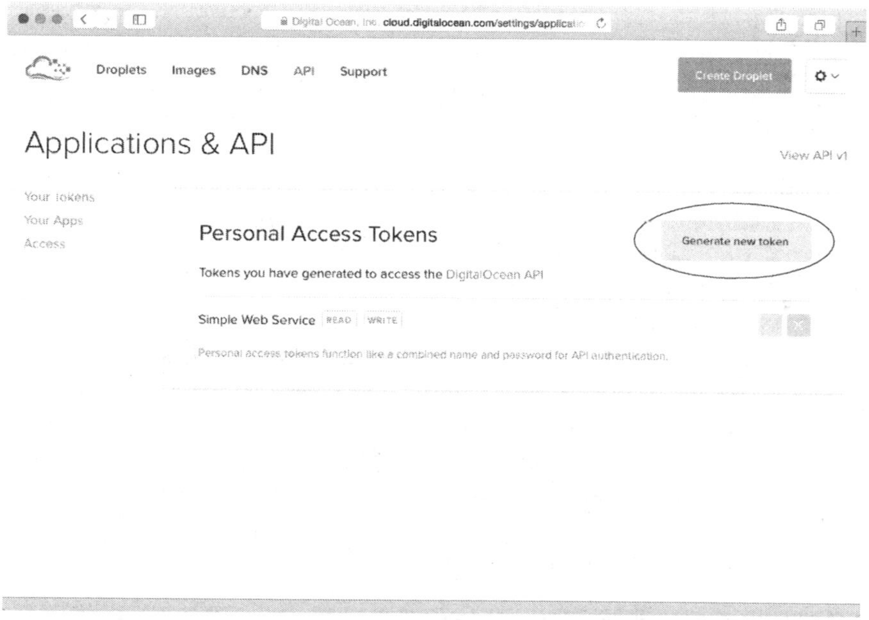


**Figure 10.8 Generating a personal access token on Digital Ocean is as easy as clicking the Generate New Token button.**

To create a Docker host on Digital Ocean through Docker Machine, execute this command on the console:

```
docker-machine create --driver digitalocean --digitalocean-access-token
    <tokenwsd
Creating CA: /home/sausheong/.docker/machine/certs/ca.pem
Creating client certificate: /home/sausheong/.docker/machine/certs/cert.pem
```

```
Creating SSH key...
Creating Digital Ocean droplet...
To see how to connect Docker to this machine, run: docker-machine env wsd
```

Once the remote Docker host is created, the next step is to connect to it. Remember, your Docker client is currently connected to the local Docker host. You need to connect it to our Docker host on Digital Ocean, called wsd. The response from Docker Machine gives you a hint how to do it. You should run:

```
docker-machine env wsd
export DOCKER_TLS_VERIFY="1"
export DOCKER_HOST="tcp://104.236.0.57:2376"
export DOCKER_CERT_PATH="/home/sausheong/.docker/machine/machines/wsd"
export DOCKER_MACHINE_NAME="wsd"
# Run this command to configure your shell:
# eval "$(docker-machine env wsd)"
```

The command tells you the environment settings for our Docker host on the cloud. To configure the client to point to this Docker host, you need to change your environment settings to match it. Here's a quick way to do this:

```
eval "$(docker-machine env wsd)"
```

As simple as that, you're connected to the Docker host on Digital Ocean! How do you know that? Just run

```
docker images
```

You'll see that there are no images listed. Remember that when you were creating the container earlier in this section you created an image locally, so if you're still connected to the local Docker host, you should see at least one image. No image means you're no longer connected to the local Docker host.

Because you have no image in this new Docker host, you have to create one again. Issue the same `docker build` command from earlier:

```
docker build -t ws-d .
```

After the command completes, you should see at least two images when you run `docker images`: the golang base image, and the new ws-d image. The final step is to run the container as you've run it before:

```
docker run --publish 80:8080 --name simple_web_service --rm ws-d
```

This command will create and start up a container on the remote Docker host. To prove that you've done it, use curl to get the post record. But wait—where's the server? It's at the same IP address that was returned when you ran `docker-machine env wsd`.

```
curl -i -X GET http://104.236.0.57/post/1
HTTP/1.1 200 OK
Content-Type: application/json
```

```
Date: Mon, 03 Aug 2015 11:35:46 GMT
Content-Length: 69

{
    "id": 2,
    "content": "My first post",
    "author": "Sau Sheong"
}
```

That's it! You've deployed our simple Go web service to the internet through a Docker container. Docker isn't the simplest way of deploying Go web applications, but it's probably going to be one of the more popular ways. Also, after you've done it once locally, you can duplicate the process almost effortlessly on multiple cloud providers, both private and public. This is the power of Docker and now you know how to use it.

I've left out a lot of details to keep the section and the chapter brief and focused. If you're interested in Docker (and it's a very interesting new tool), spend more time reading the online documentation (https://docs.docker.com) and various articles that have been written about it.

## 10.5 Comparison of deployment methods

Before I end this chapter, let's recap in a table the various types of deployment methods we discussed. There are many more other ways of deploying a web application, and table 10.1 shows only some of them.

**Table 10.1 Comparison of Go web application deployment methods**

| | Standalone | Heroku | GAE | Docker |
|---|---|---|---|---|
| Type | Public/private | Public | Public | Public/private |
| Code change | None | Low | Medium | None |
| Systems work | High | None | None | Medium |
| Maintenance | High | None | None | Medium |
| Ease of deployment | Low | High | Medium | Low |
| Platform support | None | Low | High | Low |
| Tie-in to platform | None | Low | High | Low |
| Scalability | None | Medium | High | High |
| Remarks | In this bare-bones deployment, you need to do almost everything on your own. | Heroku is a liberal public PaaS where you're able to do almost anything, with a few exceptions. | GAE is a restrictive public PaaS where you're tied into the GAE platform. | Docker is an up-and-coming technology with a lot of interest and support in both public and private deployments. |

## 10.6 Summary

- The most simple way to deploy a Go web service is to place the binary executable file(s) directly on a server, either a VM or an actual physical server, and configure Upstart to start it and keep it running continually.
- Deploying to Heroku, which is one of the simplest PaaSes around, is straightforward and involves only minor modifications, generating local dependencies using Godep and creating a Procfile. Pushing these all to Heroku's Git repository will deploy the web application.
- Deploying to GAE, Google's powerful but sandboxed PaaS, is a bit more involved, but this is compensated for by the fact that the web service deployed is very scalable. There are a number of limitations with GAE, mostly involving using services that are outside the GAE sandbox.
- Docker is a new and powerful way of deploying web services and applications. But compared to other solutions, it's much more involved. You need to dockerize your Go web service into a container, deploy it to a local Docker host, and then deploy it to a remote Docker host on the cloud.

# *appendix* *Installing and setting up Go*

## *Installing Go*

Before you can write your first line of Go code, you'll need to set up the environment. Let's start off with installing Go. The latest version of Go as of this writing is Go 1.6. To install Go, you can either download or use the official binary distributions, or you can install Go from source.

Official binary distributions are available for FreeBSD (release 8 and above), Linux (2.6.23 and above), Mac OS X (Snow Leopard and above), and Windows (XP and above). Both 32-bt (386) and 64-bit (amd64) x86 processor architectures are supported. For FreeBSD and Linux, ARM processor architecture is also supported.

To install Go, download the distribution package from https://golang.org/dl/

Choose the file appropriate for your platform. Once you have the distribution package, install Go according to your platform of choice. Note that although Go doesn't have a dependency on any source code versioning system, some Go tools like go get need it, so to make your life a bit easier you should download and install them as you're installing Go.

You can get the following source code versioning systems here:

- *Mercurial*—http://mercurial.selenic.com
- *Subversion*—http://subversion.apache.org
- *Git*—http://git-scm.com
- *Bazaar*—http://bazaar.canonical.com

### *Linux/FreeBSD*

To install on Linux or FreeBSD, you'd likely download go<VERSION>.<OS>-<ARCHITECTURE>.tar.gz. The latest Go for Linux on a 64-bit architecture is go1.3.3.linux-amd64.tar.gz.

Once you've downloaded the archive, extract it to /usr/local. Add /usr/local/go/bin to the PATH environment variable. You can do this by adding this line to your /etc/profile (for a systemwide installation) or $HOME/.profile:

```
export PATH=$PATH:/usr/local/go/bin
```

### *Windows*

You can use either the MSI installer (download the MSI file) or the zip archive. Installing from the MSI is easier—open the MSI installer and follow the instructions to install Go. By default the installer will place Go in c:\Go and set up c:\Go\bin in your PATH environment variable.

Using the zip archive is easy as well. Extract the files into a directory (for example, c:\Go) and add the bin subdirectory to your PATH variable.

### *Mac OS X*

For Mac OS X you can download the appropriate PKG file (same format as earlier) and run through the installation. The package will install the distribution to /usr/local/go and place the /usr/local/go/bin directory in your PATH environment variable. You'll need to restart your Terminal, or run this in your Terminal:

```
$ source ~/.profile
```

Alternatively you can use Homebrew to install Go. This can be as simple as

```
$ brew install go
```

## *Setting up Go*

Now that you've installed Go, you need to set it up properly. Go development tools are designed to work with code maintained in public repositories, and the model is the same regardless if you're developing an open source program or something else.

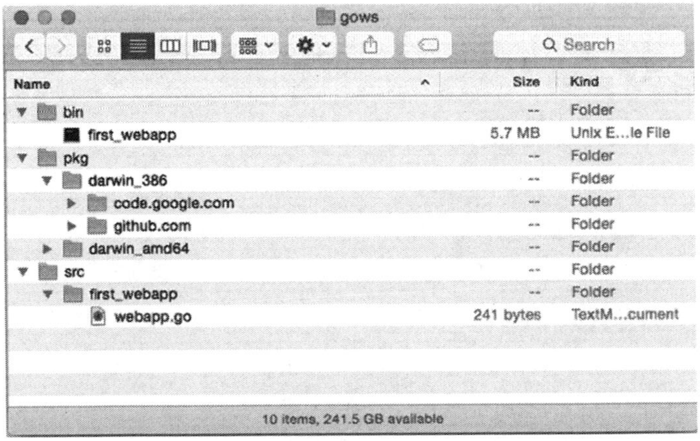


**Figure 1 Directory structure of a Go workspace**

Go code is developed in a *workspace.* A workspace is a directory with three subdirectories (see figure 1):

- src contains Go source files, which are organized in packages, with one subdirectory in the src directory representing one package.
- pkg contains package objects.
- bin contains executable binary files.

How this works is simple. When you compile Go code, it creates either packages (libraries) or binary executable files. These packages or binaries are placed in the pkg and bin directories, respectively. In figure A.1, we have the simple web application first_webapp as a subdirectory in the src directory, with the source code file webapp.go. Once you compile the source code, it generates a binary that's stored in the bin directory of the workspace.

To set up your workspace, you need to set the `GOPATH` environment variable. You can use any directory you like (except for your Go installation). Say we want to set up the workspace at $HOME/go in Linux/FreeBSD or Mac OS X. Go to the console (or Terminal in Mac OS X) and enter this:

```
$ mkdir $HOME/go
$ export GOPATH=$HOME/go
```

To set things up permanently, you can add the following lines in your ~/.profile or ~/.bashrc file (if you're using bash):

```
export GOPATH=$HOME/go
```

For convenience you should also add your workspace's bin directory to your `PATH`. Doing so will allow you to execute the binaries of your compiled Go code:

```
$ export PATH=$PATH:$GOPATH/bin
```

# index

## D

## H



## I



## J



## K



## L

## T